THE DIGESTIVE SYSTEM

THE HUMAN BODY

THE DIGESTIVE SYSTEM

EDITED BY KARA ROGERS, SENIOR EDITOR, BIOMEDICAL SCIENCES

Britannica® Educational Publishing
IN ASSOCIATION WITH
ROSEN
EDUCATIONAL SERVICES

Published in 2011 by Britannica Educational Publishing
(a trademark of Encyclopædia Britannica, Inc.)
in association with Rosen Educational Services, LLC
29 East 21st Street, New York, NY 10010.

Distributed exclusively by Rosen Educational Services.
For a listing of additional Britannica Educational Publishing titles, call toll free (800) 237-9932.

First Edition

Britannica Educational Publishing
Michael I. Levy: Executive Editor
J.E. Luebering: Senior Manager
Marilyn L. Barton: Senior Coordinator, Production Control
Steven Bosco: Director, Editorial Technologies
Lisa S. Braucher: Senior Producer and Data Editor
Yvette Charboneau: Senior Copy Editor
Kathy Nakamura: Manager, Media Acquisition
Kara Rogers: Senior Editor, Biomedical Sciences

Rosen Educational Services
Alexandra Hanson-Harding: Editor
Nelson Sá: Art Director
Cindy Reiman: Photography Manager
Matthew Cauli: Designer, Cover Design
Introduction by Catherine Vanderhoof

Library of Congress Cataloging-in-Publication Data

The digestive system / edited by Kara Rogers, senior editor. — 1st ed.
p. cm. — (The human body)
"In association with Britannica Educational Publishing, Rosen Educational Services."
Includes bibliographical references and index.
ISBN 978-1-61530-131-7 (library binding)
1. Digestive organs. 2. Digestion. I. Rogers, Kara.
QP145.D54 2011
612.3—dc22

2010001615

Manufactured in the United States of America

Cover, pp. 19, 38, 61, 86, 117, 142, 178, 209, 244, 246, 249 © www.istockphoto.com/Sebastian Kaulitzki

On page 10: The human digestive system. *Mittermeier/Taxi/Getty Images*

CONTENTS

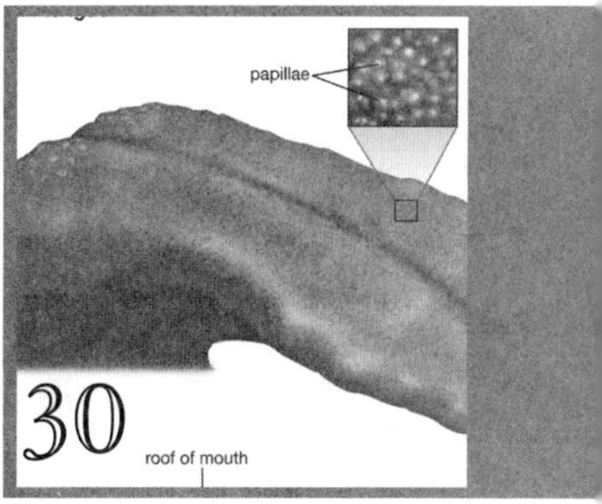
papillae
30
roof of mouth

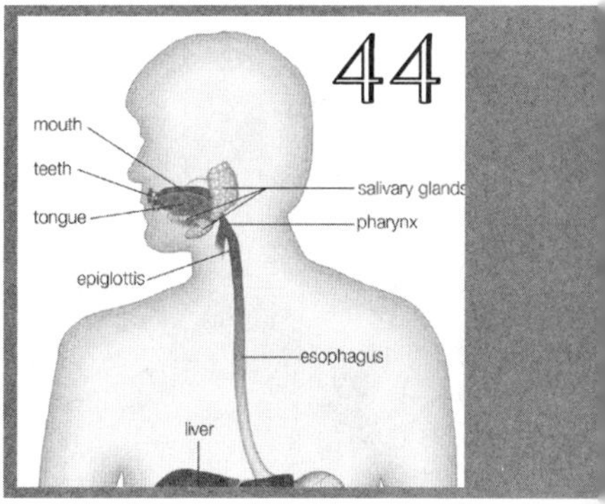
44
mouth
teeth
tongue
epiglottis
pharynx
esophagus
liver

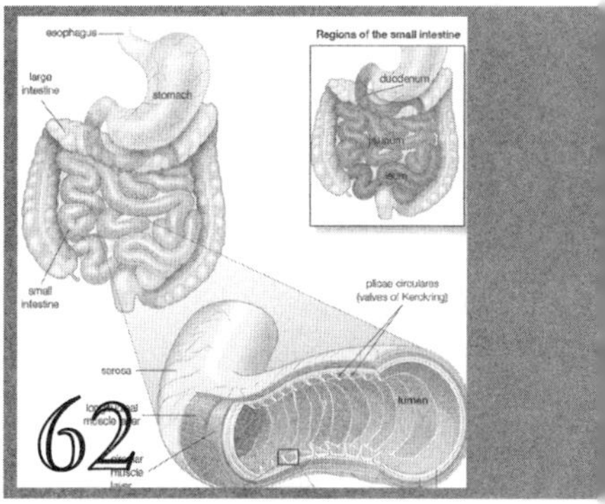
Regions of the small intestine
62

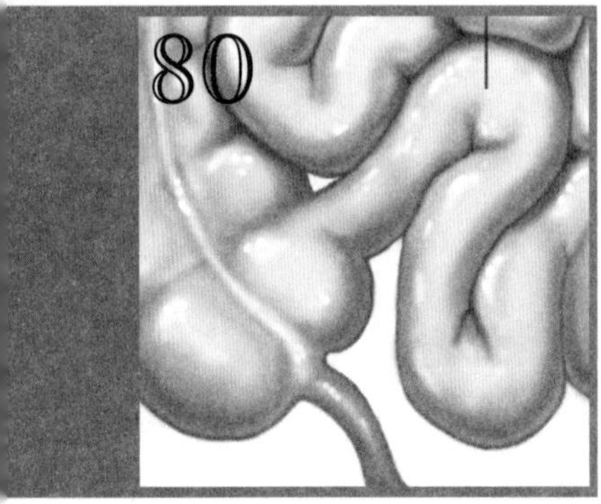
80

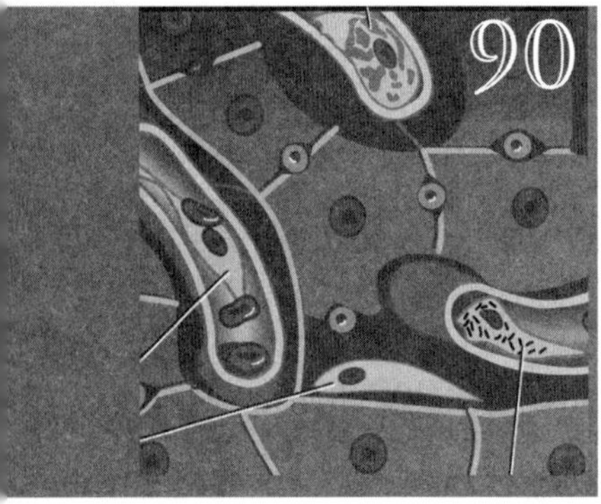
90

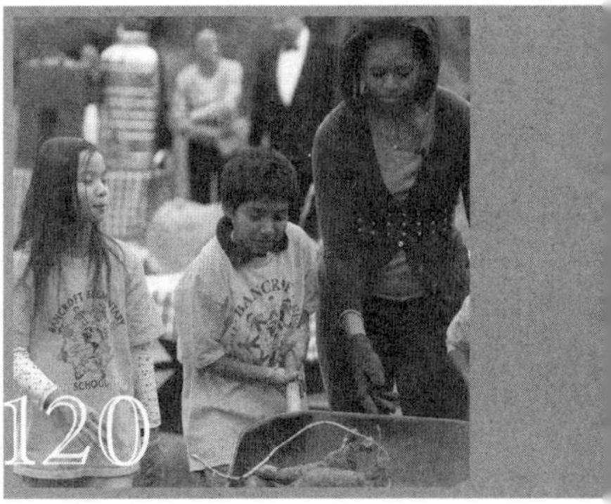

120

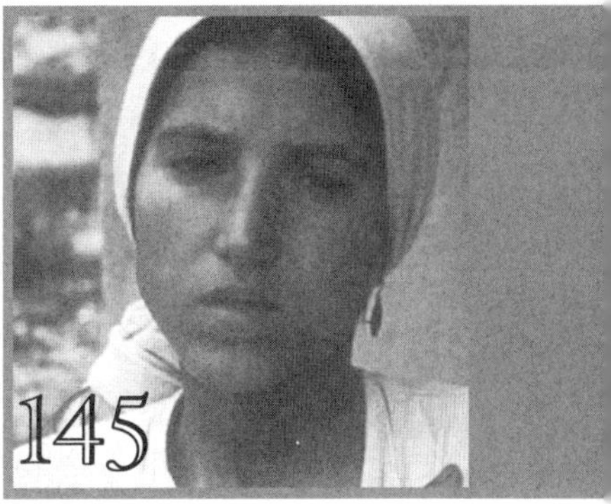

145

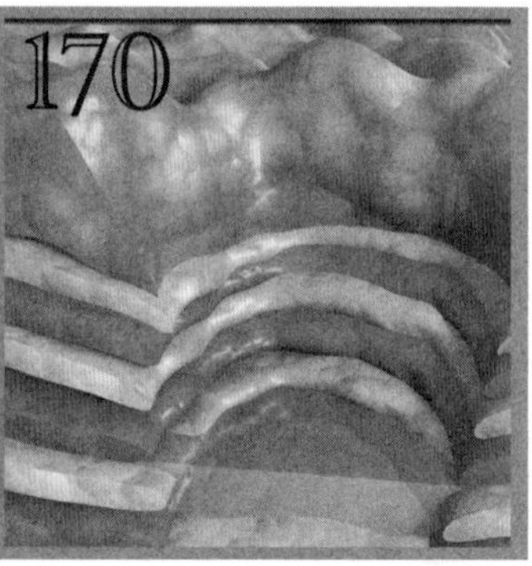
170

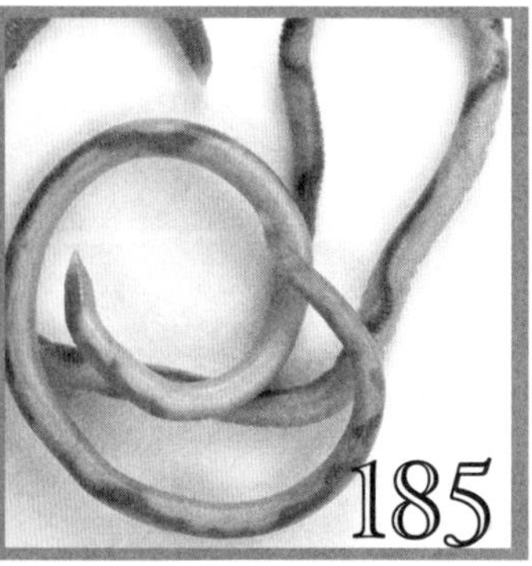
185

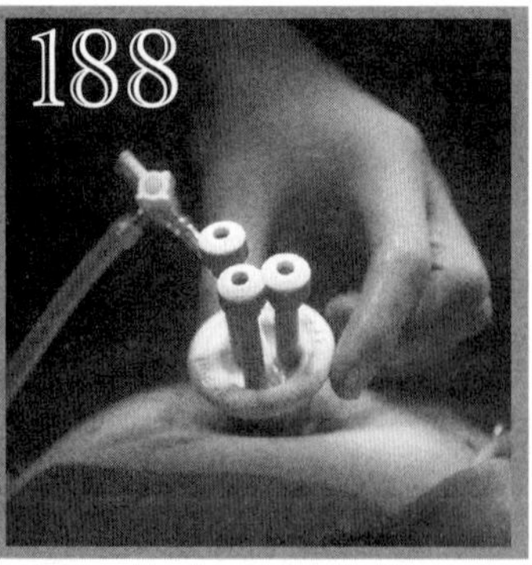
188

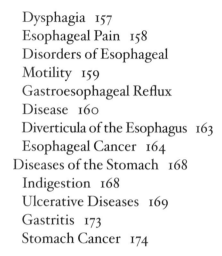

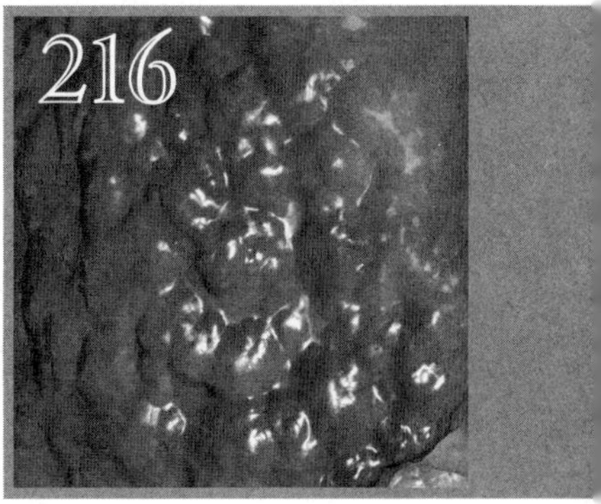
216

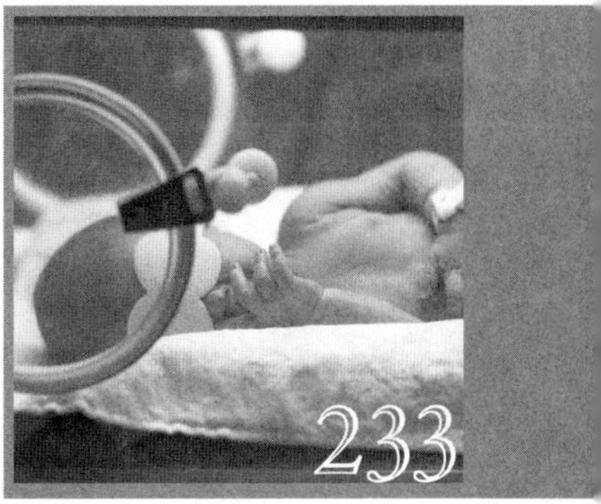
233

INTRODUCTION

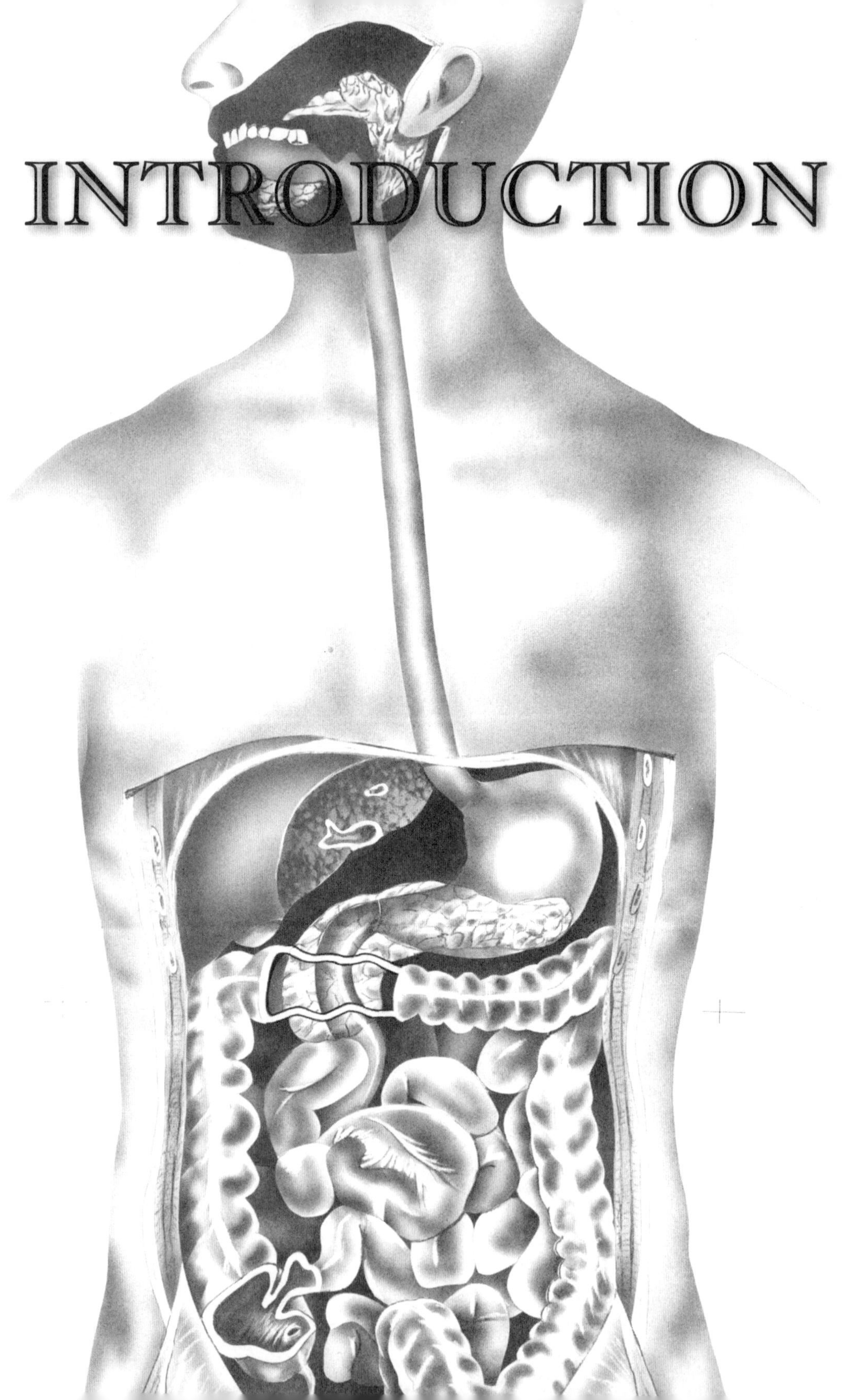

Humans eat for many different reasons: because they are hungry, because they are bored, because they are stressed, or simply because the food smells and tastes good. The biological reason for eating, however, is to replenish nutrients and to provide energy to support the body's functions. The task of the digestive system is to break down food into the elements that the body can use and to eliminate as waste whatever is left over.

One might believe that such a basic function would be well understood, with little left to learn. In fact, scientists are constantly discovering new things about how the digestive system does its job and how it interacts with other aspects of the body. Current research may help experts understand elements of health as diverse as how the digestive system affects immunity as well as its relationship to such important health concerns as heart disease, diabetes, and cancer. This book explores what happens to food in its journey through your body.

The entrance to the digestive tract is the mouth. Although little digestion of food actually takes place in the mouth, it contains important structures that aid in and begin the digestive process. These include the teeth, the tongue, and the salivary glands, which together reduce food into small particles and mix it with saliva in order to speed its progression through the digestive system. Human teeth are specifically designed for an omnivorous diet, with different shapes and surfaces for cutting and tearing meat and grinding grains and vegetables. The muscular tongue moves food around the mouth, pushing it toward the esophagus. The tongue is also covered with a mucous membrane, which contains taste buds, allowing humans to distinguish between different flavours, such as sweet, salty, sour, bitter, and umami (meaty). Saliva, which is secreted by the salivary glands, both moistens food and starts to dissolve it through the action of the enzyme amylase. The salivary glands make saliva to keep the mouth moist, but their action increases whenever chewing occurs. Salivary glands also increase their output in reaction to a stimulus that has been associated with food in the past, such as succulent odours or even a specific sight or sound related to food. So, in fact, people's mouths actually do water when expecting something tasty such as a sizzling grilled steak.

From the mouth, food passes through the esophagus, driven by the swallowing process. Swallowing is basically involuntary–once food reaches the back of the mouth the reflex to swallow takes over and cannot be retracted. Muscles in the esophagus then carry food to the stomach through a series of rhythmic contractions known as peristaltic waves. These waves continuously push the food down to the stomach. Amazingly, it takes only 10 seconds for food to move through the esophagus. When people eat in an upright position, liquids simply fall to the bottom of the esophagus and wait for the action of peristalsis to open the lower esophageal sphincter to allow their passage into the stomach.

The stomach is where the process of digestion begins in earnest. The stomach walls contain both a layer known as the gastric mucosa, which secretes gastric acid to dissolve food, and a layer of muscles, which contract to mix food and squeeze it through to the small intestine. Very few nutrients are actually absorbed into the body directly from the stomach, although it can absorb simple sugars. Liquids also pass easily between the stomach lining and the blood. Once the stomach has finished mashing and dissolving the food with digestive juices, the food exists as a semiliquid substance called chyme. At that point the duodenal bulb, where the stomach attaches to the small intestine, relaxes and opens, allowing the stomach contents to progress on the next phase of their journey.

The lower digestive tract consists of the small and large intestines, where nutrients are absorbed into the body and waste is eliminated. These two long tubes have a combined length of up to 9 metres (30 feet). In the body, they are folded and coiled in order to fit in the abdominal cavity. The long length of the intestines as well as the unique folded inner surface of the small intestine provide a large surface area, estimated to be some 4,500 square metres (5,400 square yards). This large surface area facilitates the absorption of nutrients.

The small intestine is in fact the principal organ of the digestive tract, as this is where most of the processes occur for the breakdown of carbohydrates, proteins, and fats into organic compounds, vitamins, and minerals that the body can use. The large intestine, or colon, completes the digestive process by absorbing water back into the body and compacting the remaining waste for elimination. It also contributes bacteria that help to synthesize a variety of important vitamins.

Another organ of the lower digestive tract is the appendix, a small hollow pouch attached near to where the small and large intestines are joined. Whether or not the appendix serves any function is still being studied. Removal of the appendix does not appear to interfere with normal bodily function, but some scientists suspect that it may serve as a reservoir of useful bacteria or help stimulate and develop the immune system.

Digestion is regulated by a number of important hormones, which are secreted from the liver, the pancreas, and the gastrointestinal tract, as well as from fat cells. These hormones include leptin, which controls hunger sensations by acting on cells in the hypothalamus in the brain; gastrin, which prompts the release of acid and increases muscle activity in the stomach; glucagon, which stimulates the release of glucose from the liver into the blood; and insulin, which stimulates the absorption of glucose from the blood into muscles and other tissues.

The transportation and uptake of glucose is the primary mechanism by which the body stores energy. Energy occurs in the form of glycogen in muscles and in the form of triglycerides in fat cells and is readily liberated when needed, such as during exercise or fasting. Inadequate production of insulin can lead to diabetes, in which the body is unable to effectively regulate the body's use of glucose.

A substantial part of the gastrointestinal tract is also occupied by lymphoid tissue, part of the body's immune defense system. The digestive system is one of the most critical points at which foreign and potentially dangerous substances can enter the body. The system's immune function is found primarily in the small intestine. For example, lymphocytes, a type of white blood cell, are present in the small intestine in the basement membrane, in the epithelial cells of the inner mucous layer, and in large groups of nodules known as Peyer patches. When these lymphocytes encounter a foreign substance, they respond by destroying the foreign cell or by adhering to its surface, interfering with its ability to invade tissue and rendering it harmless. Lymphocytes from the Peyer patches are also transported from the intestine back through the lymphatic system to the thoracic duct and dispersed from there throughout the body. Thus, the digestive tract also helps to maintain a reservoir of defense against infection wherever it might occur.

When all the parts of the digestive system are working as they should, carbohydrates, fats, and proteins are broken down and converted into energy for the body. This energy is used to support daily activities, to regulate body temperature, and to maintain the bodily systems that contribute to normal physiological function. In addition to the energy that food supplies, it also contains minerals and vitamins, which are dissolved and absorbed during the digestive process, and amino acids, which are necessary to the regeneration of cells. These are vital for the body's healthy functioning. A lack of vitamin D, for instance, which comes from egg yolks, fortified milk, and even sunlight, can cause rickets. A lack of iron, found in red meat, can cause anemia. Even the nondigestible dietary fibre in food plays an important role, providing roughage to stimulate bowel function and aiding in the elimination of potentially toxic or carcinogenic (cancer-causing) substances.

There are many diseases and disorders that may interfere with the proper functioning of the digestive system. Some of these conditions are congenital (present at birth). Others may be caused by infections or environmental factors or may be effects of nutritional deficiencies or of other diseases. In tropical countries, intestinal parasites such as pinworms are a frequent cause of digestive disorders. Many diseases of the digestive system are strongly linked to behavioral choices, such as alcohol and tobacco use. Among these are malignant diseases, such as cancer of the mouth, esophagus, stomach, or pancreas, and inflammatory conditions, such as pancreatitis. Worldwide, cirrhosis of the liver is one of the most frequent diseases occurring as a result of long-term, high-volume intake of alcohol.

Some diseases may also be caused by digestive malfunction. Two common examples are appendicitis and gallstones. Appendicitis is an inflammation of the appendix, usually occurring when the opening between the appendix and the large intestine becomes blocked, often by fecal matter. This prevents the appendix from emptying its contents into the intestine and leads to swelling and bacterial infection. Treatment for appendicitis is usually removal of the appendix. Gallstones are hardened deposits that form in the gallbladder, composed primarily of calcium bilirubinate (a brown-pigmented substance) and cholesterol. These stones are formed when the proportion of cholesterol in bile exceeds the level necessary to contain it in solution. At that point crystalline particles of cholesterol are formed, which may range from as small as a grain of sand to as large as a golfball in some instances. Risk factors for the formation of gallstones include obesity and high-calorie or high-cholesterol diets.

Even healthy people have occasional digestive disturbances, such as heartburn, diarrhea, and nausea. Heartburn, more technically known as gastroesophageal reflux disease (GERD), is the result of content from the stomach moving back up into the esophagus. It may occur occasionally after a large meal, but it may be aggravated by obesity or pregnancy, both of which create cramped conditions in the abdomen and put pressure on the stomach. Persistent reflux symptoms can lead to more serious diseases of the esophagus. Gastritis is an inflammation of the stomach lining that may be caused by contaminated food or by excessive alcohol intake. Traveler's diarrhea is almost always caused by ingestion of *Escherichia coli* bacteria, frequently on unwashed vegetables or in drinking water. Other types of indigestion may be the result of food sensitivities or allergies; of excessive intake of acidic foods such as coffee; of improper eating habits; or of stress. Indigestion resulting from these causes may range in severity from mild abdominal discomfort and intestinal gas to the more severe symptoms of irritable bowel syndrome, such as pain, cramping, and vomiting.

Ulcers are a relatively common disease of the stomach and can also be aggravated by stress. An ulcer is caused when the stomach lining is unable to protect itself from the stomach's own acidic gastric juices. The most common causes for erosion of the stomach lining are long-term overuse of anti-inflammatory drugs such as aspirin, known collectively as non-steroidal anti-inflammatory drugs or NSAIDS, and infection with the *Helicobacter pylori* bacterium. Globally, *H. pylori* is one of the most common causes of bacterial infection in humans, being particularly problematic in less-developed countries and even affecting roughly one-third of the U.S. population.

In this volume, readers will learn that many of the most serious diseases of the digestive system remain poorly understood and may often be difficult to diagnose. Because they all affect the digestive tract, a wide variety of diseases may manifest themselves in symptoms such as persistent diarrhea, blood in the stool, abdominal pain, nausea and vomiting, and loss of appetite. Many types of digestive disorders and cancers have been found to have some genetic component, although this may only cause a predisposition to the disease rather than being a direct cause.

Readers will also discover that, for most people, one of the most important keys to maintaining good overall health is treating the digestive system with respect. Eating a balanced diet that is high in fibre and low in fat, avoiding tobacco, using alcohol in moderation, and maintaining a healthy weight are all actions that will help to keep everything running smoothly–not just the digestive system.

CHAPTER 1

The Beginning of the Digestive Tract

The human digestive system plays a fundamental role in ensuring that all the foods and liquids we ingest are broken down into useful nutrients and chemicals. The digestive system consists primarily of the digestive tract, or the series of structures and organs through which food and liquids pass during their processing into forms that can be absorbed into the bloodstream and distributed to tissues. Other major components of the digestive system include glands that secrete juices and hormones necessary for the digestive process, as well as the terminal structures through which solid wastes pass in the process of elimination from the body.

The digestive tract begins at the lips and ends at the anus. It consists of the mouth, or oral cavity, with its teeth, for grinding the food, and its tongue, which serves to knead food and mix it with saliva. Then, there is the throat, or pharynx; the esophagus; the stomach; the small intestine, consisting of the duodenum, the jejunum, and the ileum; and the large intestine, consisting of the cecum, a closed-end sac connecting with the ileum, the ascending colon, the transverse colon, the descending colon, and the sigmoid colon, which terminates in the rectum. Glands contributing digestive juices include the salivary glands, the gastric glands in the stomach lining, the pancreas, and the liver and its adjuncts—the gallbladder and bile ducts. All of these organs and glands contribute to the physical and chemical breaking down of ingested food and to the eventual elimination of nondigestible wastes.

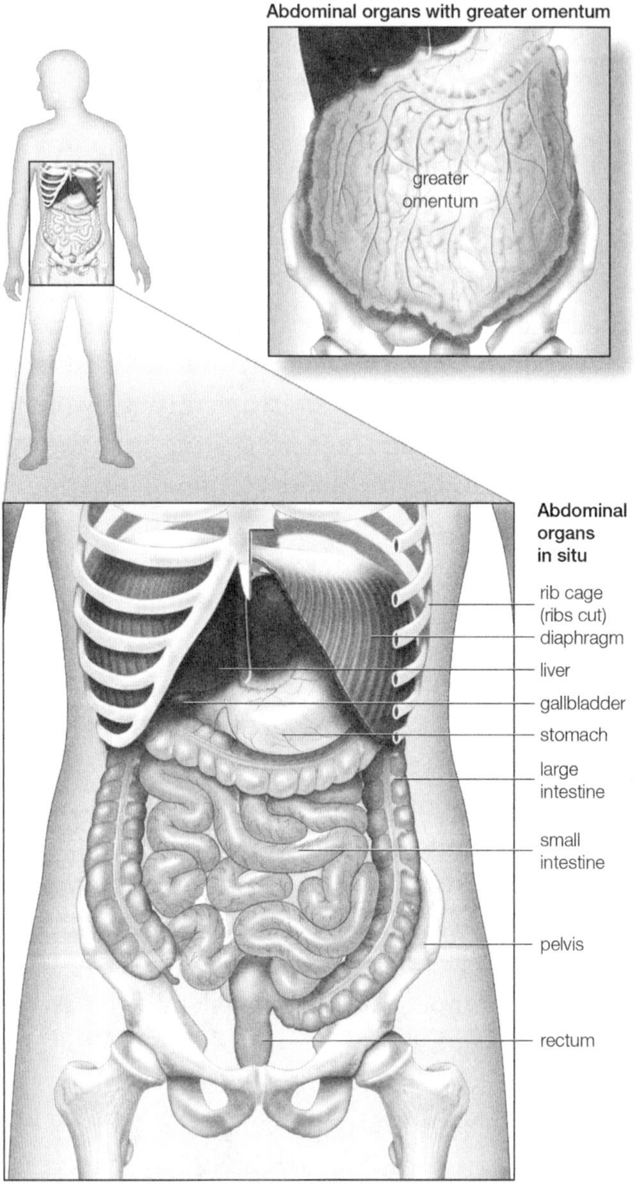

The abdominal organs are supported and protected by the bones of the pelvis and ribcage and are covered by the greater omentum, a fold of peritoneum that consists mainly of fat. Encyclopædia Britannica, Inc.

MOUTH AND ORAL STRUCTURES

Little digestion of food actually takes place in the mouth. However, through the process of mastication, or chewing, food is prepared in the mouth for transport through the upper digestive tract into the stomach and small intestine, where the principal digestive processes take place. Chewing is the first mechanical process to which food is subjected. Movements of the lower jaw in chewing are brought about by the muscles of mastication—the masseter, the temporal, the medial and lateral pterygoids, and the buccinator. The sensitivity of the periodontal membrane that surrounds and supports the teeth, rather than the power of the muscles of mastication, determines the force of the bite.

Mastication is not essential for adequate digestion. Chewing does aid digestion, however, by reducing food to small particles and mixing it with the saliva secreted by the salivary glands. The saliva lubricates and moistens dry food, while chewing distributes the saliva throughout the food mass. The movement of the tongue against the hard palate and the cheeks helps to form a rounded mass, or bolus, of food.

The Lips and Cheeks

The lips are soft, pliable anatomical structures that form the mouth margin. They are composed of a surface epidermis (skin), connective tissue, and a muscle layer. The edges of the lips are covered with reddish skin, sometimes called the vermilion border, and abundantly provided with sensitive nerve endings. The reddish skin is a transition layer between the outer, hair-bearing epidermis and the inner mucous membrane, or mucosa. The mucosa is rich in

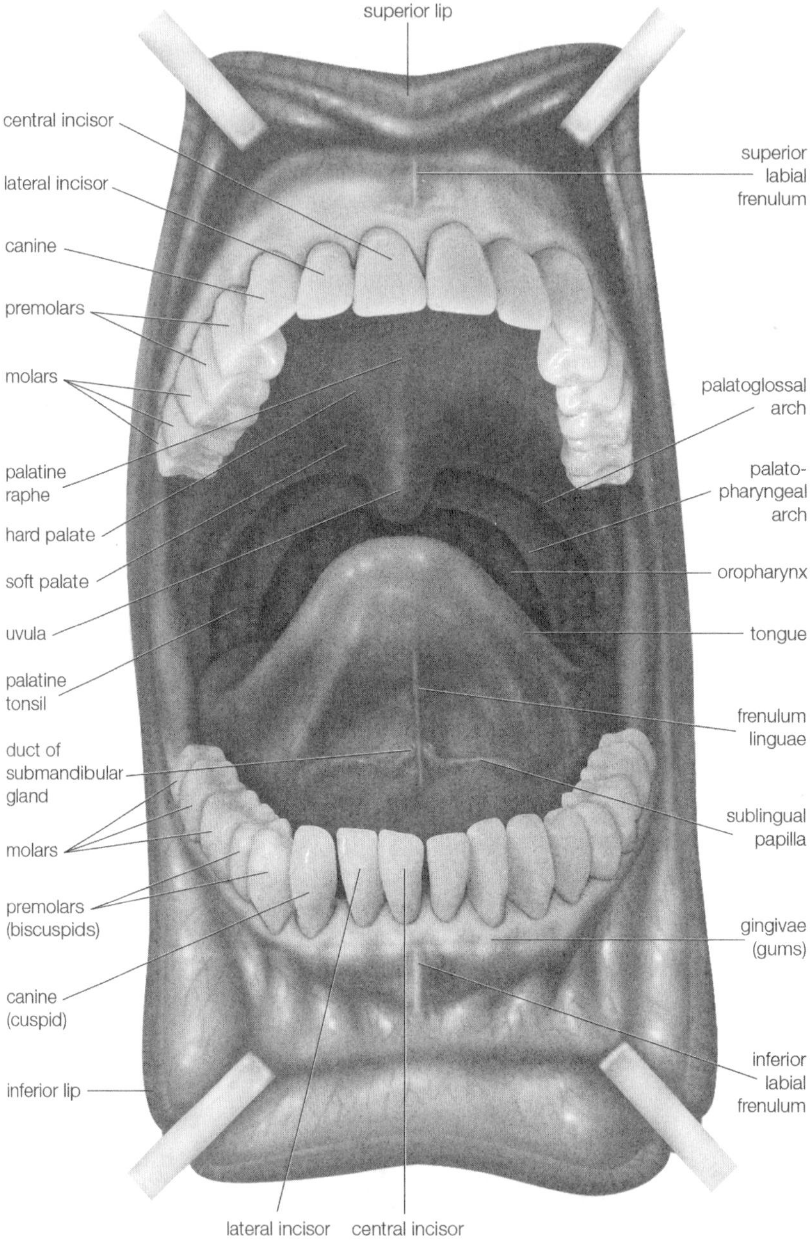

Anterior view of the oral cavity. Encyclopædia Britannica, Inc.

mucus-secreting glands, which together with saliva ensure adequate lubrication for the purposes of speech and mastication.

In newborn infants the inner surface is much thicker, with sebaceous glands and minute projections called papillae. These structural adaptations seem to aid the process of sucking. Most of the substance of each lip is supplied by the orbicularis oris muscle, which encircles the opening. This muscle and others that radiate out into the cheeks make possible the lips' many variations in shape and expression.

The cheeks, the sides of the mouth, are continuous with the lips and have a similar structure. A distinct fat pad is found in the subcutaneous tissue (the tissue beneath the skin) of the cheek. This pad is especially large in infants and is known as the sucking pad. On the inner surface of each cheek, opposite the second upper molar tooth, is a slight elevation that marks the opening of the parotid duct, leading from the parotid salivary gland, which is located in front of the ear. Just behind this gland are four to five mucus-secreting glands, the ducts of which open opposite the last molar tooth.

The lips are susceptible to diseases such as herpes simplex (fever blisters, or cold sores) and leukoplakia (white patches, which can be precancerous). In elderly men, ulcers on the vermilion border of the lower lip are frequently cancerous. The borders also may become cracked and inflamed from excessive drying by the weather, chemical irritants, inadequate moistening because of infection, or in reaction to antibiotics.

The Mouth

The mouth, which is also known as the oral (or buccal) cavity, is the orifice through which food and air enter the body. The mouth opens to the outside at the lips and empties into the throat at the rear. Its boundaries are defined by the lips, cheeks, hard and soft palates, and glottis. It is divided into two sections: the vestibule, the area between the cheeks and the teeth, and the oral cavity proper. The latter section is mostly filled by the tongue, a large muscle firmly anchored to the floor of the mouth by the frenulum linguae. In addition to its primary role in the intake and initial digestion of food, the mouth and its structures are essential in humans to the formation of speech.

The chief structures of the mouth are the teeth, which tear and grind ingested food into small pieces that are suitable for digestion; the tongue, which positions and mixes food and also carries sensory receptors for taste; and the palate, which separates the mouth from the nasal cavity, allowing separate passages for air and for food. All these structures, along with the lips, are involved in the formation of speech sounds by modifying the passage of air through the mouth.

The oral cavity and vestibule are entirely lined by mucous membranes containing numerous small glands that, along with the three pairs of salivary glands, bathe the mouth in fluid, keeping it moist and clear of food and other debris. Specialized membranes form both the gums (gingivae), which surround and support the teeth, and the surface of the tongue, on which the membrane is rougher in texture, containing many small papillae that hold the taste buds. The mouth's moist environment and the enzymes within its secretions help to soften food, facilitating swallowing and beginning the process of digestion.

The roof of the mouth is concave and is formed by the hard and soft palate. The hard palate is formed by the horizontal portions of the two palatine bones and the palatine portions of the maxillae, or upper jaws. The hard palate is covered by a thick, somewhat pale mucous membrane that is continuous with that of the gums and is bound to the upper jaw and palate bones by firm fibrous tissue. The soft palate is continuous with the hard palate in front. Posteriorly, it is continuous with the mucous membrane covering the floor of the nasal cavity. The soft palate is composed of the palatine aponeurosis—a strong, thin, fibrous sheet—and the glossopalatine and pharyngopalatine muscles. A small projection called the uvula hangs free from the posterior of the soft palate.

The floor of the mouth can be seen only when the tongue is raised. In the midline is the frenulum linguae which—in addition to its function in anchoring the tongue to the floor of the mouth—binds each lip to the gums. On each side of this is a slight fold called a sublingual papilla, from which the ducts of the submandibular salivary glands open. Running outward and backward from each sublingual papilla is a ridge (the plica sublingualis) that marks the upper edge of the sublingual (under the tongue) salivary gland and onto which most of the ducts of that gland open.

The Gums

The gums, also known as the gingivae, are made up of connective tissue covered with mucous membrane. The mucous membrane is connected by thick fibrous tissue to the membrane surrounding the bones of the jaw. The gum membrane rises to form a collar around the base of the crown (exposed portion) of each tooth. Thus, the gums are attached to and surround the necks of the teeth and adjacent alveolar bone.

Healthy gums are pink, stippled, and tough and have a limited sensitivity to pain, temperature, and pressure. The gums are separated from the alveolar mucosa, which is red, by a scalloped line that approximately follows the contours of the teeth. The edges of the gums around the teeth are free and extend as small wedges into the spaces between the teeth (interdental papillae). Internally, fibres of the periodontal membrane enter the gum and hold it tightly against the teeth. Changes in colour, loss of stippling, or abnormal sensitivity are early signs of gum inflammation, or gingivitis.

Gum tissue is rich in blood vessels and receives branches from the alveolar arteries. These vessels—called alveolar because of their relationship to the alveoli dentales, or tooth sockets—also supply blood to the teeth and the spongy bone of the upper and lower jaws, in which the teeth are lodged. Before the erupting teeth enter the mouth cavity, gum pads develop; these are slight elevations of the overlying oral mucous membrane. When tooth eruption is complete, the gum embraces the neck region of each tooth.

The Teeth

The teeth are hard, white structures found in the mouth. Usually used for mastication, the teeth of different vertebrate species are sometimes specialized. The teeth of snakes, for example, are very thin and sharp and usually curve backward. They function in capturing prey but not in chewing, because snakes swallow their food whole. The teeth of carnivorous mammals, such as cats and dogs, are more pointed than those of primates, including humans. The canines are long, and the premolars lack flat grinding surfaces, being more adapted to cutting and shearing (often the more posterior molars are lost). On the other hand, herbivores such as cows and horses have very large, flat premolars and molars with complex ridges and cusps; the canines are often totally absent.

The differences in the shapes of teeth are functional adaptations. Few animals can digest cellulose, yet the plant cells used as food by herbivores are enclosed in cellulose cell walls that must be broken down before the cell contents can be exposed to the action of digestive enzymes. By contrast, the animal cells in meat are not encased in nondigestible matter and can be acted upon directly by digestive enzymes. Consequently, chewing is not so essential for carnivores as it is for herbivores. Humans, who are omnivores (eaters of plants and animal tissue), have teeth that belong, functionally and structurally, somewhere between the extremes of specialization attained by the teeth of carnivores and herbivores.

Each tooth consists of a crown and one or more roots. The crown is the functional part of the tooth that is visible above the gum. The root is the unseen portion that supports and fastens the tooth in the jawbone. The shapes of the crowns and the roots vary in different parts of the mouth and from one animal to another. The teeth on one side of the jaw are essentially a mirror image of those located on the opposite side. The upper teeth differ from the lower and are complementary to them.

Tooth Structure

All true teeth have the same general structure and consist of three layers. In mammals an outer layer of enamel—which is wholly inorganic and is the hardest tissue in the body—covers part or all of the crown of the tooth. The middle layer of the tooth is composed of dentine, which is less hard than enamel and similar in composition to bone. The dentine forms the main bulk, or core, of each tooth and extends almost the entire length of the tooth, being covered by enamel on the crown portion and by cementum on the roots. Dentine is nourished by the pulp, which is the innermost portion of the tooth.

The pulp consists of cells, tiny blood vessels, and a nerve and occupies a cavity located in the centre of the tooth. The pulp canal is long and narrow with an enlargement, called the pulp chamber, in the coronal end. The pulp canal extends almost the whole length of the tooth and communicates with the body's general nutritional and nervous systems through the apical foramina (holes) at the end of the roots. Below the gumline extends the root of the tooth, which is covered at least partially by cementum. The latter is similar in structure to bone but is less hard than dentine. Cementum affords a thin covering to the root and serves as a medium for attachment of the fibres that hold the tooth to the surrounding tissue (periodontal membrane). Gum is attached to the adjacent alveolar bone and to the cementum of each tooth by fibre bundles.

Tooth Form and Function

Like most other mammals, humans have two successive sets of teeth during life. The first set of teeth are called primary, or deciduous, ones, and the second set are called permanent ones. Humans have 20 primary and 32 permanent teeth.

Primary teeth differ from permanent teeth in being smaller, having more pointed cusps, being whiter and more prone to wear, and having relatively large pulp chambers and small, delicate roots. The primary teeth begin to appear about six months after birth, and the primary dentition is complete by age $2^1/_2$. Shedding begins about age 5 or 6 and is finished by age 13. The primary teeth are shed when their roots are resorbed as the permanent teeth push toward the mouth cavity in the course of their growth.

In humans the primary dentition consists of 20 teeth—four incisors, two canines, and four molars in each jaw. The primary molars are replaced in the adult dentition by the premolars, or bicuspid teeth. The 12 adult molars of the permanent dentition erupt (emerge from the gums) behind the primary teeth and do not replace any of these, giving a total of 32 teeth in the permanent dentition. The permanent dentition is thus made up of four incisors, two canines, four premolars, and six molars in each jaw.

Incisor teeth are the teeth at the front of the mouth, and they are adapted for plucking, cutting, tearing, and holding. The biting portion of an incisor is wide and thin, making a chisel-shaped cutting edge. The upper incisors have a delicate tactile sense that enables them to be used for identifying objects in the mouth by nibbling. Next to the incisor on each side is a canine, or cuspid tooth. It frequently is pointed and rather peglike in shape and, like the incisors, has the function of cutting and tearing food.

Premolars and molars have a series of elevations, or cusps, that are used for breaking up particles of food. Behind each canine are two premolars, which can both cut and grind food. Each premolar has two cusps (hence the name bicuspid). The molars, by contrast, are used exclusively for crushing and grinding. They are the teeth farthest back in the mouth. Each molar typically has four or five cusps. The third molar in humans tends to be variable in size, number of roots, cusp pattern, and eruption. The number of roots for each type of tooth varies from one for incisors, canines, and premolars to two or three for molars.

The Tongue

The tongue is located on the floor of the mouth and is an organ that is capable of various muscular movements. In

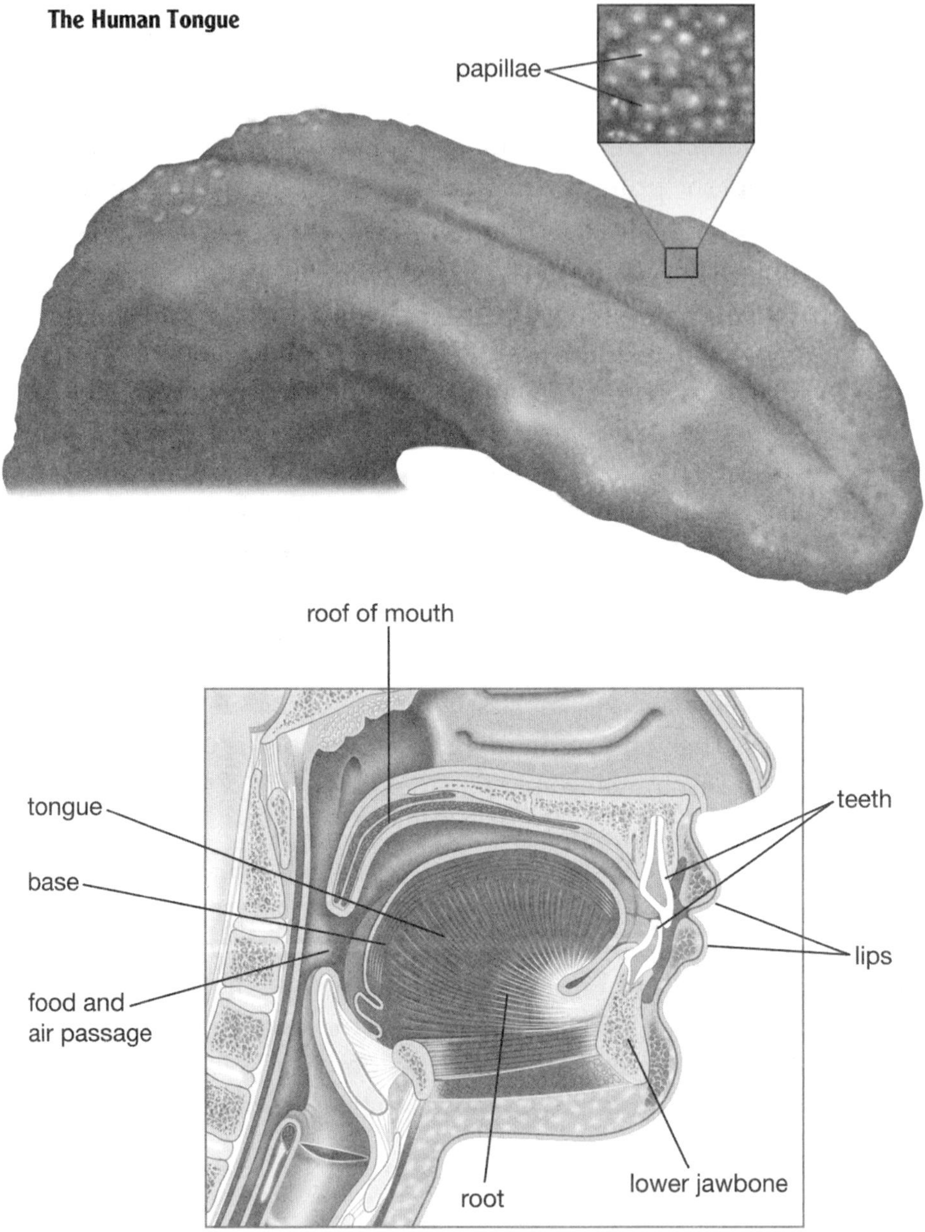

Taste buds on the human tongue exhibit sensitivity to specific tastes.
Encyclopædia Britannica, Inc.

some animals (e.g., frogs) the tongue is elongated and adapted to capturing insect prey. The tongues of certain reptiles function primarily as sensory organs, whereas cats and some other mammals use their tongues as instruments for grooming and cleaning. In mammals the tongue aids in creating negative pressure within the oral cavity that enables sucking, which is especially important for the ability of human infants and other newborn mammals to feed in the first hours and days of life. The tongue is also an important accessory organ in chewing and swallowing. In conjunction with the cheeks, it is able to guide and maintain food between the upper and lower teeth until mastication is complete. The tongue also is a major bearer of taste buds, is an aid to speech in humans, and has glands capable of producing some of the saliva necessary for swallowing.

The mammalian tongue consists of a mass of interwoven, striated (striped) muscles interspaced with glands and fat and covered with mucous membrane, which varies in different regions. The tongue is attached to the lower jaw, the hyoid bone (a U-shaped bone between the lower jaw and the larynx), the skull, the soft palate, and the pharynx by its extrinsic muscles. It is bound to the floor of the mouth and to the epiglottis (a plate of cartilage that serves as a lid for the larynx) by folds of mucous membrane.

In humans the front tips and margins of the tongue usually touch the teeth, aiding in swallowing and speech. The top surface, or dorsum, contains numerous projections of the mucous membrane called papillae. They contain taste buds, which are sensitive to chemical constituents of food, and serous glands that secrete some of the fluid in saliva.

The base, or upper rear portion, of the tongue has no papillae, but aggregated lymphatic tissue (lingual tonsils)

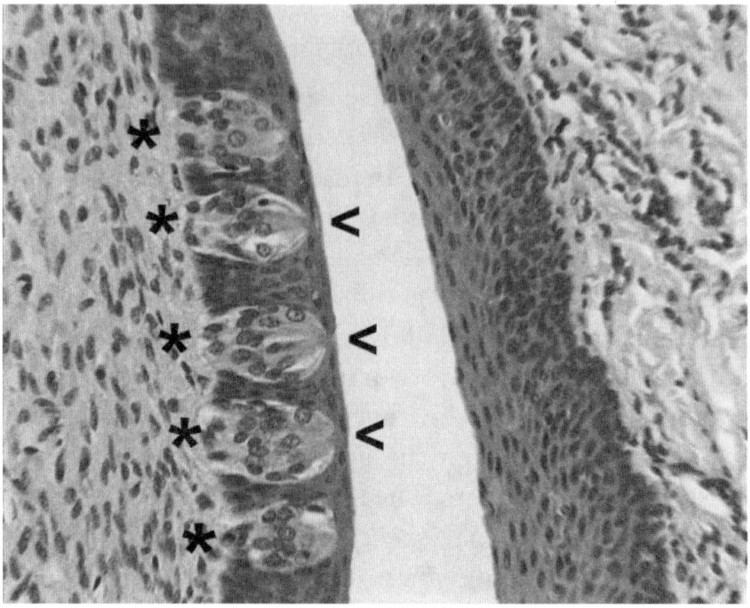

Circumvallate papillae, located on the surface of the back part of the tongue, contain taste buds (indicated by asterisks). Specialized hairlike structures (microvilli) located at the surface of taste buds in minute openings called taste pores (indicated by arrows) detect dissolved chemicals ingested in food, leading to the activation of receptor cells in the taste buds and the sensation of taste. Uniformed Services University of the Health Sciences (USUHS)

and serous and mucus-secreting glands are present. The inferior, or under, surface leads from the tip of the tongue to the floor of the mouth. Its mucous membrane is smooth, devoid of papillae, and purple in colour from the many blood vessels present. The root, the remainder of the underside that lies on the mouth's floor, contains bundles of nerves, arteries, and muscles that branch to the other tongue regions.

An important function of the tongue is taste sensation, which is derived from taste receptor cells located in clusters within taste buds. Taste buds are able to transmit information about taste and flavour to the nervous system. In humans there may be anywhere from 50 to 150 taste receptor cells within an individual taste bud. Taste buds are innervated by nerves that respond to chemicals from food in solution, thereby providing the sensation of taste. There are five fundamental taste sensations: salty, sweet, sour (acid), bitter, and umami, which represents the taste of amino acids. Each receptor cell is sensitive to a particular taste—for example, responding only to salt or only to umami. The total flavour of a food comes from the combination of taste, smell, touch, texture or consistency, and temperature sensations.

Among the disorders to which the tongue is subject are cancer, leukoplakia (white patches), fungus infection, congenital defects, and a variety of symptoms caused by disease elsewhere in the body. Surgical removal of this organ makes speech and swallowing difficult.

The Salivary Glands

Food is tasted and mixed with saliva that is secreted by several sets of glands. Besides the many minute glands that secrete saliva, there are three major pairs of salivary glands: the parotid, the submandibular, and the sublingual glands. The parotid glands, the largest of the pairs, are located at the side of the face, below and in front of each ear. The parotid glands are enclosed in sheaths that limit the extent of their swelling when inflamed, as in mumps. The submandibular glands, which are rounded in shape, lie near the inner side of the lower jawbone, in front of the sternomastoid muscle (the prominent muscle of the jaw). The sublingual glands lie directly under the mucous membrane covering the floor of the mouth beneath the tongue.

The salivary glands are of the type called racemose, from the Latin *racemosus* ("full of clusters"), because of the

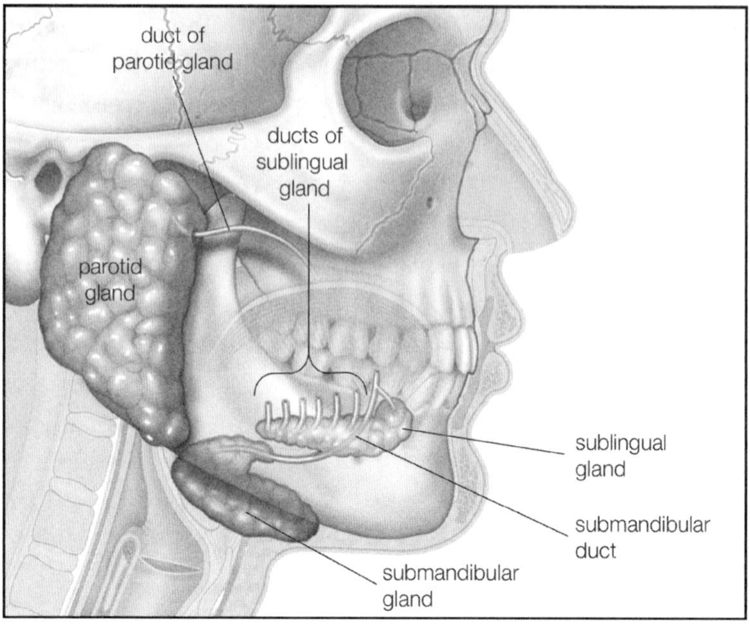

The three major pairs of salivary glands. Encyclopædia Britannica, Inc.

clusterlike arrangement of their secreting cells in rounded sacs, called acini, attached to freely branching systems of ducts. The walls of the acini surround a small central cavity known as an alveolus. In the walls of the acini are pyramidal secreting cells and some flat, star-shaped contractile cells called myoepithelial, or basket, cells. The latter cells are thought to contract, like the similar myoepithelial cells of the breast, which by their contraction expel milk from the milk ducts.

The secreting cells may be of the serous or the mucous type. The latter type secretes mucin, the chief constituent of mucus; the former, a watery fluid containing the enzyme amylase. The secreting cells of the parotid glands are of the serous type. Those of the submandibular glands, of both serous and mucous types, with the serous cells outnumbering the mucous cells by four to one. The acini of the sublingual glands are composed primarily of mucous cells.

The salivary glands are controlled by the two divisions of the autonomic nervous system, the sympathetic and the parasympathetic. The parasympathetic nerve supply regulates secretion by the acinar cells and causes the blood vessels to dilate. Functions regulated by the sympathetic nerves include secretion by the acinar cells, constriction of blood vessels, and, presumably, contraction of the myoepithelial cells. Normally secretion of saliva is constant, regardless of the presence of food in the mouth. The amount of saliva secreted in 24 hours usually amounts to 1–1.5 litres (about 0.3–0.4 gallon). When something touches the gums, the tongue, or some region of the mouth lining, or when chewing occurs, the amount of saliva secreted increases. The stimulating substance need not be food—dry sand in the mouth or even moving the jaws and tongue when the mouth is empty increases the salivary flow.

This coupling of direct stimulation to the oral mucosa with increased salivation is known as the unconditioned salivary reflex. When an individual learns that a particular sight, sound, smell, or other stimulus is regularly associated with food, that stimulus alone may suffice to stimulate increased salivary flow. This response is known as the conditioned salivary reflex.

SALIVA

Saliva is a thick, colourless, opalescent fluid that is constantly present in the mouth. It has numerous functions, though the most important relate to its ability to dissolve food and to lubricate the segments of the upper digestive tract. When saliva dissolves some of the chewed food, it not only eases the passage of food to the stomach but also creates a solution that stimulates the taste buds. The lubricating actions of saliva also serve to moisten the inside of the mouth to help with speech.

The composition of saliva varies, but its principal components are water, inorganic ions similar to those commonly found in blood plasma, and a number of organic constituents, including salivary proteins, free amino acids, and the enzymes lysozyme and amylase (ptyalin). Although saliva is slightly acidic, the bicarbonates and phosphates contained within it serve as buffers and maintain the pH, or hydrogen ion concentration, of saliva relatively constant under ordinary conditions.

Amylase is a starch-digesting enzyme that initiates the process of enzymatic hydrolysis, which in turn dissolves food. Amylase splits starch (a polysaccharide containing many sugar molecules bound in a continuous chain) into molecules of the double sugar maltose. Many carnivores, such as dogs and cats, have no amylase in their saliva. Therefore, their natural diet contains very little starch.

The concentrations of bicarbonate, chloride, potassium, and sodium in saliva are directly related to the rate of their flow. There is also a direct relation between bicarbonate concentration and the partial pressure of carbon dioxide in the blood. The concentration of chloride in the blood varies from 5 millimoles per litre at low flow rates to 70 millimoles per litre when the flow rate is high. The sodium concentrations in similar circumstances vary from 5 millimoles per litre to 100 millimoles per litre. The concentration of potassium in the blood is often higher than that in the blood plasma, up to 20 millimoles per litre, which accounts for the sharp and metallic taste of saliva when flow is brisk.

The constant flow of saliva keeps the oral cavity and teeth moist and comparatively free from food residues, sloughed epithelial cells, and foreign particles. Laboratory studies of saliva have demonstrated that it inhibits the growth of bacteria. Indeed, lysozyme, the other enzyme occurring in saliva, has the ability to lyse, or dissolve, certain bacteria. The secretion of saliva also provides a mechanism whereby certain organic and inorganic substances can be excreted from the body, including mercury, lead, potassium iodide, bromide, morphine, ethyl alcohol, and certain antibiotics such as penicillin, streptomycin, and chlortetracycline.

Although saliva is not essential to life, its absence results in a number of inconveniences, including dryness of the oral mucous membrane, poor oral hygiene because of bacterial overgrowth, a greatly diminished sense of taste, and difficulties with speech.

CHAPTER 2

THE PASSAGE OF FOOD TO THE STOMACH

The passage of food into the stomach and the breakdown of food into progressively smaller particles within the stomach are processes facilitated by muscular contractions. For example, muscles aid in swallowing and pushing food through the pharynx (throat). Likewise, a series of rhythmic muscle contractions serves to move ingested products downward through the esophagus, toward the stomach. Upon entering the stomach, foods are exposed to gastric juices, which help to dissolve the particles. The powerful grinding contractions of the stomach muscle mix the gastric contents, churning them into a semifluid mass known as chyme, which is then able to advance to the lower portions of the digestive tract.

The active role of the stomach in digestion helps to convert foods into chemical forms that the body can utilize. The efficiency by which it does this enables the body to extract an abundance of nutrients from chyme, especially as it advances through the intestines, where specialized transporters in the epithelial lining readily absorb and transfer nutrients to the bloodstream for distribution to the body's tissues.

SWALLOWING

Swallowing is the act of passing food from the mouth, by way of the pharynx and esophagus, to the stomach. Three stages are involved in swallowing food.

The first begins in the mouth. There, food is mixed with saliva for lubrication and placed on the back of the tongue. The mouth closes, and the soft portion of the roof of the mouth (soft palate) rises so that the passageway between the nasal and oral cavities is closed off. The tongue rolls backward, propelling food into the oral pharynx, a chamber behind the mouth that functions to transport food and air.

Once food enters the pharynx, the second stage of swallowing begins. Respiration is temporarily inhibited as the larynx, or voice box, rises to close the glottis (the opening to the air passage). Pressure within the mouth and pharynx pushes food toward the esophagus. At the beginning of the esophagus there is a muscular constrictor, the upper esophageal sphincter (or cricopharyngeal muscle), which relaxes and opens when food approaches. Food passes from the pharynx into the esophagus. The upper esophageal sphincter then immediately closes, preventing flow of food back into the mouth.

Once food is in the esophagus, the final phase of swallowing begins. The larynx lowers, the glottis opens, and breathing resumes. From the time food leaves the mouth until it passes the upper sphincter, only about one second of time elapses, during which all these body mechanisms spontaneously occur. After passing the upper sphincter, movements in the esophagus carry food to the stomach. Rhythmic muscular contractions (peristaltic waves) and pressure within the esophagus push the food downward. Folds in the esophageal wall stretch out as materials pass by them and again contract once they have passed. At the lower end of the esophagus, the lower esophageal sphincter relaxes and food enters the stomach. The sphincter then closes again to prevent reflux of gastric juices and food materials.

Swallowing is basically an involuntary reflex; one cannot swallow unless there is saliva or some substance to be swallowed. Initially, food is voluntarily moved to the rear of the oral cavity, but once food reaches the back of the mouth, the reflex to swallow takes over and cannot be retracted.

Swallowing is influenced by bodily position. Liquids swallowed when the body is in an upright or horizontal position flow by gravity rapidly to the stomach. In the head-down position, however, liquids remain at the beginning of the esophagus, and several swallows and peristaltic waves may be necessary to evacuate the liquid. If a person swallows food connected to a string with counterweights attached outside of the body, he can only overcome 5 to 10 grams (.17–.35 ounces) of weight resistance. Dogs can swallow food with a resistance of 50 to 500 grams (1.76–17.6 ounces). Essentially, the swallowing capacity of humans is much weaker than that of other animals. The temperature of foods also affects a person's swallowing capacity. Very cold liquids (1–3 °C [34–37 °F]) slow down or completely stop peristaltic movement in the esophagus. In contrast, liquids at high temperature (58–61 °C [136–142 °F]) increase peristaltic movements.

Afflictions affecting swallowing include paralysis of the pharynx, failure of the esophageal sphincters to open properly, and spastic contractions of the esophageal muscle walls. Any of these may be caused by physical or psychological complications.

THE PHARYNX

The pharynx, or throat, is the passageway leading from the mouth and nose to the esophagus and larynx. The pharynx permits the passage of swallowed solids and

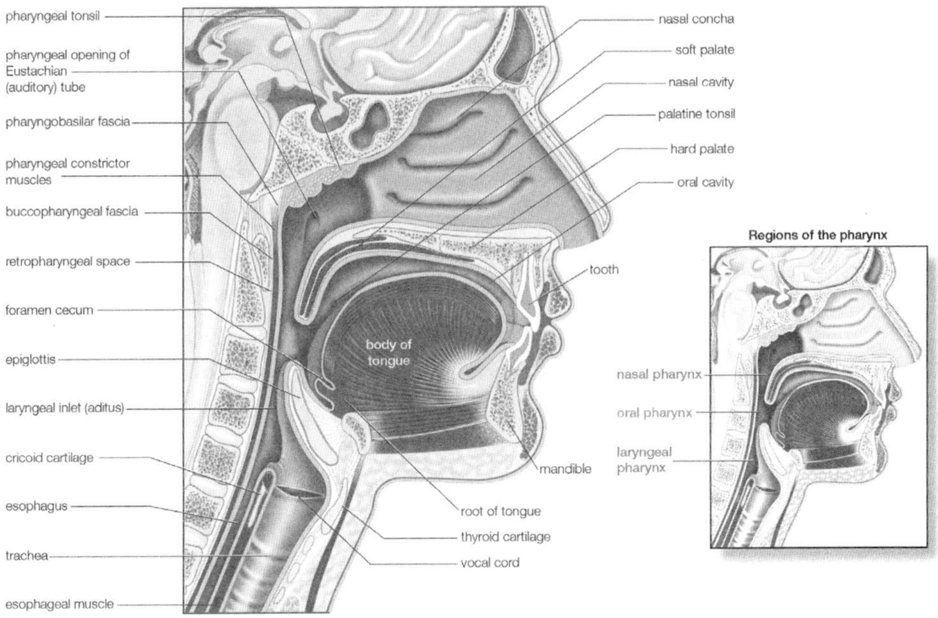

Sagittal section of the pharynx. Encyclopædia Britannica, Inc.

liquids into the esophagus, or gullet, and conducts air to and from the trachea, or windpipe, during respiration. The pharynx also connects on either side with the cavity of the middle ear by way of the Eustachian tube and provides for equalization of air pressure on the eardrum membrane, which separates the cavity of the middle ear from the external ear canal.

The pharynx has roughly the form of a flattened funnel. It is attached to the surrounding structures but is loose enough to permit gliding of the pharyngeal wall against them in the movements of swallowing. The principal muscles of the pharynx, involved in the mechanics of swallowing, are the three pharyngeal constrictors, which overlap each other slightly and form the primary musculature of the side and rear pharyngeal walls.

There are three main divisions of the pharynx: the oral pharynx, the nasal pharynx, and the laryngeal pharynx. The latter two are airways, whereas the oral pharynx is shared by both the respiratory and digestive tracts. On either side of the opening between the mouth cavity and the oral pharynx is a palatine tonsil, so called because of its proximity to the palate. Each palatine tonsil is located between two vertical folds of mucous membrane called the glossopalatine arches. The nasal pharynx, above, is separated from the oral pharynx by the soft palate. Another pair of tonsils are located on the roof of the nasal pharynx. The pharyngeal tonsils, also known as the adenoids, are part of the body's immune system. When the pharyngeal tonsils become grossly swollen (which often occurs during childhood) they occlude the airway. The laryngeal pharynx and the lower part of the oral pharynx are hidden by the root of the tongue.

The first stage of swallowing consists of passage of the bolus into the pharynx. Entry of the bolus into the nasal pharynx is prevented by the elevation of the soft palate against the posterior pharyngeal wall. As the bolus is forced into the pharynx, the larynx moves upward and forward under the base of the tongue. The superior pharyngeal constrictor muscles contract, initiating a rapid pharyngeal peristaltic, or squeezing, contraction that moves down the pharynx, propelling the bolus in front of it. The walls and structures of the lower pharynx are elevated to engulf the oncoming mass of food. The epiglottis, a lidlike covering that protects the entrance to the larynx, diverts the bolus to the pharynx. The upper esophageal sphincter, which has kept the esophagus closed until this point, relaxes as the bolus approaches and allows it to enter the upper esophagus. The pharyngeal peristaltic contraction continues into the esophagus and becomes the primary esophageal peristaltic contraction.

THE ESOPHAGUS

The esophagus is a relatively straight muscular tube through which food passes from the pharynx to the stomach. It is about 25 centimeters (10 inches) in length; the width varies from 1.5 to 2 cm (about 1 inch). Anatomically, it lies behind the trachea and heart and in front of the spinal column; it passes through the muscular diaphragm before entering the stomach. In addition to the muscular sphincters that close off both of its ends, the esophagus also contains four longitudinal layers of tissue, which play a role in enabling the tube to contract or expand to allow for the passage of food.

The four esophageal layers are the mucosa, submucosa, muscularis, and tunica adventitia. The mucosa is made up of stratified squamous epithelium containing numerous mucous glands. The submucosa is a thick, loose fibrous layer connecting the mucosa to the muscularis. Together the mucosa and submucosa form long longitudinal folds, so that a cross section of the esophagus opening would be star-shaped.

The muscularis is composed of an inner layer, in which the fibres are circular, and an outer layer of longitudinal fibres. Both muscle groups are wound around and along the alimentary tract, but the inner one has a very tight spiral, so that the windings are virtually circular, whereas the outer one has a very slowly unwinding spiral that is virtually longitudinal. The outer layer of the esophagus, the tunica adventitia, is composed of loose fibrous tissue that connects the esophagus with neighbouring structures. Except during the act of swallowing, the esophagus is normally

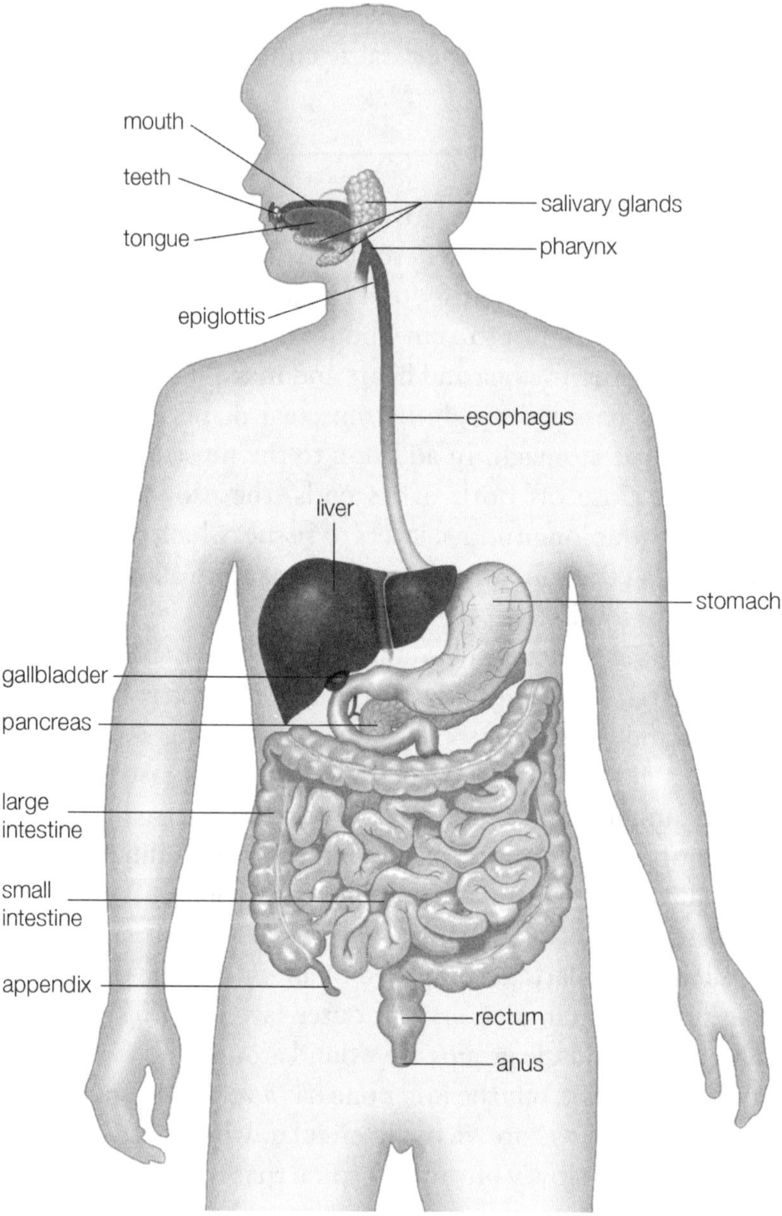

The human digestive system as seen from the front.
Encyclopædia Britannica, Inc.

empty, and its lumen, or channel, is essentially closed by the longitudinal folds of the mucosal and submucosal layers.

The upper third of the esophagus is composed of striated (voluntary) muscle. The middle third is a mixture of striated and smooth (involuntary) muscle, and the lower third consists only of smooth muscle. The two sphincter muscles of the esophagus act like drawstrings in closing channels. Both sphincters normally remain closed except during the act of swallowing. The upper esophageal sphincter (or cricopharyngeus muscle) is located at the level of the cricoid cartilage (a single ring-like cartilage forming the lower part of the larynx wall). The lower esophageal sphincter encircles the 3 to 4 cm (1.2 to 1.6 inches) of the esophagus that pass through an opening in the diaphragm called the diaphragmatic hiatus. The lower esophageal sphincter is maintained in tension at all times, except in response to a descending contraction wave, at which point it relaxes momentarily to allow the release of gas (belching) or vomiting. The lower esophageal sphincter has an important role, therefore, in protecting the esophagus from the reflux of gastric contents with changes in body position or with alterations of intragastric pressure.

Transport through the esophagus is accomplished by the primary esophageal peristaltic contractions, which originate in the pharynx. Transport of material through the esophagus takes approximately 10 seconds. When the bolus arrives at the junction with the stomach, the lower esophageal sphincter relaxes and the bolus enters the stomach. If the bolus is too large, or if the peristaltic contraction is too weak, the bolus may become arrested in the middle or lower esophagus. When this occurs, secondary peristaltic contractions originate around the bolus in response to the local distension of the esophageal wall and propel the bolus into the stomach.

When a liquid is swallowed, its transport through the esophagus depends somewhat on the position of the body and the effects of gravity. When swallowed in a horizontal or head-down position, liquids are handled in the same manner as solids, with the liquid moving immediately ahead of the advancing peristaltic contraction. (The high pressures and strong contractions of the esophageal peristaltic wave make it possible for animals with very long necks, such as the giraffe, to transport liquids through the esophagus for many feet.) When the body is in the upright position, however, liquids enter the esophagus and fall by gravity to the lower end. There they await the arrival of the peristaltic contraction and the opening of the lower esophageal sphincter (8 to 10 seconds) before being emptied into the stomach.

Disorders of the esophagus include ulceration and bleeding; heartburn, caused by gastric juices in the esophagus; achalasia, an inability to swallow or to pass food from the esophagus to the stomach, caused by destruction of the nerve endings in the walls of the esophagus; scleroderma, a collagen disease; and spasms of the esophageal muscles.

In some vertebrates the esophagus is not merely a tubular connection between the pharynx and the stomach but rather may serve as a storage reservoir or an ancillary digestive organ. In many birds, for example, an expanded region of the esophagus anterior to the stomach forms a thin-walled crop, which is the bird's principal organ for the temporary storage of food. Some birds use the crop to carry food to their young.

Ruminant mammals, such as the cow, are often said to have four "stomachs." Actually, the first three of these chambers (rumen, reticulum, and omasum) are thought to be derived from the esophagus. Vast numbers of bacteria and protozoans live in the rumen and reticulum. When food enters these chambers, the microbes begin to digest and ferment it, breaking down not only protein, starch, and fats but cellulose as well. The larger, coarser material is periodically regurgitated as the cud, and after further chewing the cud is reswallowed. Slowly the products of microbial action, and some of the microbes themselves, move into the cow's true stomach and intestine, where further digestion and absorption take place. Since the cow, like other mammals, has no cellulose-digesting enzymes of its own, it relies upon the digestive activity of these symbiotic microbes in its digestive tract. Much of the cellulose in the cow's herbivorous diet, which otherwise would have no nutritive value, is thereby made available to the cow.

THE STOMACH

The stomach receives ingested food and liquids from the esophagus and retains them for grinding and mixing with gastric juice so that food particles are smaller and more soluble. The main functions of the stomach are to commence the digestion of carbohydrates and proteins, to convert the meal into chyme, and to discharge the chyme into the small intestine periodically as the physical and chemical condition of the mixture is rendered suitable for the next phase of digestion.

The stomach is located in the left upper part of the abdomen immediately below the diaphragm. In front of the stomach are the liver, part of the diaphragm, and the anterior abdominal wall. Behind it are the pancreas, the left kidney, the left adrenal gland, the spleen, and the colon. The stomach is more or less concave on its right side, convex on its left. The concave border is called the

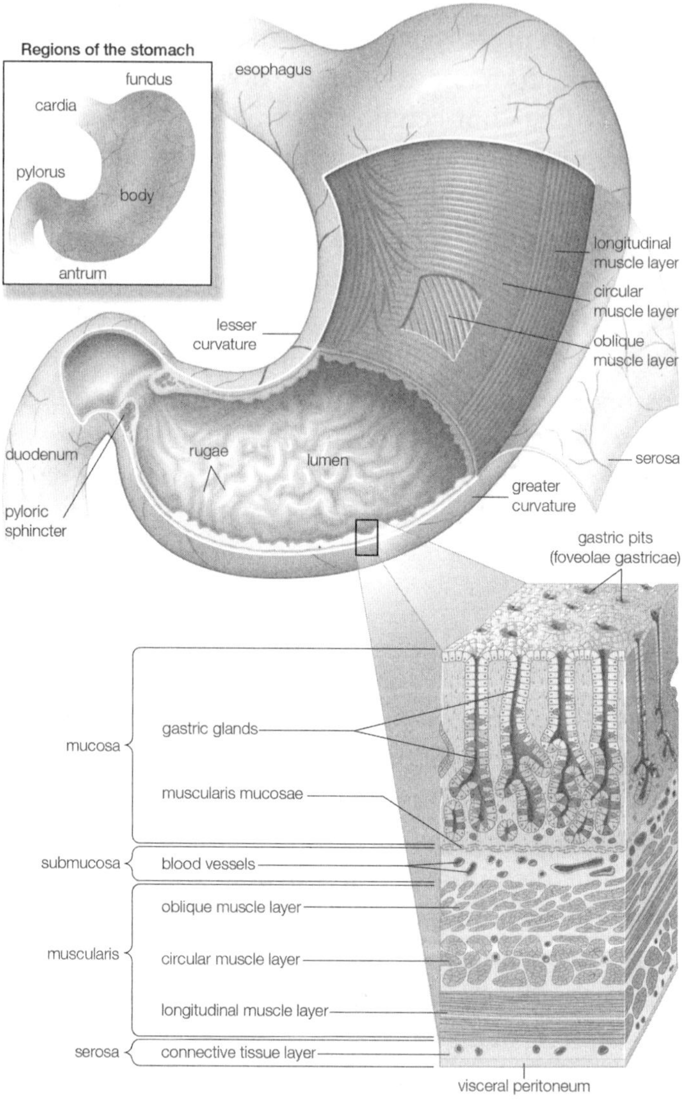

The stomach has three layers of muscle: an outer longitudinal layer, a middle circular layer, and an inner oblique layer. The inner lining consists of four layers: the serosa, the muscularis, the submucosa, and the mucosa. The mucosa is densely packed with gastric glands, which contain cells that produce digestive enzymes, hydrochloric acid, and mucus. Encyclopædia Britannica, Inc.

lesser curvature; the convex border, the greater curvature. When the stomach is empty, its mucosal lining is thrown into numerous longitudinal folds, known as rugae. These tend to disappear when the stomach is distended.

The cardia is the opening from the esophagus into the stomach. The uppermost part of the stomach, located above the entrance of the esophagus, is the fundus. The fundus adapts to the varying volume of ingested food by relaxing its muscular wall. It frequently contains a gas bubble, especially after a meal. The largest part of the stomach is known simply as the body. It serves primarily as a reservoir for ingested food and liquids. The antrum, the lowermost part of the stomach, is somewhat funnel-shaped, with its wide end joining the lower part of the body and its narrow end connecting with the pyloric canal, which empties into the duodenum (the upper division of the small intestine). The pyloric portion of the stomach (antrum plus pyloric canal) tends to curve to the right and slightly upward and backward and thus gives the stomach its J-shaped appearance. The pylorus, the narrowest portion of the stomach, is the outlet from the stomach into the duodenum. It is approximately 2 cm (almost 1 inch) in diameter and is surrounded by thick loops of smooth muscle.

The muscles of the stomach wall are arranged in three layers, or coats. The external coat, called the longitudinal muscle layer, is continuous with the longitudinal muscle coat of the esophagus. Longitudinal muscle fibres are divided at the cardia into two broad strips. The one on the right, the stronger, spreads out to cover the lesser curvature and the adjacent posterior and anterior walls of the stomach. Longitudinal fibres on the left radiate from the esophagus over the dome of the fundus to cover the greater curvature and continue on to the pylorus, where they join the longitudinal fibres coming down over the lesser curvature. The longitudinal layer continues on into the duodenum, forming the longitudinal muscle of the small intestine.

The middle, or circular muscular layer, the strongest of the three muscular layers, completely covers the stomach. The circular fibres of this coat are best developed in the lower portion of the stomach, particularly over the antrum and pylorus. At the pyloric end of the stomach, the circular muscle layer becomes greatly thickened to form the pyloric sphincter. This muscular ring is slightly separated from the circular muscle of the duodenum by connective tissue. The innermost layer of smooth muscle, called the oblique muscular layer, is strongest in the region of the fundus and progressively weaker as it approaches the pylorus.

The stomach is capable of dilating to accommodate more than one litre (about one quart) of food or liquids without increasing pressure on the stomach. This receptive relaxation of the upper part of the stomach to accommodate a meal is partly due to a neural reflex that is triggered when hydrochloric acid comes into contact with the mucosa of the antrum, possibly through the release of the hormone known as vasoactive intestinal polypeptide. The distension of the body of the stomach by food activates a neural reflex that initiates the muscle activity of the antrum.

Blood and Nerve Supply of the Stomach

Many branches of the celiac trunk bring arterial blood to the stomach. The celiac trunk is a short, wide artery that branches from the abdominal portion of the aorta, the main vessel conveying arterial blood from the heart to the systemic circulation. Blood from the stomach is returned to the venous system through the portal vein, which carries the blood to the liver.

The nerve supply to the stomach is provided by both the parasympathetic and sympathetic divisions of the autonomic nervous system. The parasympathetic nerve fibres are carried in the vagus, or 10th cranial, nerve. As the vagus nerve passes through the opening in the diaphragm together with the esophagus, branches of the right vagus nerve spread over the posterior part of the stomach, while the left vagus nerve supplies the anterior part. Sympathetic branches from a nerve network called the celiac, or solar, plexus accompany the arteries of the stomach into the muscular wall.

Stomach Contractions

Three types of motor activity of the stomach have been observed. The first is a small contraction wave of the stomach wall that originates in the upper part of the stomach and slowly moves down over the organ toward the pyloric sphincter. This type of contraction produces a slight indentation of the stomach wall. Retrograde waves frequently sweep from the pyloric sphincter to the antrum and up to its junction with the body of the stomach, which results in a back-and-forth movement of the gastric contents that has a mixing and crushing effect.

The second type of motor activity is also a contracting wave, but it is peristaltic in nature. The contraction originates in the upper part of the stomach as well and is slowly propagated over the organ toward the pyloric sphincter. This type of gastric contraction produces a deep indentation in the wall of the stomach. As the peristaltic wave approaches the antrum, the indentation completely obstructs the stomach lumen, or cavity, and thus compartmentalizes it. The contracting wave then moves over the antrum, propelling the material ahead of it through the pyloric sphincter into the duodenum. This type of contraction serves as a pumping mechanism for emptying the contents of the gastric antrum through the pyloric sphincter. Both the mixing and the peristaltic contractions of the stomach occur at a constant rate of three contractions per minute when recorded from the gastric antrum. A wave of peristalsis sweeps along the lower half of the stomach and along the entire intestine to the proximal colon at two-hour intervals after meals. These peristaltic waves can be halted by eating and can be induced by the hormone motilin.

The third type of gastric motor activity is best described as a tonic, or sustained, contraction of all the stomach muscles. The tonic contraction decreases the size of the stomach lumen, as all parts of the gastric wall seem to contract simultaneously. This activity accounts for the stomach's ability to accommodate itself to varying volumes of gastric content. The tonic contraction is independent of the other two types of contractions. However, mixing contractions and peristaltic contractions normally occur simultaneously with the tonic contraction. As food is broken down, smaller particles flow through the pyloric sphincter, which opens momentarily as a peristaltic wave descends through the antrum toward it. This permits "sampling" of the gastric contents by the duodenum.

Gastric Mucosa

The inner surface of the stomach is lined by a mucous membrane known as the gastric mucosa. The mucosa is always covered by a layer of thick mucus that is secreted by tall columnar epithelial cells. Gastric mucus is a glycoprotein that serves two purposes: the lubrication of food masses in order to facilitate movement within the stomach and the formation of a protective layer over the lining epithelium of the stomach cavity. This protective layer is a defense mechanism the stomach has against being digested by its own protein-lyzing enzymes, and it is facilitated by the secretion of bicarbonate into the surface layer from the underlying mucosa.

The acidity, or hydrogen ion concentration, of the mucous layer measures pH7 (neutral) at the area immediately adjacent to the epithelium and becomes more acidic (pH2) at the luminal level. When the gastric mucus is removed from the surface epithelium, small pits, called foveolae gastricae, may be observed with a magnifying glass. There are approximately 90 to 100 gastric pits per square millimetre (58,000 to 65,000 per square inch) of surface epithelium. Three to seven individual gastric glands empty their secretions into each gastric pit. Beneath the gastric mucosa is a thin layer of smooth muscle called the muscularis mucosae, and below this, in turn, is loose connective tissue, the submucosa, which attaches the gastric mucosa to the muscles in the walls of the stomach.

The gastric mucosa contains six different types of cells. In addition to the tall columnar surface epithelial cells, there are five common cell types found in the various gastric glands.

(1) Mucoid cells secrete gastric mucus and are common to all types of gastric glands. Mucoid cells are the main cell type found in the gastric glands in the cardiac and pyloric areas of the stomach. The necks of the glands in the body and fundic parts of the stomach are lined with mucoid cells.

(2) Zymogenic, or chief, cells are located predominantly in gastric glands in the body and fundic portions of the stomach. These cells secrete pepsinogen, from which the proteolytic (protein-digesting) enzyme pepsin is formed. There are two varieties of pepsinogen, known as pepsinogen I and pepsinogen II. Both are produced in the mucous and zymogenic cells in the glands of the body of the stomach, but the mucous glands located elsewhere in the stomach produce only pepsinogen II. Those stimuli that cause gastric acid secretion—in particular, vagal nerve stimulation—also promote the secretion of the pepsinogens.

(3) Gastrin cells, also called G cells, are located throughout the antrum. These endocrine cells secrete the acid-stimulating hormone gastrin as a response to lowered acidity of the gastric contents when food enters the stomach and gastric distention. Gastrin then enters the bloodstream and is carried in the circulation to the mucosa of the body of the stomach, where it binds to receptor sites on the outer membrane of the parietal cells. The gastrin-receptor complex that is formed triggers an energy-consuming reaction moderated by the presence of the enzyme ATPase, bound to the membrane that leads to the production and secretion of hydrogen ions in the parietal cells.

(4) Parietal, or oxyntic, cells, found in the glands of the body and fundic portions of the stomach, secrete hydrogen ions that combine with chloride ions to form hydrochloric acid (HCl). The acid that is produced drains into the lumen of the gland and then passes through to the stomach. This process occurs only when one or more types of receptors on the outer membrane of the parietal cell are bound to histamine, gastrin, or acetylcholine. Prostaglandins,

hormonelike substances that are present in virtually all tissues and body fluids, inhibit the secretion of hydrochloric acid. The drugs omeprazole (Losec™ or Prilosec™) and lansoprazole (Prevacid™) also inhibit acid secretion by the parietal cells and are used as treatments for peptic ulcer. Parietal cells produce most of the water found in gastric juice. They also produce glycoproteins called intrinsic factor, which are essential to the maturation of red blood cells, vitamin B_{12} absorption, and the health of certain cells in the central and peripheral nervous systems.

(5) Endocrine cells called enterochromaffin-like cells because of their staining characteristics are scattered throughout the body of the stomach. Enterochromaffin-like cells secrete several substances, including the hormone serotonin.

Gastric Secretion

The gastric mucosa secretes 1.2 to 1.5 litres (about 0.3 to 0.4 gallon) of gastric juice per day. Gastric juice renders food particles soluble, initiates digestion (particularly of proteins), and converts the gastric contents to a semiliquid mass called chyme, thus preparing it for further digestion in the small intestine. Gastric juice is a variable mixture of water, hydrochloric acid, electrolytes (sodium, potassium, calcium, phosphate, sulfate, and bicarbonate), and organic substances (mucus, pepsins, and protein). This juice is highly acidic because of its hydrochloric acid content, and it is rich in enzymes.

The stomach walls are protected from digestive juices by the membrane on the surface of the epithelial cells bordering the lumen of the stomach. This membrane is rich in lipoproteins, which are resistant to attack by acid.

The gastric juice of some mammals (e.g., calves) contains the enzyme rennin, which clumps milk proteins and thus takes them out of solution and makes them more susceptible to the action of a proteolytic enzyme.

The process of gastric secretion can be divided into three phases (cephalic, gastric, and intestinal) that depend upon the primary mechanisms that cause the gastric mucosa to secrete gastric juice. The phases of gastric secretion overlap, and there is an interrelation and some interdependence between the neural and humoral pathways.

The cephalic phase of gastric secretion occurs in response to stimuli received by the senses—that is, taste, smell, sight, and sound. This phase of gastric secretion is entirely reflex in origin and is mediated by the vagus nerve. Gastric juice is secreted in response to vagal stimulation, either directly by electrical impulses or indirectly by stimuli received through the senses. Ivan Petrovich Pavlov, the Russian physiologist, originally demonstrated this method of gastric secretion in a now-famous experiment with dogs.

The gastric phase is mediated by the vagus nerve and by the release of gastrin. The acidity of the gastric contents after a meal is buffered by proteins so that overall it remains around pH3 (acidic) for approximately 90 minutes. Acid continues to be secreted during the gastric phase in response to distension and to the peptides and amino acids that are liberated from protein as digestion proceeds. The chemical action of free amino acids and peptides excites the liberation of gastrin from the antrum into the circulation. Thus, there are mechanical, chemical, and hormonal factors contributing to the gastric secretory response to eating. This phase continues until the food has left the stomach.

The intestinal phase is not fully understood because of a complex stimulatory and inhibitor process. Amino acids and small peptides that promote gastric acid secretion are infused into the circulation, however, at the same time chyme inhibits acid secretion. The secretion of gastric acid is an important inhibitor of gastrin release. If the pH of the antral contents falls below 2.5, gastrin is not released. Some of the hormones that are released from the small intestine by products of digestion (especially fat), in particular glucagon and secretin, also suppress acid secretion.

Chyme

Chyme is a thick semifluid mass of partially digested food and digestive secretions that is formed in the stomach and intestine during digestion. Once food is in the small intestine, it stimulates the pancreas to release fluid containing a high concentration of bicarbonate. This fluid neutralizes the highly acidic gastric juice, which would otherwise damage the membrane lining of the intestine, resulting in a duodenal ulcer. Other secretions from the pancreas, gallbladder, liver, and glands in the intestinal wall add to the total volume of chyme.

Muscular contractions of the stomach walls help to mix food and digestive substances together in forming chyme. As particles of food become small enough, they are passed at regular intervals into the small intestine. Once in the intestine, more enzymes are added and mixing continues. When food particles are sufficiently reduced in size and composition, they are absorbed by the intestinal wall and transported to the bloodstream.

Some food material is passed from the small intestine to the large intestine, or colon. In the colon, chyme is acted upon by bacteria that break down the proteins, starches, and some plant fibres not totally digested by the other organs. In both the small and the large intestine, water is normally absorbed so the chyme gradually gets thicker. As chyme passes through the stomach and intestine, it picks up cellular debris and other types of waste products. When all of the nutrients have been absorbed from chyme, the remaining waste material passes to the end of the large intestine, the sigmoid colon and rectum, to be stored as fecal matter until it is ready to be excreted from the body.

Gastrin

Gastrin is a digestive hormone that is secreted by the wall of the pyloric end of the stomach. In humans, gastrin occurs in three forms: as a 14-, 17-, and 34-amino-acid polypeptide. These forms are produced from a series of enzymatic reactions that cleave the larger proteins into their smaller forms.

Gastrin is released into the bloodstream when food enters the stomach and is carried by the circulatory system to the gastric cells in the stomach wall, where it triggers the secretion of gastric juice. This juice consists primarily of hydrochloric acid, which helps break apart fibrous matter in food and kills bacteria that may have been ingested, and pepsinogen, which is a precursor of the protein-splitting enzyme pepsin. Gastrin also increases the motility of the stomach, thereby helping to churn food and eventually to empty the stomach. To a lesser degree, gastrin also increases the motility of the upper small intestine and the gallbladder.

The medical importance of gastrin lies in the fact that there are pancreatic islet-cell tumours called gastrinomas that secrete large quantities of gastrin (hypergastrinemia). Hypergastrinemia stimulates the production of gastric acid, which causes severe peptic ulcer disease and diarrhea. Gastrinomas are one component of the syndrome of multiple endocrine neoplasia type 1 (MEN1) and are also the defining tumour type of a rare disorder known as Zollinger-Ellison syndrome, which may occur sporadically or as a part of MEN1. Treatment consists of surgically removing the tumour or treating the patient with a drug that inhibits gastric acid secretion (a proton pump inhibitor).

Gastric Absorption and Emptying

Although the stomach absorbs few of the products of digestion, it can absorb many other substances, including glucose and other simple sugars, amino acids, and some fat-soluble substances. The pH of the gastric contents determines whether some substances are absorbed. At a low pH, for example, the environment is acidic and aspirin is absorbed from the stomach almost as rapidly as water, but, as the pH of the stomach rises and the environment becomes more basic, aspirin is absorbed more slowly.

Water moves freely from the gastric contents across the gastric mucosa into the blood. The net absorption of water from the stomach is small, however, because water moves just as easily from the blood across the gastric mucosa to the lumen of the stomach. The absorption of water and alcohol can be slowed if the stomach contains foodstuffs and especially fats, probably because gastric emptying is delayed by fats, and most water in any situation is absorbed from the small intestine.

The rate of emptying of the stomach depends upon the physical and chemical composition of the meal. Fluids empty more rapidly than solids, carbohydrates more rapidly than proteins, and proteins more rapidly than fats. When food particles are sufficiently reduced in size and are nearly soluble and when receptors in the duodenal bulb (the area of attachment between the duodenum and the stomach) have a fluidity and a hydrogen ion concentration of a certain level, the duodenal bulb and the second part of the duodenum relax, allowing emptying of the stomach to start.

During a duodenal contraction, the pressure in the duodenal bulb rises higher than that in the antrum. The pylorus prevents reflux into the stomach by shutting. The vagus nerve has an important role in the control of emptying, but there is some indication that the sympathetic division of the autonomic nervous system is also involved. Several of the peptide hormones of the digestive tract also have an effect on intragastric pressure and gastric movements, but their role in physiological circumstances is unclear.

CHAPTER 3

ANATOMY OF THE LOWER DIGESTIVE TRACT

Once food has been processed into chyme, it is able to move from the stomach into the lower digestive tract. This portion of the digestive tract consists of the small intestine and the large intestine. The combined length of these two segments is about 8.2 to 9.1 metres (27 to 30 feet). In order to fit within the abdominal cavity, the small intestine is folded repeatedly, forming a winding passageway that provides a large surface area for the absorption of nutrients. The large intestine, which is much shorter and wider than the small intestine, travels around the outside edge of the latter in a series of four sections, thereby surrounding it in a sort of square frame. The primary functions of the lower digestive tract include the absorption of nutrients from chyme and the compaction of the remaining waste contents into fecal matter, which is ultimately eliminated from the body.

THE SMALL INTESTINE

The small intestine is the principal organ of the digestive tract. Its primary functions include the mixing and transport of intraluminal contents, the production of enzymes and other constituents essential for digestion, and the absorption of nutrients. Most of the processes that solubilize carbohydrates, proteins, and fats and reduce them to relatively simple organic compounds occur in the small intestine.

The small intestine, which is 670 to 760 cm (22 to 25 feet) in length and 3 to 4 cm (1.2 to 1.6 inches) in diameter, is the

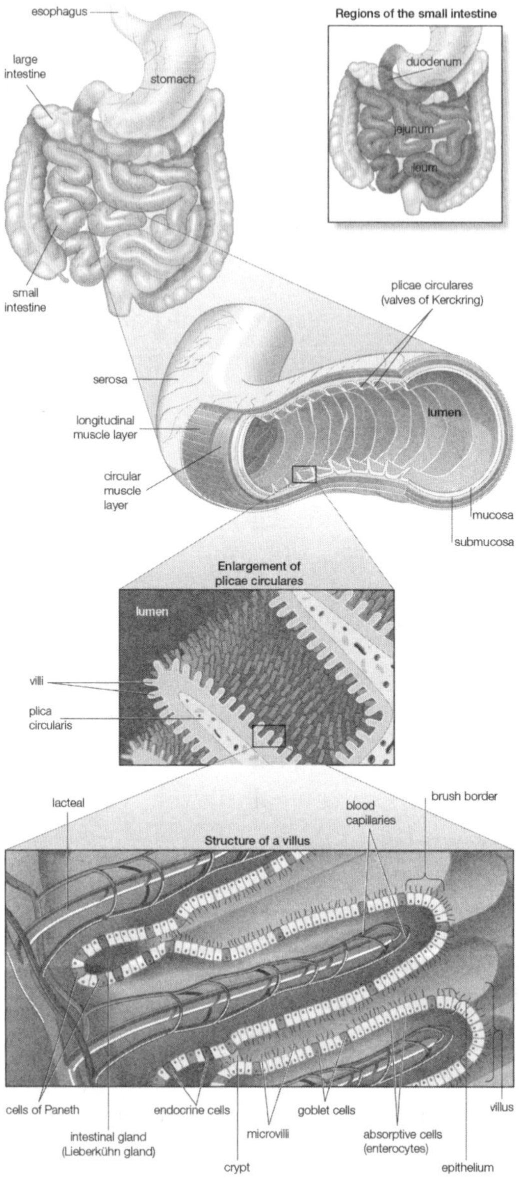

The inner wall of the small intestine is covered by numerous folds of mucous membrane called plicae circulares. The surface of these folds contains tiny projections called villi and microvilli, which further increase the total area for absorption. Absorbed nutrients are moved into circulation by blood capillaries and lacteals, or lymph channels. Encyclopædia Britannica, Inc.

longest part of the digestive tract. It begins at the pylorus, the juncture with the stomach, and ends at the ileocecal valve, the juncture with the colon. The main functional segments of the small intestine are the duodenum, the jejunum, and the ileum.

The duodenum is 23 to 28 cm (9 to 11 inches) long and forms a C-shaped curve that encircles the head of the pancreas. Unlike the rest of the small intestine, it is retroperitoneal (that is, it is behind the peritoneum, the membrane lining the abdominal wall). Its first segment, known as the duodenal bulb, is the widest part of the small intestine. It is horizontal, passing backward and to the right from the pylorus, and lies somewhat behind the wide end of the gallbladder. The second part of the duodenum runs vertically downward in front of the hilum of the right kidney (the point of entrance or exit for blood vessels, nerves, and the ureters). It is into this part through the duodenal papilla (papilla of Vater) that the pancreatic juice and bile flow. The third part of the duodenum runs horizontally to the left in front of the aorta and the inferior vena cava (the principal channel for return to the heart of venous blood from the lower part of the body and the legs), while the fourth part ascends to the left side of the second lumbar vertebra (at the level of the small of the back), then bends sharply downward and forward to join the second part of the small intestine, the jejunum. An acute angle, called the duodenojejunal flexure, is formed by the suspension of this part of the small intestine by the ligament of Treitz.

The jejunum forms the upper two-fifths of the rest of the small intestine. It, like the ileum, has numerous convolutions and is attached to the posterior abdominal wall by the mesentery, an extensive fold of serous-secreting membrane. The ileum is the remaining three-fifths of the small intestine, though there is no absolute point at which the jejunum ends and the ileum begins. In broad terms, the jejunum occupies the upper and left part of the abdomen below the subcostal plane (that is, at the level of the 10th rib), while the ileum is located in the lower and right part. At its termination the ileum opens into the large intestine.

The arrangement of the muscular coats of the small intestine is uniform throughout the length of the organ. The inner, circular layer is thicker than the outer, longitudinal layer. The outermost layer of the small intestine is lined by the peritoneum.

Blood and Nerve Supply of the Small Intestine

The superior mesenteric artery (a branch of the abdominal aorta) and the superior pancreaticduodenal artery (a branch of the hepatic artery) supply the small intestine with blood. These vessels run between layers of the mesentery, the membrane that connects the intestines with the wall of the abdominal cavity, and give off large branches that form a row of connecting arches from which branches arise to enter the wall of the small bowel. The blood from the intestine is returned by means of the superior mesenteric vein, which, with the splenic vein, forms the portal vein, which drains into the liver.

The small intestine has both sympathetic and parasympathetic innervation. The vagus nerve provides parasympathetic innervation. Sympathetic innervation is provided by branches from the superior mesenteric plexus, a nerve network underneath the solar plexus that follows the blood vessels into the small intestine and finally terminates in the Auerbach plexus, which is located between the circular and longitudinal muscle coats, and the Meissner plexus, which is located in the submucosa.

Numerous fibrils, both adrenergic (sympathetic) and cholinergic (parasympathetic), connect these two plexuses.

Contractions and Motility of the Small Intestine

The contractions of the circular and longitudinal muscles are regulated by electrical impulses that begin with the passage of calcium ions into the muscle cell. The duodenal pacemaker sends electrical impulses down the small intestine at a rate of 11 cycles per minute in the duodenum, gradually decreasing to 8 cycles per minute in the ileum. These electrical changes are propagated in the longitudinal muscle layer of the wall of the small intestine.

Occurring simultaneously with the slow-wave electrical activity may be fast, spikelike electrical charges. This type of electrical activity originates in the circular muscle layer of the intestinal wall and occurs when the circular layer contracts. The depolarization of the muscle cell membranes, or an excess of positive charges on the inside of the cell, causes the myofibrils (the contracting components of the myofilaments that constitute the muscle tissues) to contract. The rate of these contractions is governed by the rate of depolarization of the muscle cell membrane. The two spiral muscle layers then contract, causing the motor activity that permits the mixing and transporting of the food in the small intestine.

The primary purposes of the movements of the small intestine are to provide mixing and transport of intraluminal contents. A characteristic of small intestine motility is the inherent ability of the smooth muscle constituting the wall of the intestine to contract spontaneously and rhythmically. This phenomenon is independent of any extrinsic nerve supply to the small intestine. In the myenteric plexus (a network of nerve fibres in the wall of the intestine), there are several other messenger substances and receptors capable of modulating smooth muscle activity, including somatostatin, serotonin (5-hydroxytryptamine), and the enkephalins. With at least seven such substances in and around the smooth muscle, there is some confusion as to their respective roles. The contractions of the small intestine create pressure gradients from one adjacent segment of the organ to another. The pressure gradients, in turn, are primarily responsible for transport within the small intestine.

Within the small intestine, two types of motor activity have been recognized: segmenting contractions and peristaltic contractions. The predominant motor action of the small intestine is the segmenting contraction, which is a localized circumferential contraction, principally of the circular muscle of the intestinal wall. Segmenting contractions mix, separate, and churn the intestinal chyme. The contraction involves only a short segment of the intestinal wall, less than 1 to 2 cm (about 1 inch), and constricts the lumen, tending to divide its contents. As the chyme moves from the duodenum to the ileum, there is a gradual decrease in the number of segmenting contractions. This has been described as the "gradient" of small intestine motility.

Although segmenting contractions usually occur in an irregular manner, they can occur in a regular or rhythmic pattern and at a maximum rate for that particular site of the small intestine (rhythmic segmentation). Rhythmic segmentation may occur only in a localized segment of small intestine, or it may occur in a progressive manner, with each subsequent segmenting contraction occurring slightly below the preceding one (progressive segmentation).

A peristaltic contraction may be defined as an advancing ring, or wave, of contraction that passes along a segment of the gastrointestinal tract. It normally occurs only over a short segment (approximately every 6 cm [2.4 inches]) and moves at a rate of about 1 or 2 cm per minute. This type of motor activity in the small intestine results in the transport of intraluminal contents downward, usually one segment at a time.

When an inflammatory condition of the small bowel exists, or when irritating substances are present in the intraluminal contents, a peristaltic contraction may travel over a considerable distance of the small intestine; this is called the peristaltic rush. Diarrhea due to common infections is frequently associated with peristaltic rushes. Most cathartics (e.g., laxatives) produce their diarrheic effect by irritating the intestinal mucosa or by increasing the contents, particularly with fluid.

Absorption in the Small Intestine

Although the small intestine is only 3 to 4 cm (1.2 to 1.6 inches) in diameter and approximately 7 metres (23 feet) in length, it has been estimated that its total absorptive surface area is approximately 4,500 square metres (5,400 square yards). This enormous absorptive surface is provided by the unique structure of the mucosa, which is arranged in concentric folds that have the appearance of transverse ridges. These folds, known as plicae circulares, are approximately 5 to 6 cm (2 inches) long and about 3 mm (0.1 inch) thick.

Plicae circulares are present throughout the small intestine except in the first portion, or bulb, of the duodenum, which is usually flat and smooth, except for a few longitudinal folds. Also called valves of Kerckring, the plicae circulares are largest in the lower part of the duodenum and in the upper part of the jejunum. They become smaller and finally disappear in the lower part of the ileum.

The folds usually run one-half to two-thirds of the way around the intestinal wall. Occasionally, a single fold may spiral the wall for three or four complete turns. It has been estimated that the small intestine contains approximately 800 plicae circulares and that they increase the surface area of the lining of the small bowel by five to eight times the outer surface area.

Another feature of the mucosa that greatly multiplies its surface area is that of tiny projections called villi. The villi usually vary from 0.5 to 1 mm (0.02 to 0.04 inch) in height. Their diameters vary from approximately one-eighth to one-third their height. The villi are covered by a single layer of tall columnar cells called goblet cells because of their rough resemblance to empty goblets after they have discharged their contents. Goblet cells are found scattered among the surface epithelial cells covering the villi and are a source of mucin, the chief constituent of mucus.

At the base of the mucosal villi are depressions called intestinal glands, or Lieberkühn glands. The cells that line these glands continue up and over the surface of the villi. In the bottom of the glands, epithelial cells called cells of Paneth are filled with alpha granules, or eosinophilic granules, so called because they take up the rose-coloured stain eosin. Though they may contain lysozyme, an enzyme toxic to bacteria, and immunoglobins, their precise function is uncertain.

There are three other cell types in the Lieberkühn glands: goblet cells, endocrine cells, and undifferentiated cells, which have the potential to undergo changes for the purpose of replacing losses of any cell type. The main functions of the undifferentiated cells in these glands are cell renewal and secretion. Undifferentiated cells have an average life of 72 hours before becoming exhausted and being cast off.

The appearance and shape of the villi vary in different levels of the small intestine. In the duodenum the villi are closely packed, large, and frequently leaflike in shape. In the jejunum the individual villus measures between 350 and 600 μm in height (there are about 25,000 μm in an inch) and has a diameter of 110 to 135 μm. The inner structure of the individual villus consists of loose connective tissue containing a rich network of blood vessels, a central lacteal (or channel for lymph), smooth muscle fibres, and scattered cells of various types. The smooth muscle cells surround the central lacteal and provide for the pumping action required to initiate the flow of lymph out of the villus. A small central arteriole (minute artery) branches at the tip of the villus to form a capillary network; the capillaries, in turn, empty into a collecting venule that runs to the bottom of the villus.

A remarkable feature of the mucosa villi is the rough, specialized surface of the epithelial cells. This plasma membrane, known as the brush border, is thicker and richer in proteins and lipids than is the plasma membrane on the epithelial cells at the side and base of the villus. Water and solutes pass through pores in the surface epithelium of the mucosa by active transport and solvent drag; i.e., solutes are carried in a moving stream of water that causes an increased concentration of solute on the side of the membrane from which the water had originally come. The size of the pores is different in the ileum from in the jejunum. This difference accounts for the various rates of absorption of water at the two sites.

The enterocytes are joined near their apex by a contact zone known as a "tight junction." These junctions are believed to have pores that are closed in the resting state and dilated when absorption is required. The brush border is fused to a layer of glycoprotein, known as the "fuzzy coat," where certain nutrients are partly digested. It consists of individual microvilli approximately 0.1 μm in diameter and 1 μm in height; each epithelial cell may have as many as 1,000 microvilli. The microvilli play an important role in the digestion and absorption of intestinal contents by enlarging the absorbing surface approximately 25 times. They also secrete the enzymes disaccharidase and peptidase that hydrolyze disaccharides and polypeptides to monosaccharides and dipeptides to amino acids, respectively.

Molecular receptors for specific substances are found on the microvilli surfaces at different levels in the small intestine. This may account for the selective absorption of particular substances at particular sites—for example, intrinsic-factor-bound vitamin B_{12} in the terminal ileum. Such receptors may also explain the selective absorption of iron and calcium in the duodenum and upper jejunum. Furthermore, there are transport proteins in the microvillus membrane associated with the passage of sodium ions, D-glucose, and amino acids. Actin is found in the core of the microvillus, and myosin is found in the brush border. Because contractility is a function of these proteins, the microvilli have motor activity that presumably initiates the stirring and mixing actions within the lumen of the small intestine.

Beneath the mucosa of the small intestine, as beneath that of the stomach, are the muscularis and the submucosa. The submucosa consists of loose connective tissue and contains many blood vessels and lymphatics. Brunner glands, located in the submucosa of the duodenum, are composed of acini (round sacs) and tubules that are twisting and have multiple branching. These glands empty into the base of Lieberkühn glands in the duodenum. Their exact function is not known, but they do secrete a clear fluid that contains mucus, bicarbonate, and a relatively weak proteolytic (protein-splitting) enzyme. In the submucosa of the jejunum, there are solitary nodules (lumps) of lymphatic tissue; there is more lymphatic tissue in the ileum, in aggregates of nodules known as Peyer patches.

Paneth Cells

Paneth cells, also called Davidoff cells, are a specialized type of epithelial cell found in the mucous-membrane lining of the small intestine and of the appendix, at the base of tubelike depressions known as Lieberkühn glands. Named for the 19th-century Austrian physiologist Joseph Paneth, the cell has one nucleus at its base and densely packed secretory granules throughout the rest of its body. The cells' function is not totally known, nor is their manner of discharging their granules.

Paneth cells secrete large amounts of protein-rich material and are thought to secrete the enzyme peptidase, which breaks peptide molecules into amino acids suitable for assimilation by the body. In humans the granules are found to contain carbohydrates, proteins, and zinc. In mice a specific protein, lysozyme, known to destroy some bacteria, is believed to be present in the granules. This suggests that the Paneth cell might also have an antibacterial function.

Argentaffin Cells

Argentaffin cells are round or partly flattened cells occurring in the lining tissue of the digestive tract and containing granules thought to be of secretory function. These epithelial cells, though common throughout the digestive tract, are most concentrated in the small intestine and appendix. The cells locate randomly within the mucous membrane lining of the intestine and in tubelike depressions in that lining known as the Lieberkühn glands.

The granules of argentaffin cells contain a chemical called serotonin, which stimulates smooth muscle contractions. Functionally, it is believed that serotonin diffuses out of the argentaffin cells into the walls of the digestive tract, where neurons leading to the muscles are stimulated to produce the wavelike contractions of peristalsis. Peristaltic movements encourage the passage of food substances through the intestinal tract.

Peyer Patches

Peyer patches are nodules of lymphatic cells. They are formed when lymphatic cells aggregate into bundles or patches, which occurs usually only in the lowest portion (ileum) of the small intestine. Peyer patches are named for the 17th-century Swiss anatomist Hans Conrad Peyer.

Peyer patches are round or oval and are located in the mucous membrane lining of the intestine. They can be seen by the naked eye as elongated thickened areas, and their surface is free of the projections (villi) and depressions (Lieberkühn glands) that characterize the intestinal wall. Usually there are only 30 to 40 patches in each individual. In young adults they may be more numerous, and as a person ages they tend to become less prominent.

The full function of Peyer patches is not known, but they do play a role in immunologic response and contain B and T cells similar to those found in peripheral lymph nodes. In typhoid fever, these patches may become sites of inflammation, in which case they may develop into ulcerations, hemorrhages, or perforations.

Secretions of the Small Intestine

There are many sources of digestive secretions into the small intestine. Secretions into the small intestine are controlled by nerves, including the vagus, and hormones.

The most effective stimuli for secretion are local mechanical or chemical stimulations of the intestinal mucous membrane. Such stimuli always are present in the intestine in the form of chyme and food particles. The gastric chyme that is emptied into the duodenum contains gastric secretions that will continue their digestive processes for a short time in the small intestine.

One of the major sources of digestive secretion is the pancreas, a large gland that produces both digestive enzymes and hormones. The pancreas empties its secretions into the duodenum through the major pancreatic duct (duct of Wirsung) in the duodenal papilla (papilla of Vater) and the accessory pancreatic duct a few centimetres away from it. Pancreatic juice contains enzymes that digest proteins, fats, and carbohydrates. Secretions of the liver are delivered to the duodenum by the common bile duct via the gallbladder and are also received through the duodenal papilla.

The composition of the succus entericus, the mixture of substances secreted into the small intestine, varies somewhat in different parts of the intestine. Except in the duodenum, the quantity of the fluid secreted is minimal, even under conditions of stimulation. In the duodenum, for example, where the Brunner glands are located, the secretion contains more mucus. In general, the secretion of the small intestine is a thin, colourless or slightly straw-coloured fluid, containing flecks of mucus, water, inorganic salts, and organic material. The inorganic salts are those commonly present in other body fluids, with the bicarbonate concentration higher than it is in blood. Aside from mucus, the organic matter consists of cellular debris and enzymes, including a pepsinlike protease (from the duodenum only), an amylase, a lipase, at least two peptidases, sucrase, maltase, enterokinase, alkaline phosphatase, nucleophosphatases, and nucleocytases.

THE LARGE INTESTINE

The large intestine, or colon, serves as a reservoir for the liquids emptied into it from the small intestine. It has a much larger diameter than the small intestine (approximately 2.5 cm, or 1 inch, as opposed to 6 cm, or 2.4 inches, in the large intestine), but at 150 cm (5 feet), it is less than one-quarter the length of the small intestine. The primary functions of the colon are to absorb water; to maintain osmolality, or level of solutes, of the blood by excreting and absorbing electrolytes (substances, such as sodium and chloride, that in solution take on an electrical charge) from the chyme; and to store fecal material until it can be evacuated by defecation. The colon also contains large numbers of bacteria that synthesize niacin (nicotinic acid), thiamin (vitamin B_1) and vitamin K, vitamins that are essential to several metabolic activities as well as to the function of the central nervous system.

The large intestine secretes mucus, which aids in lubricating the intestinal contents and facilitates their transport through the bowel. Each day approximately 1.5 to 2 litres (about 0.4 to 0.5 gallon) of chyme pass through the ileocecal valve that separates the small and large intestines. The chyme is reduced by absorption in the colon to around 150 ml (5 fluid ounces). The residual indigestible matter, together with sloughed-off mucosal cells, dead bacteria, and food residues not digested by bacteria, constitute the feces.

The large intestine can be divided into the cecum, ascending colon, transverse colon, descending colon, and sigmoid colon. The cecum, the first part of the large intestine, is a sac with a closed end that occupies the right iliac fossa, the hollow of the inner side of the ilium (the upper part of the hipbone). Guarding the opening of the ileum (the terminal portion of the small intestine) into the cecum is the ileocecal valve.

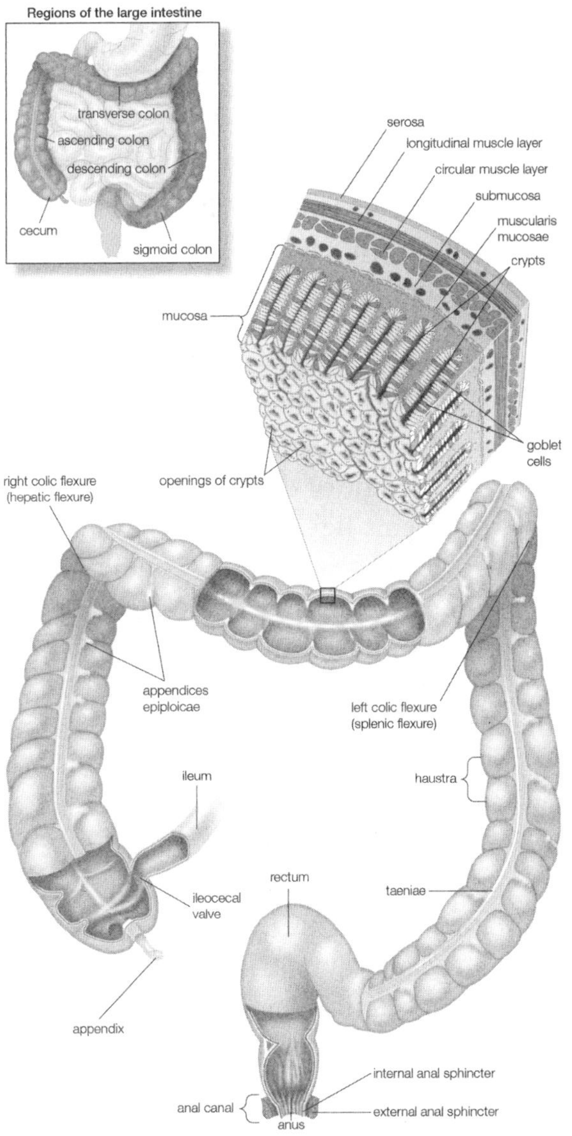

The mucosa of the large intestine is punctuated with numerous crypts that absorb water and are lined with mucus-secreting goblet cells. At the lower end of the rectum, the circular and longitudinal muscle layers terminate in the internal and external anal sphincters. Encyclopædia Britannica, Inc.

The circular muscle fibres of the ileum and those of the cecum combine to form the circular sphincter muscle of the ileocecal valve. The ascending colon extends up from the cecum at the level of the ileocecal valve to the bend in the colon called the hepatic flexure, which is located beneath and behind the right lobe of the liver. Behind, it is in contact with the rear abdominal wall and the right kidney. The ascending colon is covered by peritoneum except on its posterior surface.

The transverse colon is variable in position, depending largely on the distention of the stomach, but usually is located in the subcostal plane—that is, at the level of the 10th rib. On the left side of the abdomen, it ascends to the bend called the splenic flexure, which may make an indentation in the spleen. The transverse colon is bound to the diaphragm opposite the 11th rib by a fold of peritoneum.

The descending colon passes down and in front of the left kidney and the left side of the posterior abdominal wall to the iliac crest (the upper border of the hipbone). The descending colon is more likely than the ascending colon to be surrounded by peritoneum.

The sigmoid colon is commonly divided into iliac and pelvic parts. The iliac colon stretches from the crest of the ilium, or upper border of the hipbone, to the inner border of the psoas muscle, which lies in the left iliac fossa. Like the descending colon, the iliac colon is usually covered by peritoneum. The pelvic colon lies in the true pelvis (lower part of the pelvis) and forms one or two loops, reaching across to the right side of the pelvis and then bending back and, at the midline, turning sharply downward to the point where it becomes the rectum.

The layers that make up the wall of the colon are similar in some respects to those of the small intestine; there are distinct differences, however. The external aspect of the colon differs markedly from that of the small intestine because of features known as the taeniae, haustra, and appendices epiploicae. The taeniae are three long bands of longitudinal muscle fibres, about 1 cm (0.4 inch) in width, that are approximately equally spaced around the circumference of the colon. Between the thick bands of the taeniae, there is a thin coating of longitudinal muscle fibres. Because the taeniae are slightly shorter than the large intestine, the intestinal wall constricts and forms circular furrows of varying depths called haustra, or sacculations. The appendices epiploicae are collections of fatty tissue beneath the covering membrane. On the ascending and descending colon, they are usually found in two rows, whereas on the transverse colon they form one row.

The inner surface of the colon has many crypts that are lined with mucous glands and numerous goblet cells, and it lacks the villi and plicae circulares characteristic of the small intestine. It contains many solitary lymphatic nodules but no Peyer patches. Characteristic of the colonic mucosa are deep tubular pits, increasing in depth toward the rectum.

The inner layer of muscle of the large intestine is wound in a tight spiral around the colon, so that contraction results in compartmentalization of the lumen and its contents. The spiral of the outer layer, on the other hand, follows a loose undulating course, and contraction of this muscle causes the contents of the colon to shift forward and backward. The bulk of the contents, in particular the amount of undigested fibre, influences these muscular activities.

Blood and Nerve Supply of the Large Intestine

The arterial blood supply to the large intestine is supplied by branches of the superior and inferior mesenteric arteries (both of which are branches of the abdominal aorta) and the hypogastric branch of the internal iliac artery (which supplies blood to the pelvic walls and viscera, the genital organs, the buttocks, and the inside of the thighs). The vessels form a continuous row of arches from which vessels arise to enter the large intestine.

Venous blood is drained from the colon from branches that form venous arches similar to those of the arteries. These eventually drain into the superior and inferior mesenteric veins, which ultimately join with the splenic vein to form the portal vein. The innervation of the large intestine is similar to that of the small intestine.

Contractions and Motility of the Large Intestine

Local contractions and retrograde propulsions ensure mixing of the contents and good contact with the mucosa. Colonic motility is stimulated by mastication and by the presence of fat, unabsorbed bile salts, bile acids, and the peptide hormones gastrin and cholecystokinin. The hormones secretin, glucagon, and vasoactive intestinal peptide act to suppress motility. The electrical activity of the muscles of the colon is more complex than that of the small intestine.

Variations from the basic rhythmic movements of the colon are present in the lower (distal) half of the colon and in the rectum. Slow-wave activity that produces contractions from the ascending colon to the descending colon occurs at the rate of 11 cycles per minute, and slow-wave activity in the sigmoid colon and rectum occurs at 6 cycles per minute. Local contractions migrate distally in the colon at the rate of 4 cm (1.6 inches) per second. Retrograde, or reverse, movements occur mainly in the upper (proximal) colon.

The Appendix

The appendix is a vestigial hollow tube that is closed at one end and is attached at the other end to the cecum, a pouch-like beginning of the large intestine into which the small intestine empties its contents. It is not clear whether the appendix serves any useful purpose in humans. Suspected functions include housing and cultivating beneficial gut flora that can repopulate the digestive system following an illness that wipes out normal populations of these flora; providing a site for the production of endocrine cells in the fetus that produce molecules important in regulating homeostasis; and serving a possible role in immune function during the first three decades of life by exposing leukocytes (white blood cells) to antigens in the gastrointestinal tract, thereby stimulating antibody production that may help modulate immune reactions in the gut. While the specific functions of the human appendix remain unclear, there is general agreement among scientists that the appendix is gradually disappearing from the human species over evolutionary time. The appendix is of medical significance because its blockage can lead to appendicitis, a painful and potentially dangerous inflammation.

The appendix is usually 8 to 10 cm (3 to 4 inches) long and less than 1.3 cm (0.5 inch) wide. The cavity of the appendix is much narrower where it joins the cecum than it is at its closed end. The appendix has muscular walls that are ordinarily capable of expelling into the cecum the mucous secretions of the appendiceal walls or any of the intestinal contents that have worked their way into the structure. If anything blocks the opening of the appendix or prevents it from expelling its contents into the cecum, appendicitis may occur. The most common obstruction in the opening is a fecalith, a hardened piece of fecal matter.

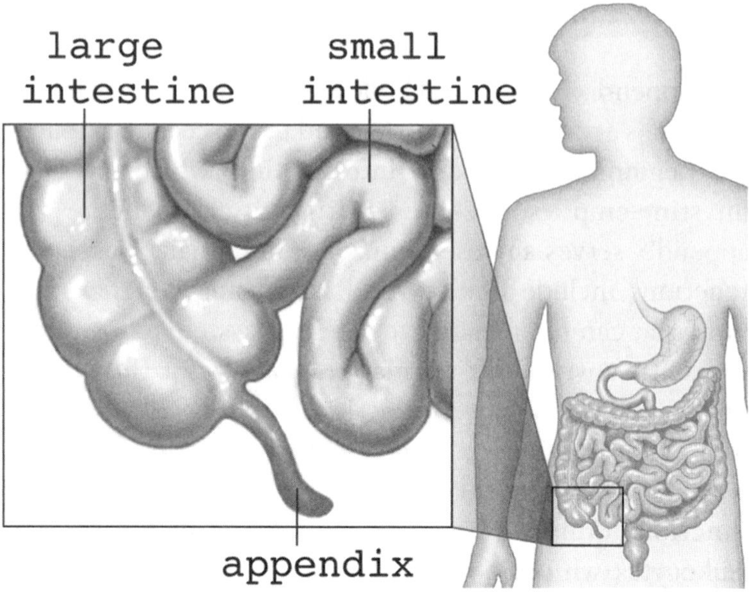

The appendix is a hollow tube that is closed at one end and is attached at the other end to the cecum at the beginning of the large intestine.
Encyclopædia Britannica, Inc.

Swelling of the lining of the appendiceal walls themselves can also block the opening.

When the appendix is prevented from emptying itself, a series of events occurs. Fluids and its own mucous secretions collect in the appendix, leading to edema, swelling, and the distention of the organ. As the distention increases, the blood vessels of the appendix become closed off, which causes the necrosis (death) of appendiceal tissue. Meanwhile, the bacteria normally found in this part of the intestine begin to propagate in the closed-off pocket, worsening the inflammation. The appendix, weakened by necrosis and subject to increasing pressure from within by the distention, may burst, spilling its contents into the abdominal cavity and infecting the membranes that line the cavity and cover the abdominal organs. Fortunately, peritonitis is usually prevented by the protective mechanisms of the body. The omentum, a sheet of fatty tissue, often wraps itself around the inflamed appendix, and an exudate that normally develops in the areas of inflammation behaves like glue and seals off the appendix from the surrounding peritoneal cavity.

The Rectum

The rectum, which is a continuation of the sigmoid colon, begins in front of the midsacrum (the sacrum is the triangular bone near the base of the spine and between the two hipbones). It ends in a dilated portion called the rectal ampulla, which in front is in contact with the rear surface of the prostate in the male and with the posterior vaginal wall in the female. Posteriorly, the rectal ampulla is in front of the tip of the coccyx (the small bone at the very base of the spine).

At the end of the pelvic colon, the mesocolon, the fold of peritoneum that attaches the colon to the rear wall of the abdomen and pelvis, ceases, and the rectum is then covered by peritoneum only at its sides and in front. Lower down, the rectum gradually loses the covering on its sides until only the front is covered. About 7.5 cm (3 inches) from the anus, the anterior peritoneal covering is also folded back onto the bladder and the prostate or the vagina.

Near the termination of the sigmoid colon and the beginning of the rectum, the colonic taeniae spread out to form a wide external longitudinal muscle coat. At the lower end of the rectum, muscle fibres of the longitudinal and circular coats tend to intermix. The internal circular muscle coat terminates in the thick rounded internal anal sphincter muscle. The smooth muscle fibres of the external longitudinal muscle coat of the rectum terminate by interweaving with striated muscle fibres of the levator ani, or pelvic diaphragm, a broad muscle that forms the floor of the pelvis. A second sphincter, the external anal sphincter, is composed of striated muscle and is divided into three parts known as the subcutaneous, superficial, and deep external sphincters. Thus, the internal sphincter is composed of smooth muscle and is innervated by the autonomic nervous system, while the external sphincters are of striated muscle and have somatic (voluntary) innervation provided by nerves called the pudendal nerves.

The mucosal lining of the rectum is similar to that of the sigmoid colon but becomes thicker and better supplied with blood vessels, particularly in the lower rectum. Arterial blood is supplied to the rectum and anus by branches from the inferior mesenteric artery and the right and left internal iliac arteries. Venous drainage from the anal canal and rectum is provided by a rich network of veins called the internal and external hemorrhoidal veins.

Two to three large crescentlike folds known as rectal valves are located in the rectal ampulla. These valves are caused by an invagination, or infolding, of the circular muscle and submucosa. The columnar epithelium of the rectal mucosa, innervated by the autonomic nervous system, changes to the stratified squamous (scalelike) type, innervated by the peripheral nerves, in the lower rectum a few centimetres above the pectinate line, which is the junction between the squamous mucous membrane of the lower rectum and the skin lining the lower portion of the anal canal.

Once or twice in 24 hours, a mass peristaltic movement shifts the accumulated feces onward from the descending and sigmoid sectors of the colon. The rectum is normally empty, but when it is filled with gas, liquids, or solids to the extent that the intraluminal pressure is raised to a certain level, the impulse to defecate occurs.

The musculus puborectalis forms a sling around the junction of the rectum with the anal canal and is maintained in a constant state of tension. This results in an angulation of the lower rectum so that the lumen of the rectum and the lumen of the anal canal are not in continuity, a feature essential to continence. Continuity is restored between the lumina of the two sectors when the sling of muscle relaxes, and the longitudinal muscles of the distal and pelvic colon contract. The resulting shortening of the distal colon tends to elevate the pelvic colon and obliterates the angle that it normally makes with the rectum. The straightening and shortening of the passage facilitates evacuation.

The act of defecation is preceded by a voluntary effort, which, in turn, probably gives rise to stimuli that magnify the visceral reflexes, although these originate primarily in the distension of the rectum. Centres that control defecation reflexes are found in the hypothalamus of the brain, in two regions of the spinal cord, and in the ganglionic plexus of the intestine. As the result of these reflexes, the internal anal sphincter relaxes.

The Anal Canal

The anal canal is the terminal portion of the digestive tract, distinguished from the rectum because of the transition of its internal surface from a mucous membrane layer (endodermal) to one of skinlike tissue (ectodermal). The anal canal is 2.5 to 4 cm (1 to 1.6 inches) in length; its diameter is narrower than that of the rectum to which it connects. The canal is divided into three areas: the upper part, with longitudinal folds called rectal columns; the lower portion, with internal and external constrictive muscles (sphincters) to control evacuation of feces; and the anal opening itself.

The anal canal connects with the rectum at the point where it passes through a muscular pelvic diaphragm. The upper region has 5 to 10 rectal columns, each column containing a small artery and vein. These are the terminal portions of the blood vessels that furnish the rectal and anal areas; they are susceptible to enlargement, commonly known as hemorrhoids. The mucous membrane of the upper portion is similar to that in the rest of the large intestine. It contains mucus-producing and absorptive cells.

The lower portions of the anal columns are joined by small concentric circular folds of the mucous membrane known as anal valves. Between the valves are small anal sinuses that open to lymph ducts and glands. These sometimes become abscessed and infected, especially in persons who have chronic diarrhea, constipation, or diabetes mellitus. The internal wall of the anal canal is first lined by moist, soft skin that lacks hair or glands; it then becomes a tough (keratinized) layer of skin containing hair and glands. The keratinized layer is continuous with the skin of the anal opening and external body. Both the upper and lower portions of the anal canal have circular and longitudinal muscle layers that allow expansion and contraction of the canal. The anal opening is keratinized skin that has several folds while contracted. When open, the folds allow the skin to stretch without tearing. In the skin around the anal opening but not immediately adjacent to it are glands that give off perspiration.

The lower anal canal and the anal opening are composed of two muscular constrictions that regulate fecal passage. The internal sphincter is part of the inner surface of the canal. It is composed of concentric layers of circular muscle tissue and is not under voluntary control. The external sphincter is a layer of voluntary (striated) muscle encircling the outside wall of the anal canal and anal opening. One can cause it to expand and contract at will, except during the early years of life when it is not yet fully developed. Nerves in the anal canal cause sphincter response and the sensation of pain. The lower part of the canal is very sensitive to heat, cold, cutting, and abrasion.

Waste products pass to the anal canal from the rectum. Nerve responses from the rectum cause the internal sphincter to relax while the external one contracts. Shortly thereafter the external sphincter also relaxes and allows fecal discharge. The pelvic diaphragm and longitudinal muscles draw the anus and rectum up over the passing feces so that they are not extruded (prolapsed) out of the anal opening with the feces. Numerous blood vessels surround the anal canal and may be subject to enlargement and rupture. This condition, commonly called a hemorrhoid, or pile, may cause pain, bleeding, and projection of the vessels from the anus.

CHAPTER 4

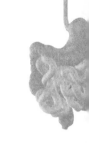

Digestive Glands and Hormones

The secretion of hormones and other substances from the digestive glands plays an important role in coordinating the activities of digestion and in facilitating the utilization of nutrients by the body's tissues. Digestive hormones send important signals to the brain that convey different types of information, such as that concerning hunger or satiety. The secretion of substances such as bile is fundamental to the breakdown of certain types of food; bile functions specifically in the digestion of fats. Examples of digestive glands include the liver and the pancreas, which secretes two hormones—insulin and glucagon—that are central to the metabolism of carbohydrates.

THE LIVER

The liver is not only the largest gland in the body but also the most complex in function. The liver consists of a spongy mass of wedge-shaped lobes, with tissue made up of cells tunneled through with bile ducts and blood vessels. This arrangement underlies the ability of the liver to perform its many important functions. The major functions of the liver are to participate in the metabolism of protein, carbohydrates, and fat; to synthesize cholesterol and bile acids; to initiate the formation of bile; to engage in the transport of a pigment known as bilirubin; to metabolize and transport certain drugs; to control transport and storage of carbohydrates, vitamins, and other substances; to synthesize blood-clotting factors; to remove wastes and toxic

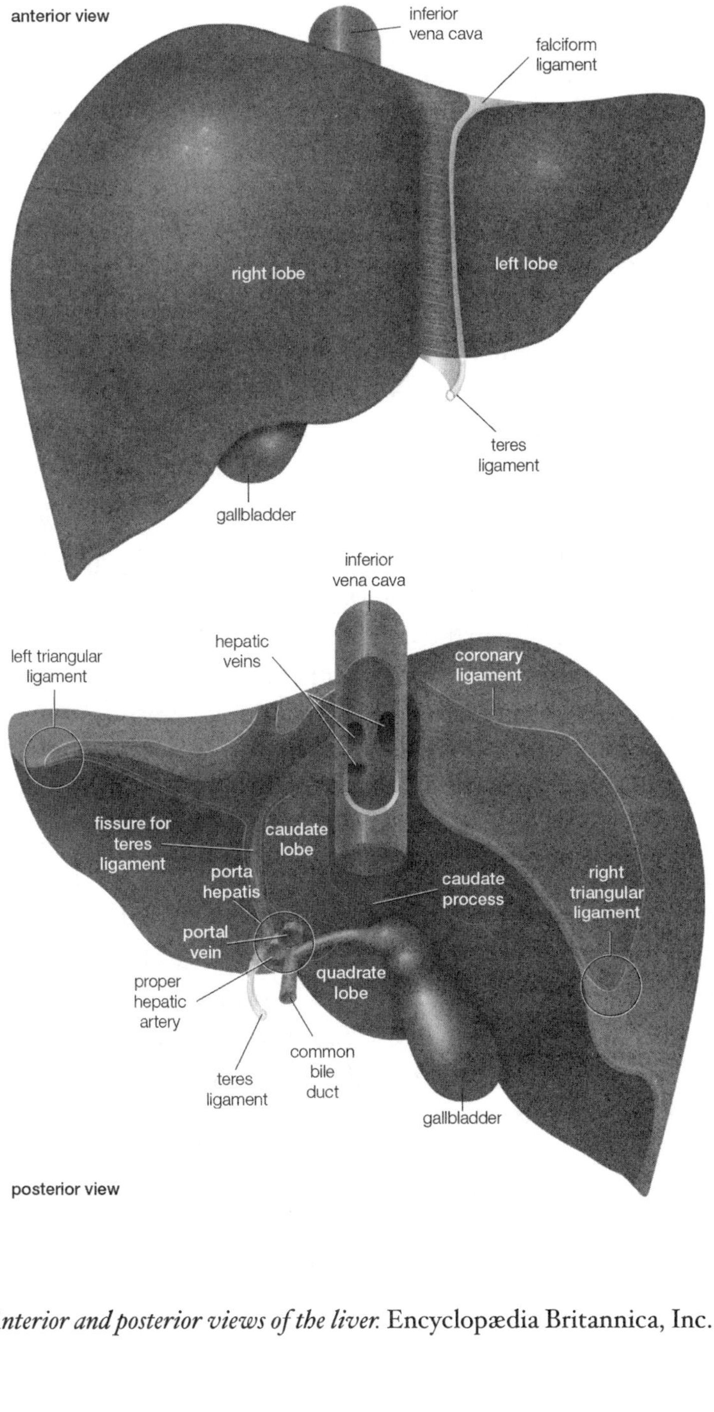

Anterior and posterior views of the liver. Encyclopædia Britannica, Inc.

matter from the blood; to regulate blood volume; and to destroy old red blood cells.

The cells of the liver synthesize a number of enzymes. They also play a role in the conversion of nutrients entering the liver from the intestine into forms that are usable by the body cells or that can be stored for future use. Fats are converted into fatty acids and then into carbohydrates or ketone bodies and transported by the blood to the tissues, where they are further metabolized. Sugars are converted into glycogen, which remains stored in the liver until it is needed for energy production. It is then reconverted into glucose and released into the bloodstream. The liver manufactures blood serum proteins, including albumin and several clotting factors, and supplies them to the blood. The liver also metabolizes nitrogenous waste products and detoxifies poisonous substances, preparing them for elimination in the urine or feces.

The liver lies under the lower right rib cage and occupies much of the upper right quadrant of the abdomen, with a portion extending into the upper left quadrant. The organ weighs from 1.2 to 1.6 kg (2.6 to 3.5 pounds) and is somewhat larger in men than in women. Its greatest horizontal measurement ranges from 20 to 22 cm (approximately 8 inches); vertically, it extends 15 to 18 cm (about 6 to 7 inches), and in thickness it ranges from 10 to 13 cm (about 4 to 5 inches). The liver is divided into two unequal lobes: a large right lobe and a smaller left lobe. The left lobe is separated on its anterior (frontal) surface by the dense falciform (sickle-shaped) ligament that connects the liver to the undersurface of the diaphragm. On the inferior surface of the liver, the right and left lobes are separated by a groove containing the teres ligament, which runs to the navel. Two small lobes, the caudate and the quadrate, occupy a portion of the inferior surface of the right lobe. The entire liver, except for a small portion that abuts the right leaf of the diaphragm, is enveloped in a capsule of tissue that is continuous with the parietal peritoneum that lines the abdominopelvic walls and diaphragm.

The major blood vessels enter the liver on its inferior surface in a centrally placed groove called the porta hepatis, which anatomically separates the quadrate and caudate lobes. The liver has two sources of blood supply. Fully oxygenated blood comes from the hepatic artery, which is a major branch of the celiac axis (the main artery that crosses the abdomen) after its emergence from the abdominal aorta. Partially oxygenated blood is supplied by the large portal vein, which in turn receives all venous blood from the spleen, pancreas, gallbladder, lower esophagus, and the remainder of the gastrointestinal tract, including the stomach, small intestine, large intestine, and upper portion of the rectum.

The portal vein is formed by the juncture of the splenic vein with the superior mesenteric vein. At the porta hepatis, a groove that separates the two lobes of the liver at the right side, the portal vein divides into two large branches, each going to one of the major lobes of the liver. The porta hepatis is also the exit point for the hepatic ducts. These channels are the final pathway for a network of smaller bile ductules interspersed throughout the liver that serve to carry newly formed bile from liver cells to the small intestine via the biliary tract.

The microscopic anatomy of the liver reveals a uniform structure of clusters of cells called lobules, where the vital functions of the liver are carried out. Each lobule, measuring about 1 mm (0.04 inch) in diameter, consists of numerous cords of rectangular liver cells, or hepatocytes, that radiate from central veins, or terminal hepatic venules, toward a thin layer of connective tissue that

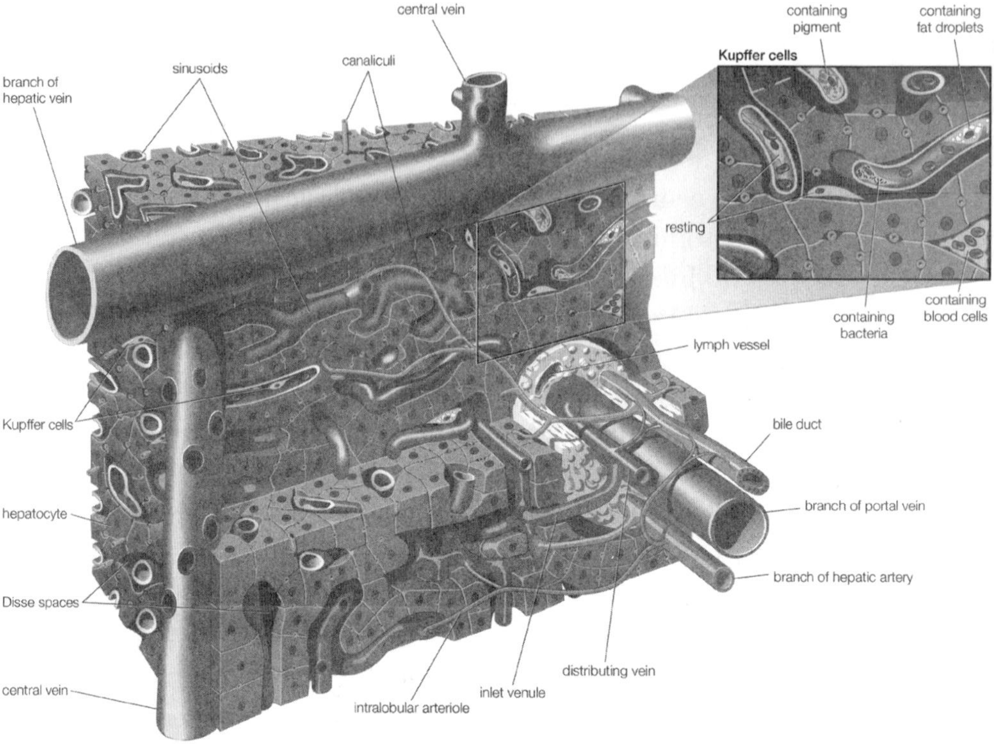

Liver cells, or hepatocytes, have direct access to the liver's blood supply through small capillaries called sinusoids. Hepatocytes carry out many metabolic functions, including the production of bile. Kupffer cells line the liver's vascular system; they play a role in blood formation and the destruction of cellular debris. Encyclopædia Britannica, Inc.

separates the lobule from other neighbouring lobules. The cords of liver cells are one cell thick and are separated from one another on several surfaces by spaces called sinusoids, or hepatic capillaries. Sinusoids are lined by thin endothelial cells that have openings through which finger-like projections (microvilli) of the hepatocytes extend, allowing direct accessibility of the hepatocyte to the bloodstream in the sinusoids.

The other major cell of the liver, the Kupffer cell, adheres to the wall of the sinusoid and projects into its lumen. It functions as a phagocyte (a cell that engulfs and destroys foreign material or other cells). Small spaces (Disse spaces) are present in places between the hepatocyte and the sinusoidal endothelium, probably for the transport of lymph. On neighbouring surfaces the hepatocytes are bound to one another by dense, tight junctions. These are perforated by small channels, called canaliculi, which are the terminal outposts of the biliary system, receiving bile from the hepatocyte. They eventually join with other canaliculi, forming progressively larger bile ducts that eventually emerge from the porta hepatis as the hepatic duct.

Hepatocytes occupy about 80 percent of the volume of the liver, and their cytoplasm (the area surrounding the nucleus) contains many mitochondria, which provide the energy needed for the many synthetic and metabolic functions of the liver cell. The cytoplasm also contains a series of long tubules, called the endoplasmic reticulum, which provides many enzymes essential to liver function. Some of the membranes of the endoplasmic reticulum appear granular, or rough, owing to the presence of ribosomes, which are responsible for forming specific polypeptide (protein) chains after having had the amino group removed (deamination) and having been converted into glucose through a process called gluconeogenesis. The ammonia released from gluconeogenesis is converted to urea in the hepatocyte by way of the urea cycle.

The nonribosomal, or smooth, endoplasmic reticulum is where cytochromes (combinations of heme from hemoglobin with various proteins) and certain enzymes undertake the important hepatic functions of drug and hormonal metabolism and also cholesterol synthesis. Hepatocytes also conjugate with carbohydrate components of bilirubin and other fat-soluble metabolic and foreign compounds and thereby are made soluble in water. Bilirubin is the product of hemoglobin metabolism that is formed in the bone marrow and the lymphatic tissue and is carried to the liver after becoming bound to plasma albumin. It is released at the hepatocytic sinusoidal membrane and is transported to the smooth endoplasmic reticulum, where it is conjugated with one or two molecules of glucuronic acid and thereby becomes soluble in water and excretable in bile.

The Golgi apparatus, a series of tubular structures between the endoplasmic reticulum and the canaliculus, acts as a transport station for newly made proteins and other hepatocytic products before they are conveyed to other parts of the cell or out of the cell entirely. Lysosomes, another important cytoplasmic constituent, are responsible for the intracellular storage of pigments, such as iron or copper, and for the digestion of certain contents, such as glycogen or foreign particles. The nucleus of the hepatocyte guides replication of the cell and transmits genetic material in the form of messenger ribonucleic acid (mRNA) from deoxyribonucleic acid (DNA) to organelles located in the cytoplasm.

The production of bile is a defining characteristic of the liver. Each day the liver secretes about 800 to 1,000 ml (about 1 quart) of bile, which contains bile salts needed for the digestion of fats in the diet. The presence of fat in the duodenum stimulates the flow of bile out of the gallbladder and into the small intestine. Senescent (worn-out) red blood cells are destroyed in the liver, spleen, and bone marrow. Bilirubin, formed in the process of hemoglobin breakdown, is released into the bile, creating its characteristic greenish orange colour, and is excreted from the body through the intestine.

A common sign of impaired liver function is jaundice, a yellowness of the eyes and skin arising from excessive bilirubin in the blood. Jaundice can result from an abnormally high level of red blood cell destruction (hemolytic jaundice), defective uptake or transport of bilirubin by the hepatic cells (hepatocellular jaundice), or a blockage in the bile duct system (obstructive jaundice). Failure of hepatic cells to function can result from hepatitis, cirrhosis, tumours, vascular obstruction, or poisoning. Symptoms may include weakness, low blood pressure, easy bruising and bleeding, tremor, and accumulation of fluid in the abdomen. Blood tests can reveal abnormal levels of bilirubin, cholesterol, serum proteins, urea, ammonia, and various enzymes. A specific diagnosis of a liver problem can be established by performing a needle biopsy.

The liver is subject to a variety of other disorders and diseases. Abscesses can be caused by acute appendicitis; those occurring in the bile ducts may result from gallstones or may follow surgery. The parasite that causes amebic dysentery, a protozoan called *Entamoeba histolytica*, can produce liver abscesses as well. Various other parasites prevalent in different parts of the world also infect the liver. Liver cancer is common, occurring mostly as secondary tumours originating elsewhere in the body. Glycogen-storage diseases, a group of hereditary disorders, generate a buildup of glycogen in the liver and an insufficient supply of glucose in the blood. Certain drugs may damage the liver, producing jaundice.

THE BILIARY TRACT

The biliary tract begins with the appearance of two large ducts, the right and left hepatic ducts, at the porta hepatis. Just below the porta hepatis, these 1- to 2-cm (about

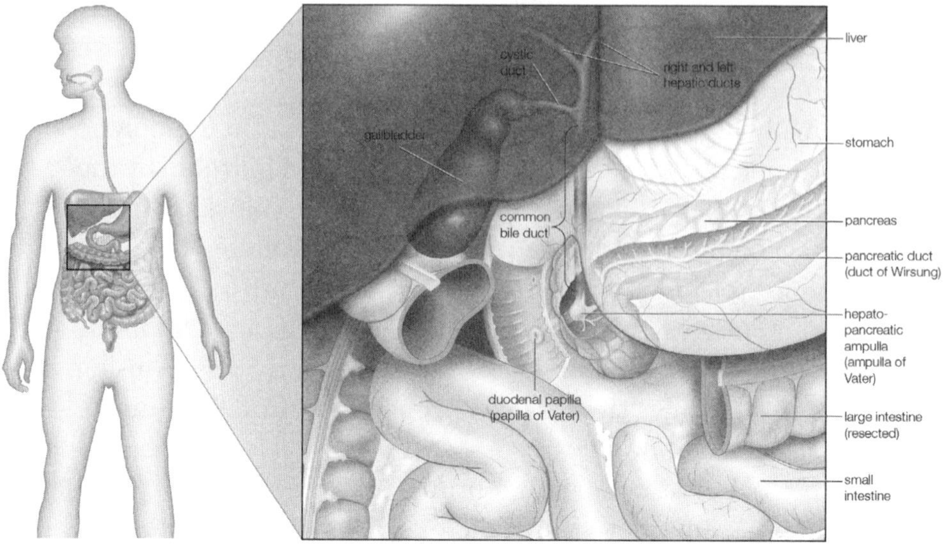

The gallbladder and bile ducts in situ. Encyclopædia Britannica, Inc.

half-inch) ducts join to form the hepatic duct, which proceeds for another 2 to 3 cm and is joined by the cystic duct, leading from the gallbladder. The resulting common bile duct progresses downward through the head of the pancreas. There it is joined by the main pancreatic duct (duct of Wirsung) at a slightly dilated area called the hepatopancreatic ampulla (ampulla of Vater), which lies in the wall of the inner curve of the descending duodenum, and terminates in the lumen of the duodenum at a 2- to 3-cm elevation called the duodenal papilla (papilla of Vater).

The common bile duct averages about 10 cm (about 4 inches) in length, and flow of bile from its lower end into the intestine is controlled by the muscular action of the hepatopancreatic sphincter (sphincter of Oddi), located in the duodenal papilla. The cystic duct varies from 2 to 3 cm in length and terminates in the gallbladder. Throughout its length, the cystic duct is lined by a spiral mucosal elevation, called the valvula spiralis (valve of Heister).

The Gallbladder

The gallbladder is a muscular membranous sac that stores and concentrates bile. Situated beneath the liver, the gallbladder is pear-shaped and has a capacity of about 50 ml (1.7 fluid ounces). The inner surface of the gallbladder wall is lined with mucous-membrane tissue similar to that of the small intestine. Cells of the mucous membrane have hundreds of microscopic projections called microvilli, which increase the area of fluid absorption. The absorption of water and inorganic salts from the bile by the cells of the mucous membrane causes the stored bile to be about 5 times—but sometimes as much as 18 times—more concentrated than when it was produced in the liver.

Contraction of the muscle wall in the gallbladder is stimulated by the vagus nerve of the parasympathetic system and by the hormone cholecystokinin, which is produced in the upper portions of the intestine. The contractions result in the discharge of bile through the bile duct into the duodenum of the small intestine.

If food is present in the small intestine, bile that is flowing from the two lobes of the liver into the hepatic and common bile ducts will continue directly into the duodenum. If the small intestine is empty, however, the sphincter of Oddi will be closed, and bile flowing down the common duct will accumulate and be forced back up the tube until it reaches the open cystic duct. The bile flows into the cystic duct and gallbladder, where it is stored and concentrated until needed. When food enters the duodenum, the common duct's sphincter opens, the gallbladder contracts, and bile enters the duodenum to aid in the digestion of fats.

The gallbladder is commonly subject to many disorders, particularly the formation of solid deposits called gallstones. Despite its activity, it can be surgically removed without serious effect.

Bile

Bile, also known as gall, is a greenish yellow secretion that is produced in the liver and passed to the gallbladder for concentration, storage, or transport into the first region of the small intestine, the duodenum. Its function is to aid in the digestion of fats in the duodenum. Bile is composed of bile acids and salts, phospholipids, cholesterol, pigments, water, and electrolyte chemicals that keep the total solution slightly acidic (with a pH of about 5 to 6). Bile is continually secreted from the cells of the liver into the common bile duct and gallbladder; once in the gallbladder it becomes highly concentrated. The amount of bile secreted into the duodenum is controlled by the hormones cholecystokinin, secretin, gastrin, and somatostatin and also by the vagus nerve.

Bile salts are composed of the salts of four different kinds of free bile acids (cholic, deoxycholic, chenodeoxycholic, and lithocholic acids). Each of these acids may in turn combine with glycine or taurine to form more complex acids and salts. Bile salts and acids can be synthesized from cholesterol or extracted from the bloodstream by the liver. They pass from the liver into the small intestine, where they act as detergents to emulsify fat and reduce the surface tension on fat droplets to prepare them for the action of pancreatic and intestinal fat-splitting enzymes. The salts are large, negatively charged ions that are not readily absorbed by the upper region of the small intestine. Consequently, they remain in the small intestine until most of the fat is digested.

In the lower small intestine, the salts and acids are absorbed and passed back into the bloodstream until they are once again extracted by the liver. This cycle, from the liver to the small intestine and blood and then back to the liver, is called enterohepatic circulation. Some salts and acids are lost during this process; these are replaced in the liver by continual synthesis from cholesterol. The rate of synthesis is directly related to the amount of acids and salts lost. Bile salts do not normally reach the colon. When they do, however, they may inhibit the absorption of water and sodium, causing a watery diarrhea.

Bile salts and acids are transported in a fluid that contains water, sodium, chloride, and bicarbonates. This fluid is produced in the liver, and it serves to neutralize hydrochloric acid passed from the stomach into the small intestine. Water-insoluble wastes that the liver removes from blood, such as cholesterol, steroids, drugs, and hemoglobin pigments, are carried in the fluid to the excretory system. Hemoglobin pigments are broken down, producing several bile fluid compounds, including bilirubin, which has no known function other than that of a colouring agent. Traces of other substances can also be found in bile including mucus, serum proteins, lecithin, neutral fats, fatty acids, and urea.

THE PANCREAS

The pancreas is a long, narrow gland that is situated transversely across the upper abdomen, behind the stomach and the spleen. The midportion of the pancreas lies against

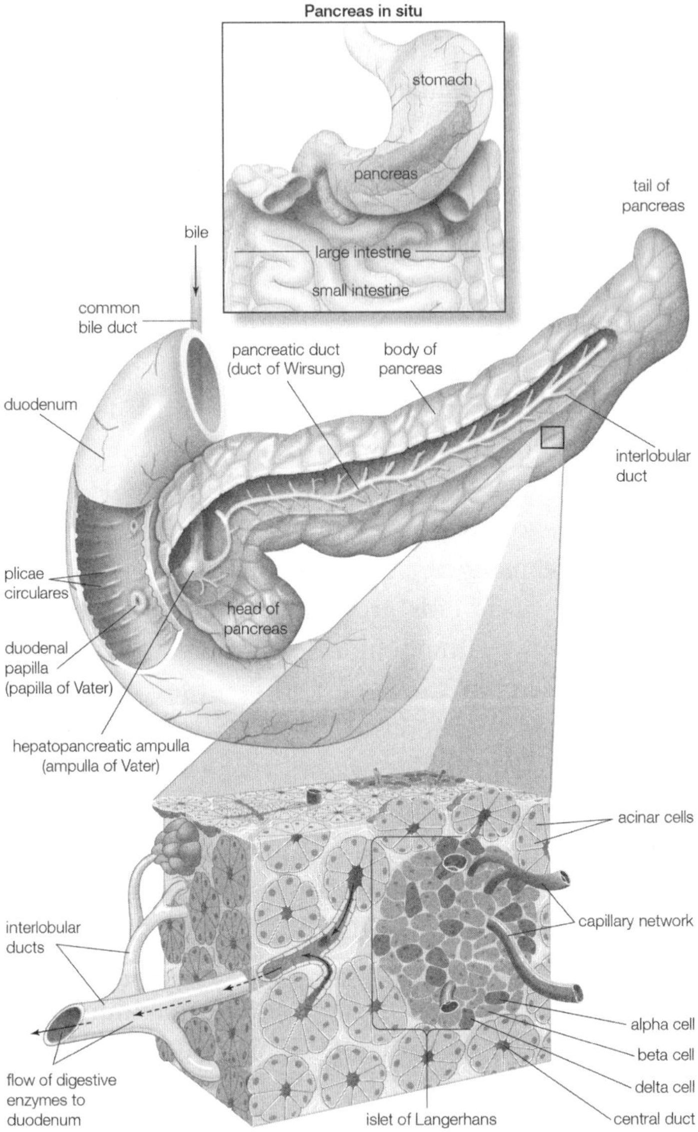

Acinar cells produce digestive enzymes, which are secreted into tiny ducts that feed into the pancreatic duct. Islets of Langerhans are clusters of cells that secrete hormones such as insulin and glucagon directly into a capillary network, which also joins the pancreatic duct. Encyclopædia Britannica, Inc.

the vertebral column, the abdominal aorta, and the inferior vena cava.

The pancreas is both an exocrine (ductal) and endocrine (ductless) gland. The exocrine tissue, called acinar tissue, produces important digestive enzyme precursors that are transmitted into the small intestine, while the endocrine tissue (contained in the islets of Langerhans) produces at least two hormones (insulin and glucagon) that are important in the regulation of carbohydrate metabolism. Two other hormones produced by the pancreas, vasoactive intestinal polypeptide and somatostatin, are pivotal elements in the control of intestinal secretion and motility.

Individual acinar cells have the shape of a truncated pyramid, arranged in groups around a central ductal lumen. These central ducts empty into progressively larger intercalated and collecting ducts that eventually join the pancreatic duct (duct of Wirsung). The pancreatic duct in turn enters the hepatopancreatic ampulla (ampulla of Vater) of the duodenum, where, in about 80 percent of instances, it is joined by the common bile duct. Occasionally the junction with the common bile duct is proximal to the ampulla, and in a few cases the pancreatic duct and the common bile duct join the duodenum separately.

Acinar Cells

The acinar cells constitute more than 95 percent of the cellular population of the exocrine pancreas. They produce a variety of digestive proteins, or enzymes, involved principally with the degradation of dietary proteins (proteases), fats (lipases), and carbohydrates (amylases) in the intestine. Other protein secretions include a trypsin inhibitor, a so-called "stone protein" that keeps calcium in solution, and various serum proteins, including albumin and immunoglobulins.

In the acinar cells almost all enzymatic proteins are synthesized on ribosomes from amino acids carried to the pancreas by the bloodstream. Enzyme precursors are conjugated in the Golgi apparatus and then concentrated into membrane-wrapped zymogen granules, which are stored in the cytoplasm before secretion. Enzymatic secretion is mediated by stimulants such as secretin, a hormone released from the duodenum by the introduction of gastric acid; cholecystokinin, released by the presence of dietary fat; amino acids; hydrochloric acid; and acetylcholine, which is produced as a response to the sensory aspects of feeding and to the physical effects of chewing and swallowing.

Upon binding of specific receptor sites on the acinar membrane with cholecystokinin or acetylcholine, the zymogen granules migrate to the apex of the acinar cell, where they are extruded into the central ductal lumen. Binding of vasoactive intestinal polypeptide or secretin to acinar receptors causes increased production of bicarbonate, sodium, water, and enzymes by acinar cells and small ductal cells. Bicarbonate is secreted in exchange for chloride, and sodium is exchanged for hydrogen, with a resultant increased acidity of the blood leaving the actively secreting pancreas. Binding of cholecystokinin causes production of bicarbonate and enzymes by the acinar cells.

In the absence of cholecystokinin and acetylcholine, as in fasting subjects or in patients being fed intravenously, the synthesis of zymogen by the acinar cells is markedly reduced. Pancreatic atrophy also occurs after removal of the pituitary gland, probably owing to the absence of growth hormone. Thus, cholecystokinin, acetylcholine,

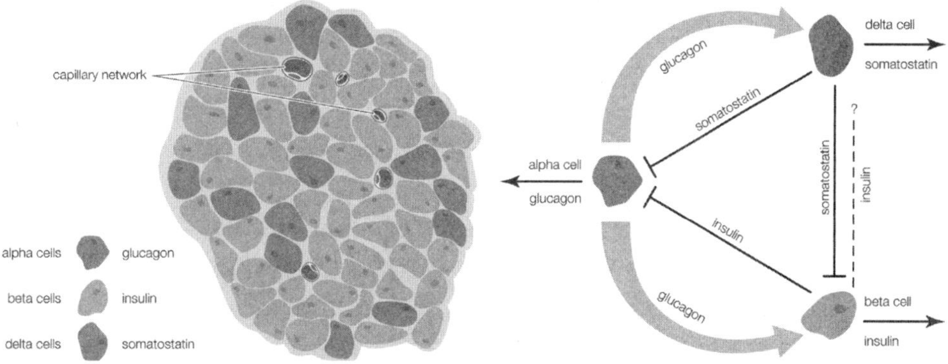

The islets of Langerhans contain alpha, beta, and delta cells that produce glucagon, insulin, and somatostatin, respectively. These hormones regulate one another's secretion through paracrine cell-cell interactions.
Encyclopædia Britannica, Inc.

and growth hormone are pancreatotrophic, or pancreas-feeding, hormones. The pancreas itself also appears to secrete an as-yet-unidentified hormone that is trophic, or nutritive, to the liver.

Islets of Langerhans

The islets, or islands, of Langerhans are irregularly shaped patches of endocrine tissue located within the pancreas of most vertebrates. They are named for the German physician Paul Langerhans, who first described them in 1869. The normal human pancreas contains about 1,000,000 islets. The islets consist of four distinct cell types, of which three (alpha, beta, and delta cells) produce important hormones. The fourth component (C cells) has no known function.

The most common islet cell, the beta cell, produces insulin, the major hormone in the regulation of carbohydrate, fat, and protein metabolism. The release of insulin from the beta cells can be triggered by growth hormone (somatotropin) or by glucagon, but the most important stimulator of insulin release is glucose. When the blood glucose level increases—as it does after a meal—insulin is released to counter it. The inability of the islet cells to make insulin or the failure to produce amounts sufficient to control blood glucose level are the causes of diabetes mellitus.

The alpha cells of the islets of Langerhans produce an opposing hormone, glucagon, which releases glucose from the liver and fatty acids from fat tissue. In turn, glucose and free fatty acids favour insulin release and inhibit glucagon release. The delta cells produce somatostatin, a strong inhibitor of somatotropin, insulin, and glucagon; its role in metabolic regulation is not yet clear. Somatostatin is also produced by the hypothalamus and functions there to inhibit secretion of growth hormone by the pituitary gland.

HORMONES OF THE GASTROINTESTINAL TRACT

Control of the activity of the specialized cells in the digestive system that are concerned with motor and secretory functions depends upon signals received at their cell membranes. These signals originate in either endocrine or nerve cells and are carried to the target cell by amino or peptide "messenger" molecules. When secreted, these substances either diffuse into the tissue spaces around the cells and affect target cells in the vicinity or are taken up in the circulating blood and delivered to target cells some distance away. In both circumstances the messengers are hormones, but those exerting their effect locally are called paracrine. Those exerting their effect at a distance are called endocrine.

The difference between paracrine signaling and endocrine signaling is illustrated by the hormones somatostatin and gastrin. Somatostatin has inhibiting effects on the production of acid in the stomach, the motor activity of the intestine, and the release of digestive enzymes from the pancreas. These effects are achieved by local diffusion of somatostatin from delta cells in the vicinity of the target tissue (delta cells are found in the islets of Langerhans, the intestines, and the stomach). On the other hand, gastrin, a hormone produced by the granular gastrin cells in the mucosa of the gastric antrum (the lower part of the stomach), is secreted into the blood. Thus, it produces its effects at a site distant from the site of its release.

Peptides are composed of a number of amino acids strung together in a chain. The amino acids occur in an ordered sequence that is peculiar to each peptide. The biological activity of the peptide (i.e., the ability to stimulate the target cells) may reside in only a fraction of the chain—for example, in a four- or five-amino-acid sequence. In other instances the entire chain must be intact to achieve this purpose.

Gastrin exemplifies the biological capability of a fraction of the molecule. These fractions have a molecular structure that fits the receptor site on the membrane of the target cell and therefore can initiate the intracellular events in the production of the acid. The gastrin cells of the antrum of the stomach primarily produce a messenger peptide consisting of 17 amino acids, whereas those in the duodenum and jejunum of the small intestine primarily produce a messenger peptide with 34 amino acids. The shorter molecule is more potent. The chain can be cleaved to only four amino acids (the tetrapeptide), however, and (provided that the sequence remains the same as in the parent molecule and the fragment is the one at the amino terminal of the whole molecule) the cleaved amino acid chain retains biological activity, although it is less potent than the larger molecules of gastrin.

Certain messenger peptides have been found to originate not in endocrine cells but in neural elements within the gastrointestinal tract, to be released during electrical discharge within the nerves. For example, vasoactive intestinal polypeptide released from nerve terminals in the brain also is abundant in the nervous structures of the gut, including the submucosal and myenteric nerve plexuses. Occasionally vasoactive intestinal polypeptide coexists with acetylcholine, the messenger molecule of the autonomic parasympathetic nervous system.

Peptides that bind with target cell receptors and stimulate the cell to react are known as agonists. Others that fit the receptor but do not initiate intracellular events are known as antagonists. The ability of antagonists to occupy receptors and thereby deny access to an agonist is the basis of the treatment of peptic ulcer disease with histamine (H_2) receptor blockers. By occupying the receptors on the parietal cells, antagonists deny histamine the opportunity to initiate the production of hydrochloric acid, one of the chief causative agents of peptic ulcers.

Similar events stimulate or suppress the production of the messenger peptides in their endocrine or neural cell of origin. For example, the discharge of granules of gastrin from the gastrin cells occurs when a meal is consumed. While the concentration of hydrogen ions (the acidity) remains low because of the buffering effect of the food, the release of gastrin continues. As digestion proceeds and the stomach begins to empty, however, the acidity increases because of the diminishing neutralizing effect of the food. When the contents of the stomach in contact with the mucosa of the antrum reach a certain level of acidity (pH of 2.5 or less), the release of gastrin stops.

Failure of this mechanism leads to inappropriate secretion of acid when the stomach is empty and may cause peptic ulcers in the duodenum. Some endocrine cells have microvilli on their surface that project into the lumen of the gland or into the main channel of the stomach or intestine. These cells probably have an ability to "sample" continuously the lumenal contents in their vicinity.

When production and secretion of a peptide hormone is excessive, it induces an increase in the number of the target cells and may increase the size of the individual cells. This is known as trophism and is similar to the increase in size of skeletal muscle in response to appropriate exercise (work hypertrophy). Such trophism is observed in certain disease states that involve the gastrointestinal hormones. Thus, when gastrin is secreted into the blood by a tumour of gastrin cells (gastrinoma) of the pancreas, it is a continuous process because there is no mechanism at that site to inhibit the secretion. This brings about a massive increase in the number of parietal cells in the stomach and an overproduction of acid. This in turn overwhelms the defenses of the mucosa of the upper gastrointestinal tract against autodigestion and results in intractable and complicated peptic ulceration.

Eighteen different endocrine cells can be identified within the gastrointestinal tract, but it is probable that several of these and their particular peptides are evolutionary vestiges that functioned in other stages of human development, while others may represent different stages of maturation of the same endocrine cell.

Insulin

As mentioned previously, insulin is a hormone that regulates the level of sugar (glucose) in the blood and that is

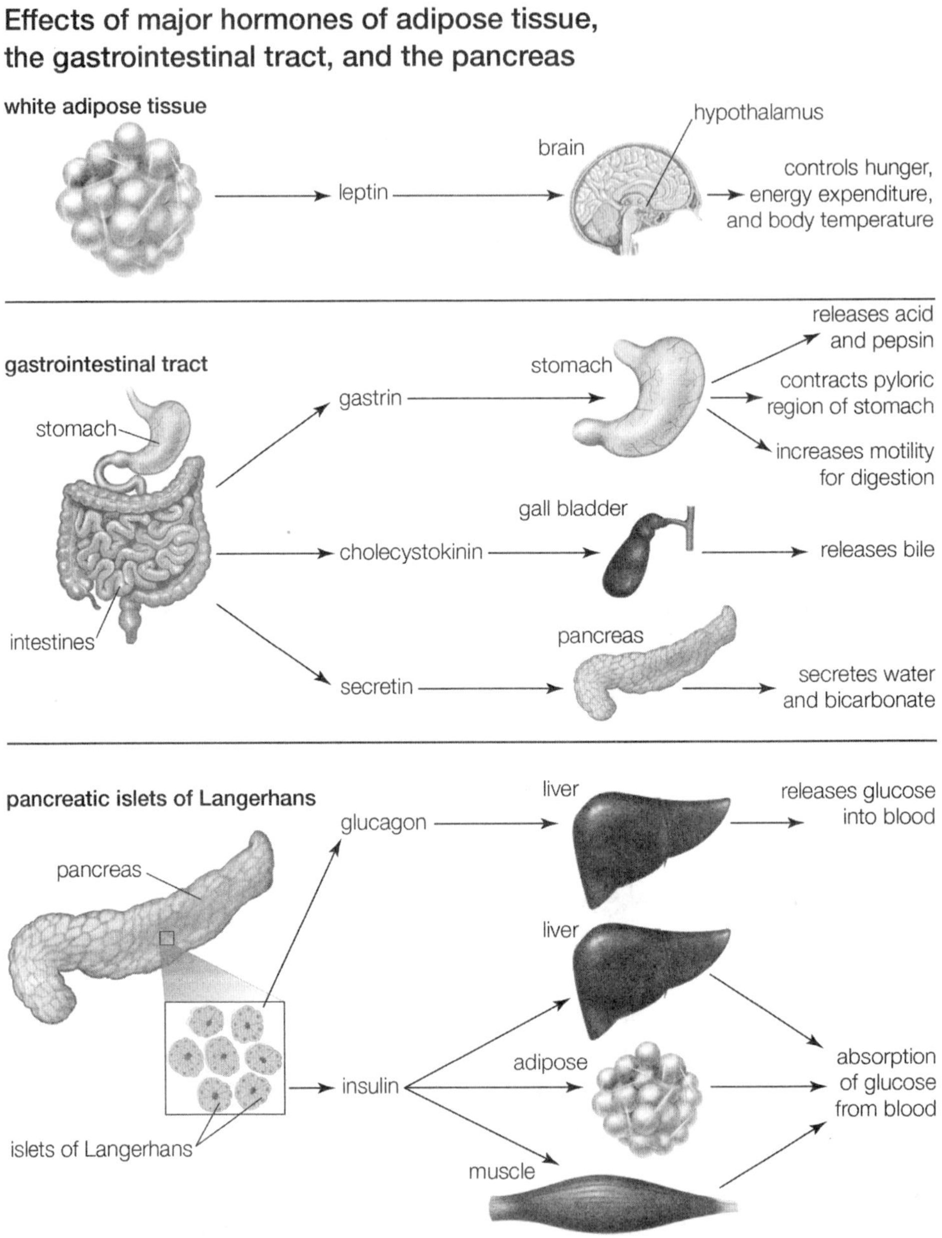

Hormones secreted from adipose tissue, the gastrointestinal tract, and the pancreatic islets of Langerhans regulate a variety of physiological processes. Encyclopædia Britannica, Inc.

produced by the beta cells of the islets of Langerhans in the pancreas. Insulin is secreted when the level of blood glucose rises—as after a meal. When the level of blood glucose falls, secretion of insulin stops, and the liver releases glucose into the blood. Insulin was first isolated as a pancreatic extract in 1921 by the Canadian scientists Sir Frederick G. Banting and Charles H. Best.

Insulin is a protein composed of two chains, an A chain (with 21 amino acids) and a B chain (with 30 amino acids), which are linked together by sulfur atoms. Insulin is derived from a 74-amino-acid prohormone molecule called proinsulin. Proinsulin is relatively inactive, and under normal conditions only a small amount of it is secreted. In the endoplasmic reticulum of beta cells, the proinsulin molecule is cleaved in two places, yielding the A and B chains of insulin and an intervening, biologically inactive C peptide. The A and B chains become linked together by two sulfur-sulfur (disulfide) bonds. Proinsulin, insulin, and C peptide are stored in granules in the beta cells, from which they are released into the capillaries of the islets in response to appropriate stimuli. These capillaries empty into the portal vein, which carries blood from the stomach, intestines, and pancreas to the liver. The pancreas of a normal adult contains approximately 200 units of insulin, and the average daily secretion of insulin into the circulation in healthy individuals ranges from 30 to 50 units.

Several factors stimulate insulin secretion, but by far the most important is the concentration of glucose in the arterial (oxygenated) blood that perfuses the islets. When blood glucose concentrations increase (i.e., following a meal), large amounts of glucose are taken up and metabolized by the beta cells, and the secretion of insulin increases. Conversely, as blood glucose concentrations decrease, the secretion of insulin decreases. However, even during fasting, small amounts of insulin are secreted. The secretion of insulin may also be stimulated by certain amino acids, fatty acids, keto acids (products of fatty acid oxidation), and several hormones secreted by the gastrointestinal tract. The secretion of insulin is inhibited by somatostatin and by activation of the sympathetic nervous system (the branch of the autonomic nervous system responsible for the fight-or-flight response).

Insulin acts primarily to stimulate glucose uptake by three tissues—adipose (fat), muscle, and liver—that are important in the metabolism and storage of nutrients. Like other protein hormones, insulin binds to specific receptors on the outer membrane of its target cells, thereby activating metabolic processes within the cells. A key action of insulin in these cells is to stimulate the translocation of glucose transporters (molecules that mediate cell uptake of glucose) from within the cell to the cell membrane.

In adipose tissue, insulin stimulates glucose uptake and utilization. The presence of glucose in adipose cells, in turn, leads to increased uptake of fatty acids from the circulation, increased synthesis of fatty acids in the cells, and increased esterification (when an acid molecule binds to an alcohol) of fatty acids with glycerol to form triglycerides, the storage form of fat. In addition, insulin is a potent inhibitor of the breakdown of triglycerides (lipolysis). This prevents the release of fatty acids and glycerol from fat cells, saving them for when they are needed by the body (e.g., when exercising or fasting). As serum insulin concentrations decrease, lipolysis and fatty acid release increase.

In muscle tissue, insulin stimulates the transport of glucose and amino acids into muscle cells. The glucose is stored as glycogen, a storage molecule that can be broken down to supply energy for muscle contraction during exercise and to supply energy during fasting. The amino acids transported into muscle cells in response to insulin stimulation are utilized for the synthesis of protein. In contrast, in the absence of insulin the protein of muscle cells is broken down to supply amino acids to the liver for transformation into glucose.

Insulin is not required for the transport of glucose into liver cells, but it has profound effects on glucose metabolism in these cells. It stimulates the formation of glycogen, and it inhibits the breakdown of glycogen (glycogenolysis) and the synthesis of glucose from amino acids and glycerol (gluconeogenesis). Therefore, the overall effect of insulin is to increase glucose storage and to decrease glucose production and release by the liver. These actions of insulin are opposed by glucagon, another pancreatic hormone produced by cells in the islets of Langerhans.

Inadequate production of insulin is responsible for the condition called diabetes mellitus. Severe diabetics require periodic injections of insulin. The first insulin injections utilized hormone extracts from pigs, sheep, and cattle, but by the early 1980s, certain strains of bacteria had been genetically modified to produce human insulin. Today the treatment of diabetes mellitus relies primarily on a form of human insulin that is made using recombinant DNA technology.

Glucagon

Glucagon is a 29-amino-acid peptide that is produced specifically by the alpha cells of the islets. It has a high degree of similarity with several glucagon-like peptides that are secreted by cells scattered throughout the gastrointestinal tract. Glucagon secretion is stimulated by the ingestion of protein, by low blood glucose concentrations (hypoglycemia), and by exercise. It is inhibited by the ingestion of carbohydrates, an effect that may be mediated by the resultant increase in blood glucose concentrations and insulin secretion. Glucagon strongly opposes the action of insulin; it raises the concentration of glucose in the blood by promoting glycogenolysis and by stimulating gluconeogenesis. By increasing the concentration of glucose in the bloodstream, glucagon plays a critical role in maintaining blood glucose concentrations during fasting and exercise.

Intestinal Glucagon

Intestinal glucagon (enteroglucagon) is secreted by L cells, which are found throughout the gastrointestinal tract, in response to the presence of carbohydrate and triglycerides in the small intestine. Intestinal glucagon modulates intestinal motility and has a strong trophic influence on mucosal structures.

Somatostatin

Somatostatin is a polypeptide that inhibits the activity of certain pancreatic and gastrointestinal hormones. Somatostatin exists in two forms: one composed of 14 amino acids and a second composed of 28 amino acids. The name *somatostatin*, essentially meaning stagnation of a body, was coined when investigators found that an extract of hypothalamic tissues inhibited the release of growth hormone from the pituitary gland. Somatostatin subsequently was found to be widely distributed throughout the central nervous system and to occur in other tissues.

In the pancreas, somatostatin is produced by the delta cells of the islets of Langerhans, where it serves to block the secretion of both insulin and glucagon from adjacent cells. Insulin, glucagon, and somatostatin act in concert to control the flow of nutrients into and out of the circulation. The relative concentrations of these hormones regulate the rates of absorption, utilization, and storage of glucose, amino acids, and fatty acids. The anatomic proximity of the beta, alpha, and delta cells in the islets of Langerhans is important. Somatostatin and glucagon appear to have a paracrine relationship, each influencing the secretion of the other, with both affecting the rate of insulin release. Somatostatin also inhibits the secretion of several gastrointestinal hormones—including gastrin, secretin, cholecystokinin, and vasoactive intestinal polypeptide. This results in the inhibition of many functions of the gastrointestinal tract, including the secretion of acid by the stomach, the secretion of digestive enzymes by the pancreas, and the absorption of nutrients by the intestine.

Few examples of somatostatin deficiency have been found. Alzheimer disease appears to cause a decrease in somatostatin levels in brain tissue, although it is not clear what role this plays in the course of the disease. In the late 1970s, a rare somatostatin-producing tumour called a somatostatinoma was first identified. Since then somatostatinomas have been well characterized. The tumours tend to develop in the pancreas, duodenum, or jejunum, and diagnosis is based on plasma levels of a substance called somatostatin-like immunoreactivity (SLI), which may be 50 times greater than normal in individuals with a somatostatinoma. The excess levels of somatostatin may cause abdominal cramps and pain, persistent diarrhea, high blood glucose concentrations, weight loss, and episodic flushing of the skin.

Serotonin

Serotonin, or 5-hydroxytryptamine, is an amine that is formed from the amino acid 5-hydroxytrytophan in the enterochromaffin cells (EC) and in other similar cells called enterochromaffin-like cells (ECL). These cells also secrete histamine and kinins, which likewise have important messenger functions in glandular secretions and on blood vessels. Serotonin acts in paracrine fashion. Both EC and ECL cells are widely distributed in the epithelial lining of the gastrointestinal tract.

Cholecystokinin

Cholecystokinin (or CCK; formerly called pancreozymin) is a digestive hormone released with secretin when food from the stomach reaches the duodenum. Cholecystokinin and pancreozymin were once considered two separate hormones because two distinct actions had been described: the release of enzymes from the pancreas, an action ascribed to pancreozymin; and the contraction of the gallbladder, which forces bile into the duodenum, an action ascribed to cholecystokinin. However, today these two actions are recognized as belonging to one enzyme, now known solely as cholecystokinin.

Cholecystokinin is secreted by cells of the upper small intestine. Its secretion is stimulated by the introduction of hydrochloric acid or fatty acids into the stomach or the duodenum. Cholecystokinin stimulates the gallbladder to contract and release stored bile into the intestine. It also stimulates the secretion of pancreatic juice and may induce satiety. There are several hypotheses regarding cholecystokinin's ability to induce satiety. One hypothesis is that meal-induced secretion of cholecystokinin activates the satiety centre of the hypothalamus in the brain so that the person feels full and stops eating. A second hypothesis is that, because cholecystokinin inhibits emptying of the stomach, the sensation of satiety may be the result of distension of the stomach.

Gastric Inhibitory Polypeptide

Gastric inhibitory polypeptide is a hormone secreted by cells of the intestinal mucosa. It acts to block the secretion of hydrochloric acid into the stomach, and it increases insulin secretion from the beta cells of the islets of Langerhans. This latter action causes an increase in serum insulin concentrations that is significantly larger after ingesting glucose than after intravenous administration of the same amount of glucose.

Pancreatic Polypeptide

Pancreatic polypeptide is a hormone consisting of 36 amino acids that is secreted by the F (or PP) cells of the islets of Langerhans. Its secretion is stimulated by eating, exercising, and fasting. It can inhibit gallbladder contraction and pancreatic exocrine secretion, but its role in the metabolism of nutrients is uncertain.

Secretin

Secretin is a digestive hormone made up of 27 amino acids that is released from the wall of the duodenum. It was discovered in 1902 by British physiologists Sir William M. Bayliss and Ernest H. Starling. Bayliss and Starling placed dilute hydrochloric acid into a segment of a dog's bowel from which the nerve supply had been severed. They then collected an extract of the bowel lining and injected it into another dog. The result was an increase in the secretion of pancreatic juice in the dog that received the injection. They named the material in the extract "secretin." With this discovery emerged the concept that chemical messages could act at distant sites to regulate bodily functions.

When hydrochloric acid passes from the stomach into the duodenum, secretin is released into the bloodstream and stimulates the acinar cells of the pancreas to secrete water and bicarbonate into the pancreatic ducts that drain into the duodenum. By this mechanism, hydrochloric acid secreted by the stomach, which can be damaging to the intestinal lining, is promptly diluted and neutralized. Secretin also inhibits the secretion of gastrin, which triggers the initial release of hydrochloric acid into the stomach, and delays gastric emptying.

Vasoactive Intestinal Polypeptide

Vasoactive intestinal polypeptide is a 28-amino-acid hormone secreted by endocrine cells or nerve endings in the gastrointestinal tract. It inhibits the release of gastrin and the secretion of acid, is a mild stimulant of bicarbonate secretion from the pancreas, and is a powerful stimulant of the secretion of water and electrolytes by the small and large intestines.

Studies have indicated that vasoactive intestinal polypeptide is capable of acting as a neurotransmitter (a chemical agent released by neurons to stimulate neighbouring neurons). This mode of action has been associated with the hormone's ability to induce a relaxation effect in some tissues. Certain other gastrointestinal hormones are suspected to act as neurotransmitters as well. These hormones include motilin, neuropeptide Y (which interacts with ghrelin to regulate appetite), gastrin-releasing peptide (bombesin-like peptide), glucagon, and somatostatin.

Some pancreatic islet-cell tumours secrete excessive amounts of vasoactive intestinal polypeptide (a condition called Verner-Morrison syndrome, or pancreatic cholera). These tumours cause severe, intractable, debilitating watery diarrhea and an associated loss of large quantities of potassium. The resulting dehydration may be life-threatening.

Endorphins and Enkephalins

Endorphins and enkephalins, each comprising five amino acids in the molecule, are present in the vagus nerves and the myenteric plexus. They have the properties of opiate (opium-derived) substances such as morphine. They bind to the same receptors and are neutralized by the opiate antagonist naloxone. There is no evidence that endorphins and enkephalins are circulating hormones, but the enkephalins may have a physiological paracrine role in modulating smooth muscle activity in the gastrointestinal tract, and endorphins may serve in modulating the release of other peptides from endocrine cells in the digestive system.

Prostaglandins

Prostaglandins are hormonelike substances involved in the contraction and relaxation of the smooth muscle of the gastrointestinal tract. Prostaglandins are also able to protect the mucosa of the alimentary tract from injury by various insults (boiling water, alcohol, aspirin, bile acids, stress) by increasing the secretion of mucus and bicarbonate from the mucosa, which in turn stimulates the migration of cells to the surface for repair and replacement of the mucosal lining.

Other Hormones of Importance

A hormone known as motilin is secreted between meals. A high level of motilin in the blood stimulates the contraction of the fundus and antrum and accelerates gastric emptying. It contracts the gallbladder and increases the squeeze pressure of the lower esophageal sphincter. A hormone called neurotensin is secreted by the N cells of the ileum in response to fat in the small intestine. Neurotensin modulates motility, relaxes the lower esophageal sphincter, and blocks the stimulation of acid and pepsin secretion by the vagus nerve.

Substance P—which is present in significant amounts in the vagus nerves and the myenteric plexus—stimulates saliva production, contraction of smooth muscle cells, and inflammatory responses in tissues, but it is uncertain whether it is anything other than an evolutionary vestige. A peptide called bombesin is found in the intrinsic nerves of the gastrointestinal tract. It stimulates the release of gastrin and pancreatic enzymes and causes contraction of the gallbladder. These functions may be secondary, however, to the release of cholecystokinin. It is uncertain if bombesin has a physiological role or if it is an evolutionary vestige, similar to substance P.

CHAPTER 5

FEATURES OF THE DIGESTIVE TRACT

Through the act of eating, or ingestion, nutrients enter the body, and it is the role of the digestive system to then render these nutrients useful to cells. Many nutrient molecules are so large and complex that they must be split into smaller molecules before they can be used by cells. This process of breaking down food into molecular particles of usable size and content is called digestion. Each segment of the digestive tract carries out a specific function in the larger process of digestion, and collectively the entire system enables the efficient extraction of nutrients and the disposal of wastes. Thus, nutrient digestion and absorption form the two major functions of the digestive system.

The digestive tract is also equipped with special features to deal with nonnutrient entities from the external environment that enter the body. For example, it is designed to facilitate the movement of gases such as air swallowed with food and methane produced by gut bacteria, and to protect against infectious organisms that may accompany food into the body. In fact, the digestive system serves as an important resource for immune defense, with unique epithelial barriers and supplies of immune cells called lymphocytes, which are constantly ready for dispatch upon entry and detection of a potentially harmful agent.

ROLE OF DIGESTION

Cells require a constant source of energy in order to function. In humans this energy comes primarily from the nutrients found in foods. Some nutrients serve as raw materials for the synthesis of cellular material. Others (e.g., many vitamins) act as regulators of chemical reactions; and still others, upon oxidation, yield energy. Not all nutrients, however, are in a form suitable for immediate use by the body. Some must undergo physical and chemical changes before they can serve as energy or cell substance. This function is fulfilled by digestion.

Once food is broken down mechanically and is converted chemically, it can be absorbed by cells and used to maintain vital bodily functions. The amount of energy derived from food depends on the nutrients that the food contains, as well as on the body's ability to absorb the chemically converted substances. The role of digestion then is to process foods to the point where they can be readily absorbed into the bloodstream and delivered to cells.

UTILIZATION OF FOOD BY THE BODY

The human body can be thought of as an engine that releases the energy present in the foods that it digests. This energy is utilized partly for the mechanical work performed by the muscles and in the secretory processes and partly for the work necessary to maintain the body's structure and functions. The performance of work is associated with the production of heat. Heat loss is controlled so as to keep body temperature within a narrow range. Unlike other engines, however, the human body is continually breaking down (catabolizing) and building up (anabolizing) its component parts. Foods supply nutrients essential to the manufacture of the new material and provide energy needed for the chemical reactions involved.

Carbohydrate, fat, and protein are, to a large extent, interchangeable as sources of energy. Typically, the energy provided by food is measured in kilocalories, or Calories. One kilocalorie is equal to 1,000 gram-calories (or small calories), a measure of heat energy. However, in common parlance, kilocalories are referred to as "calories." In other words, a 2,000-calorie diet actually has 2,000 kilocalories of potential energy. One kilocalorie is the amount of heat energy required to raise one kilogram of water from 14.5 to 15.5 °C (58.1 to 59.9°F) at one atmosphere of pressure. Another unit of energy widely used is the joule, which measures energy in terms of mechanical work. One joule is the energy expended when one kilogram is moved a distance of one metre by a force of one newton. The relatively higher levels of energy in human nutrition are more likely to be measured in kilojoules (1 kilojoule = 10^3 joules) or megajoules (1 megajoule = 10^6 joules). One kilocalorie is equivalent to 4.184 kilojoules.

The energy present in food can be determined directly by measuring the output of heat when the food is burned (oxidized) in a bomb calorimeter. However, the human body is not as efficient as a calorimeter, and some potential energy is lost during digestion and metabolism. Corrected physiological values for the heats of combustion of the three energy-yielding nutrients, rounded to whole numbers, are as follows: carbohydrate, 4 kilocalories (17 kilojoules) per gram; protein, 4 kilocalories (17 kilojoules) per gram; and fat, 9 kilocalories (38 kilojoules) per gram. Beverage alcohol (ethyl alcohol) also yields energy—7 kilocalories (29 kilojoules) per gram—although it is not essential in the diet. Vitamins, minerals, water, and other food constituents have no energy value, although many of them participate in energy-releasing processes in the body.

The energy provided by a well-digested food can be estimated if the gram amounts of energy-yielding substances (non-fibre carbohydrate, fat, protein, and alcohol) in that food are known. For example, a slice of white bread containing 12 grams of carbohydrate, 2 grams of protein, and 1 gram of fat supplies 67 kilocalories (280 kilojoules) of energy. Food composition tables and food labels provide useful data for evaluating energy and nutrient intake of an individual diet. Most foods provide a mixture of energy-supplying nutrients, along with vitamins, minerals, water, and other substances. Two notable exceptions are table sugar and vegetable oil, which are virtually pure carbohydrate (sucrose) and fat, respectively.

Throughout most of the world, protein supplies between 8 and 16 percent of the energy in the diet, although there are wide variations in the proportions of fat and carbohydrate in different populations. In more prosperous communities about 12 to 15 percent of energy is typically derived from protein, 30 to 40 percent from fat, and 50 to 60 percent from carbohydrate. On the other hand, in many poorer agricultural societies, where cereals comprise the bulk of the diet, carbohydrate provides an even larger percentage of energy,

First Lady Michelle Obama gets help from students with the harvest of the White House garden. Mark Wilson/Getty Images

with protein and fat providing less. The human body is remarkably adaptable and can survive, and even thrive, on widely divergent diets. However, different dietary patterns are associated with particular health consequences.

NUTRIENT DIGESTION

There are four means by which digestive products are absorbed: active transport, passive diffusion, facilitated diffusion, and endocytosis. Active transport involves the movement of a substance across the membrane of the absorbing cell against an electrical or chemical gradient. It is carrier-mediated; that is, the substance is temporarily bound to another substance that transports it across the cell membrane, where it is released. This process requires energy and is at risk of competitive inhibition by other substances. That is, other substances with a similar molecular structure can compete for the binding site on the carrier.

Passive diffusion requires neither energy nor a carrier. The substance merely passes along a simple concentration gradient from an area of high concentration of the substance to an area of low concentration until a state of equilibrium exists on either side of the membrane. Facilitated diffusion also requires no energy, but it involves a carrier, or protein molecule located on the outside of the cell membrane that binds the substance and carries it into the cell. The carrier may be competitively inhibited. Endocytosis takes place when the material to be absorbed, on reaching the cell membrane, is engulfed into the cell interior.

Absorption of food by the small intestine occurs principally in the middle section, or jejunum. However, the duodenum, although the shortest portion of the small intestine, has an extremely important role. The duodenum receives not only chyme saturated with gastric acid but pancreatic and liver secretions as well. It is in the duodenum that the intestinal contents are rendered isotonic with the blood plasma; i.e., the pressures and volumes of the intestinal contents are the same as those of the blood plasma, so that the cells on either side of the barrier will neither gain nor lose water.

Bicarbonate secreted by the pancreas neutralizes the acid secreted by the stomach. This brings the intestinal contents to the optimal pH, allowing the various digestive enzymes to act on their substrates at peak efficiency. A number of important gastrointestinal hormones regulate gastric emptying, gastric secretion, pancreatic secretion, and contraction of the gallbladder. These hormones, along with neural impulses from the autonomic nervous system, provide for autoregulatory mechanisms for normal digestive processes.

Most salts and minerals, as well as water, are readily absorbed from all portions of the small intestine. Sodium is absorbed by an active process, the necessary metabolic energy being provided by the epithelial cells of the mucosa of the small intestine. Sodium is moved from the lumen of the intestine across the mucosa against a concentration gradient (i.e., a progressive increase in the concentration of sodium) and an electrochemical gradient (i.e., a gradual increase in the concentration of charged ions). Sodium ions are absorbed more readily from the jejunum than from other parts of the small intestine. Chloride is readily absorbed in the small intestine, probably as a consequence of sodium absorption.

Potassium is absorbed at about 5 percent of the rate of sodium. It is thought that potassium moves across the intestinal mucosa passively or by facilitated diffusion as a consequence of water absorption. The absorption of water appears to be secondary to the absorption of electrolytes (substances that dissociate into ions in a solution). Water absorption occurs throughout the small intestine, though chiefly in the jejunum. Water moves freely across the intestinal mucosa both ways, but it tends to move in the direction of the hypertonic solution (the solution into which a net flow of water occurs) and away from the hypotonic solution (one from which a net flow of water occurs). Thus, if the contents of the lumen are hypotonic, water moves rapidly from the lumen to the blood. If the contents of the intestinal lumen are hypertonic, water moves more rapidly from the blood into the lumen. This two-way movement of water tends to maintain the intestinal contents in an isotonic state.

Carbohydrates

Carbohydrates are absorbed as monosaccharides (simple sugars such as glucose, fructose, and galactose that cannot be further broken down by hydrolysis) or as disaccharides (carbohydrates such as sucrose, lactose, maltose, and dextrin that can be hydrolyzed to two monosaccharides). These simpler molecules, however, must be obtained by the breaking down of polysaccharides, complex carbohydrates that contain many monosaccharides. Chief among these is amylose, a starch that accounts for 20 percent of dietary carbohydrate. Amylose consists of a straight chain of glucose molecules bound to their neighbours by oxygen links. The bulk of the starch is amylopectin, which has a branch chain linked in after every 25 molecules of glucose on the main chain.

Only a small amount of starch is digested by salivary amylase. Most is rapidly digested in the duodenum by pancreatic amylase. But even this enzyme has little effect on the branch chains of amylopectin and even less on the linkages in cellulose molecules. This accounts for the inability of humans to break down cellulose. There are several forms of amylase in pancreatic juice whose function is to hydrolyze complex carbohydrates to disaccharides and trisaccharides and amylopectins to dextrins. In the brush border (comprising ultrafine microvilli) and the surface membrane of the epithelial enterocytes are the disaccharidase enzymes, lactase, maltase, sucrase, and trehalase, which hydrolyze maltose and the dextrins to the monosaccharides glucose, galactose, and fructose.

Glucose—which is one of the two monosaccharide components of table sugar (sucrose) and milk sugar (lactose)—is combined with phosphate in the liver cell and is either transported to peripheral tissues for metabolic purposes or stored in the hepatocyte as glycogen, a complex polysaccharide. Specific enzyme systems are present in the hepatocyte for these conversions, as well as for the translation of other dietary monosaccharides (fructose from sucrose and galactose from lactose) into glucose. The hepatocyte (liver cell) is also able to convert certain amino acids and products of glucose metabolism (pyruvate and lactate) into glucose through gluconeogenesis.

Fructose appears to be absorbed by simple diffusion, but glucose and galactose are transported by an energy-using process, probably binding to a specific protein carrier with attached sodium ions. The sugar is released inside the enterocyte, sodium is pumped out, and the sugars then diffuse into the circulation down a concentration gradient.

Dietary Fibre

Dietary fibre, the structural parts of plants, cannot be digested by the human intestine because the necessary enzymes are lacking. Even though these nondigestible compounds pass through the gut unchanged (except for a small percentage that is fermented by bacteria in the large intestine), they nevertheless contribute to good health. Insoluble fibre does not dissolve in water and provides bulk, or roughage, that helps with bowel function (regularity) and accelerates the exit from the body of potentially carcinogenic or otherwise harmful substances in food.

Types of insoluble fibre are cellulose, most hemicelluloses, and lignin (a phenolic polymer, not a carbohydrate). Major food sources of insoluble fibre are whole grain breads and cereals, wheat bran, and vegetables. Soluble fibre, which dissolves or swells in water, slows down the transit time of food through the gut (an undesirable effect) but also helps lower blood cholesterol levels (a desirable effect). Types of soluble fibre are gums, pectins, some hemicelluloses, and mucilages. Fruits (especially citrus fruits and apples), oats, barley, and legumes are major food sources. Both soluble and insoluble fibre help delay glucose absorption, thus ensuring a slower and more even supply of blood glucose. Dietary fibre is thought to provide important protection against some gastrointestinal diseases and to reduce the risk of other chronic diseases as well.

Proteins

The digestion of protein entails breaking the complex molecule first into peptides, each having a number of amino acids, and second into individual amino acids. The pepsins are enzymes secreted by the stomach in the presence of acid that breaks down proteins (proteolysis). The pepsins account for about 10 to 15 percent of protein digestion. They are most active in the first hour of digestion, and their ability to break down protein is restricted by the necessity for an acidic environment with a pH

Meat—such as this steak—is an important source of protein. Other protein-rich foods include eggs, beans, and milk.
Miguel Mendez/AFP/Getty Images

between 1.8 and 3.5. The trypsins (proteolytic enzymes secreted by the pancreas) are much more powerful than pepsins, so the greater part of protein digestion occurs in the duodenum and upper jejunum. Therefore, even after total removal of the stomach, protein digestion usually is not impaired.

Pancreatic secretion contains inactive protease precursors that become enzymatically active after interacting with another enzyme, enterokinase, which is secreted from the microvillous component of the enterocytes in the duodenal and jejunal mucosa. Trypsinogen is activated in the intestine by enterokinase, which is liberated from duodenal lining cells by the interaction of bile acids and cholecystokinin. This activation of trypsinogen to trypsin is initiated by the cleavage from it of six terminal amino acid residues. The other proteases are activated by free trypsin. The net effect of these proteases is to reduce dietary proteins to small polypeptide chains of two to six amino acids and to single amino acids.

Trypsin activates the other pancreatic proteases, including chymotrypsin and elastase. Trypsin, chymotrypsin, and elastase are known as endopeptidases and are responsible for the initial breakdown of the protein chains to peptides by hydrolysis. The next step—the breakdown of these peptides to smaller molecules and then to individual amino acids—is brought about by the enzymic activity of carboxypeptidases, which are also secreted by the pancreas.

Peptidase activity commences outside the enterocytes (in the mucus and brush border) and continues inside the cell. A different peptidase appears to be involved in each stage of the breakdown of protein to amino acids. Likewise, the transport of different peptides involves different mechanisms. Dipeptides (peptides that release two amino acids on hydrolysis) and tripeptides (peptides that release three amino acids) are moved from the surface brush border into the cell by an energy-requiring process involving a carrier protein. Small peptides with few amino acids are absorbed directly as such. The greater part of the breakdown of peptides to amino acids takes place within the enterocyte. Curiously, small peptides are absorbed more rapidly than amino acids, and, indeed, the precise details of the mechanism for absorption of amino acids are largely unknown. It is known that some amino acids have a specific individual transport system while others share one.

Amino acids may be classified into groups, depending upon their optical rotatory characteristics (i.e., whether they rotate polarized light to the left, or levo, or to the right, or dextro) and in terms of reactivity, or acidity (pH).

Levorotatory amino acids are absorbed extremely rapidly—much more rapidly than are dextrorotatory amino acids. In fact, levorotatory amino acids are absorbed almost as quickly as they are released from protein or peptide. Neutral amino acids have certain structural requirements for active transport, and if these specific structural arrangements are disturbed, active transport will not occur. Basic amino acids, which have a pH above 7, are transported at about 5 to 10 percent of the rate of neutral levorotatory amino acids.

Fats

Almost all dietary fat is stored as triglycerides. Solubility in water is necessary in order for fat to be transferred from the lumen of the intestine to the absorptive cells. Many factors, such as the length of the fatty acid chains of the triglycerides, play an important role in determining this solubility. Triglycerides have three long chains of fatty acids (LCFA) attached to a glycerol framework, and they are insoluble in water. The remainder are medium-chain triglycerides (MCT), which can be absorbed intact by the mucosa of the small intestine.

Lipases, which include phospholipase, esterase, colipase, and lipase, function to reduce MCTs to free monoglycerides and medium-chain fatty acids (MCFA), which are more soluble in water than the LCFAs and move quickly through the cells and pass into the portal circulation and then to the liver. Lipases require the presence of bile acids in the intestinal lumen for the formation of micellar solutions of fat prior to optimal digestion.

Long-chain fatty acids attached to the triglycerides are attacked by the pancreatic enzyme lipase. Two of the three fatty acid chains are split off, leaving one attached to the glycerol (forming a monoglyceride). In the presence of excess levels of bile salts, however, this activity of pancreatic lipase is inhibited. A lipase may be present in gastric juice, but it is not capable of digesting MCFAs and LCFAs, and the proportion of small-chain fatty acids in food is small. Thus, little digestion occurs in the stomach.

Another pancreatic enzyme, colipase, binds to the bile salts, leaving lipase available to attack the triglycerides. The monoglycerides that result from these splitting processes combine into a complex called a micelle. The micelle permits fat components to be soluble in water. Because bile salts have a hydrophobic, or water-repelling region, and a hydrophilic, or water-attracting region, the micelle is formed with bile salts arranged around the outside with hydrophobic ends facing inside and hydrophobic fatty acids, monoglycerides, phospholipids, and cholesterol, as well as the fat-soluble vitamins A, D, E, and K, in the centre.

There is a layer of fluid overlying the surface cells of the mucosa of the small intestine known as the "unstirred" layer. It is across this layer that the micelles must pass to reach the cell membranes. The rate of diffusion through the unstirred layer is determined by the thickness of the layer and the gradient in concentrations of the various elements of the transport system from the lumen of the intestine to the cell membrane. Underneath the unstirred layer is a glycoprotein layer known as the "fuzzy coat," which mainly comprises mucus. Beneath the fuzz is the brush border on the surface of the cell membrane. It has a double layer of lipid that is easily penetrated by the fatty acids and monoglycerides that are soluble in lipids.

Once the micelle has passed through the fuzzy coat and the brush border, it enters the cells of the tissues that line the intestine. The micelle disintegrates, the bile salts diffuse back into the lumen, and a carrier protein picks up the fatty acids and the monoglycerides and transports them to the endoplasmic reticulum, a tubular structure rich in enzymes, in the cell interior. At this site the triglyceride is synthesized again under the influence of an enzyme catalyst called acyltransferase.

The triglycerides pass to the membrane of another tubular structure, known as the Golgi apparatus, where they are packaged into vesicles (chylomicrons). These vesicles are spheres with an outer coating of phospholipids and a small amount of apoprotein, while the interior is entirely triglyceride except for a small quantity of cholesterol. The chylomicrons migrate to the cell membrane, pass through it, and are attracted into the fine branches of the lymphatic system, the lacteals. From there the chylomicrons pass to the thoracic duct. The whole process of absorption, from the formation of micelles to the movement out of the cells and into the lacteals, takes between 10 and 15 minutes.

The medium-chain triglycerides are broken down to medium-chain fatty acids by pancreatic lipase. Medium-chain fatty acids are soluble in water and readily enter the micelles. Ultimately, after moving across the membrane of the enterocyte, they pass into the capillary tributaries of the portal vein and then to the liver.

The liver metabolizes fat by converting stored fatty acids to their energy-releasing form, acetylcoenzyme A (acetyl CoA), when hepatic glucose and glycogen stores are exhausted or unavailable for metabolic purposes (as in diabetic ketoacidosis). The liver also plays a role in the formation of storage fats (triglycerides) whenever carbohydrates, protein, or fat exceeds the requirements of tissues for glucose or the needs of the liver for glycogen. Furthermore, the liver synthesizes cell membrane components (phospholipids) and proteins (lipoproteins) that carry lipids (fats and cholesterol) in the blood.

Vitamins

Fat-soluble vitamins pass with the chylomicrons into the lymphatic system. Vitamin A, first presenting as the precursor beta-carotene, is cleaved to form retinol, which is then recombined with fatty acids before entering the chylomicron. Vitamins D and D_3 diffuse passively into the chylomicron. The absence of bile salts from the intestine—which occurs in jaundice due to obstruction of the biliary tract—severely impairs vitamin K absorption and blood clotting, with risk of hemorrhage. Vitamin E, a mixture of oils known as tocopherols, is present in eggs and is synthesized by such plants as soybeans, corn (maize), and wheat. It passes through the enterocyte with the other lipids of the micelle and is ultimately stored in the liver.

Folic Acid

Folic acid (pteroylglutamic acid) is necessary for the synthesis of nucleic acids and for cell replication. Folic acid deficiency results in an impaired maturation of red blood cells (erythrocytes). Folates are synthesized by bacteria and plants and are hydrolyzed to folic acid in the intestine. Milk and fruit are the main sources of folic acid, providing on average 500 micrograms daily. Folic acid is stored in the liver.

The hydrolysis of the folates, a necessary step to absorption, takes place on the brush borders of jejunal enterocytes and is completed on lysosomes—structures within the cell that contain various hydrolytic enzymes and are part of the intracellular digestive system. When hydrolysis of folates is disturbed, anemia develops. This process is interfered with by certain drugs, especially phenytoin, used in the management of epilepsy, and by the long-term use of sulfonamides in the suppression of disease. A methyl group is added to pteroylglutamic acid in the enterohepatic circulation in the liver and is excreted in the bile. Approximately 100 micrograms are utilized each day. The method of absorption is uncertain.

Vitamin B_{12}

Vitamin B_{12}, also called cobalamin because it contains cobalt, is essential to the formation of blood cells. It is a coenzyme that assists the enzymes responsible for moving folate into the cell interior. Vitamin B_{12} is a product of bacterial metabolism. Although bacteria in the colon also produce vitamin B_{12}, it cannot be absorbed at that site.

Vitamin B_{12} occurs in a bound form in food and is liberated by proteolytic activity in the stomach and small intestine. It then binds with intrinsic factor (IF), a glycoprotein produced by the same parietal cells that form hydrochloric acid. Intrinsic factor is essential to transport, and the B_{12} protein complex, known as transcobalamin II, is necessary to transfer the vitamin from the intestine to the rest of the body. Once the IF is attached, further proteolytic digestion of the bound vitamin is prevented. Absorption is confined to the distal 100 cm of ileum, especially the last 20 cm, where the complex binds to receptors in the brush border of the enterocytes. The process is slow; it takes three hours from its presentation in food to its appearance in the peripheral blood via the enterohepatic circulation and hepatic veins. The daily requirement of vitamin B_{12} is one microgram. Vitamin B_{12} is stored primarily in the liver.

Vitamin D

Vitamin D is essentially a hormone and is available from two sources. First, under the influence of photosynthesis made possible by ultraviolet rays from the Sun, a sterol compound from the liver (dehydrocholesterol) is converted to vitamin D_3. This supplies enough vitamin D_3 for human needs. In the absence of exposure to sunlight, dietary supplements become necessary. Eggs, liver, fortified bread, and milk are the main sources of vitamin D. Deficiency of vitamin D occurs when there is lack of sunlight and inadequate vitamin D in the diet. It may also result from disease or after resection of the small intestine, which may cause malabsorption. In these circumstances softening of bone (osteomalacia) and rickets may occur.

In the jejunum vitamin D is incorporated along with bile salts and fatty acids into the micelles. Subsequently, as the provitamin D_1, vitamin D is absorbed in the ileum and then passes into the circulation via the portal vein. A specific bloodborne protein, an alpha-1–globulin, carries it to the liver, where the process of chemical change to the active hormone begins by hydroxylation to cholecalciferol. The derivatives are conveyed from the liver to various tissues, including the skin, bone, and parathyroid glands. In the intestine vitamin D influences the permeability of the brush borders of the enterocytes to calcium.

Calcium

Calcium is required for the construction of bone. It forms part of the substance cementing together the walls of adjacent cells, and it is vital in the responsiveness to stimuli of muscle and nerve cells, which determines their excitability. The main sources of calcium are milk and milk products; meat, in which it is bound to proteins; and vegetables, in which it is bound to phytates (phytic acid) and oxalates (the salt of oxalic acid).

The absorption of calcium is influenced by conditions within the lumen of the small intestine. The acid secretion from the stomach converts the calcium to a salt, which is absorbed primarily in the duodenum. Unabsorbed calcium is precipitated in the ileum and is excreted in the feces. Lactose, the sugar of milk, aids calcium absorption, whereas excess fatty acid and high concentrations of magnesium and oxalates interfere with it.

Calcium is absorbed across the brush border of the enterocyte cell membrane by a mechanism that requires energy. Vitamin D is essential to this process, and, when it is deficient, the active transport of calcium stops. Parathyroid hormone (parathormone) and growth hormone from the pituitary gland also influence calcium absorption. An average diet contains 1,200 mg of calcium, one-third of which is absorbed. In the passage of the blood through the kidney, 99 percent of the circulating calcium is reabsorbed. Thus, in kidney failure as well as in malabsorption states, excessive losses of calcium occur. In calcium deficiency, calcium is resorbed from the bone, which thereby weakens and softens the skeletal structure.

Magnesium

An average diet contains around 300 mg of magnesium, of which two-thirds is absorbed. Half of the absorbed magnesium is excreted by the kidneys, which can regulate the amount within a range of 1 to 150 millimoles per day. This control is subject to the influences of parathormone and the thyroid hormone calcitotonin. Magnesium is important to neuromuscular transmission. It is also an important cofactor in the enzymic processes that form the matrix of bone and in the synthesis of nucleic acid. Magnesium deficiency can result from the overuse of diuretics and from chronic renal failure, chronic alcoholism, uncontrolled diabetes mellitus, and intestinal malabsorption.

Magnesium has an inverse relationship with calcium. Thus, if food is deficient in magnesium, more of the calcium in the food is absorbed. If the blood level of

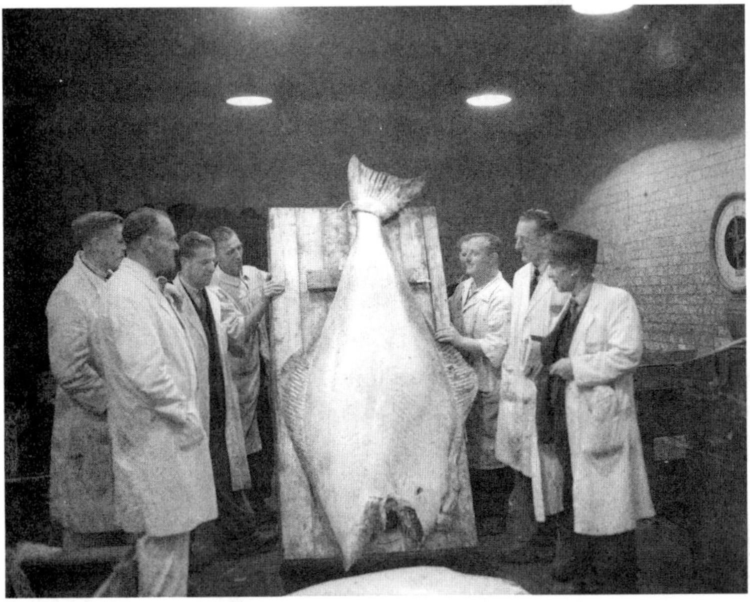

Halibut is an excellent source of magnesium. Other magnesium-rich foods include artichokes, whole wheat flour, almonds, beans, and spinach. Express/Hulton Archive/Getty Images

magnesium is low, calcium is mobilized from bone. The treatment of hypocalcemia due to malabsorption includes administration of magnesium supplements.

Iron

Iron is necessary for the synthesis of hemoglobin, the oxygen-carrying compound of the red blood cells. It also has an important role as a cofactor in intracellular metabolism. The main dietary sources are meat, eggs, nuts, and seeds. The average daily diet contains approximately 20 mg of iron. Humans are unable to excrete iron that has been absorbed in excess of the daily requirement of 1 mg.

The acid in the stomach prevents the formation of insoluble complexes, as does vitamin C. Some amino acids from dietary protein stabilize the iron in low molecular weight complexes. Phosphates and phytates of vegetable origin, some food additives, and the inhibition of acid secretion impede the absorption of iron.

Iron is almost wholly absorbed in the duodenum by a process that involves metabolic activity requiring energy. Most of the iron remains trapped in the surface enterocytes and is lost when the cells die and are shed into the intestine. The amount of iron lost seems to be related in some way to the state of the body's iron stores, although this can be overcome if very large doses of iron are taken orally. Alcohol in the stomach and duodenum increases the rate of absorption. Transport of the iron from the enterocyte is achieved by binding to a carrier, a plasma protein called transferrin. From the intestine it passes into the portal circulation and the liver. When the loss of iron is increased, as in excessive menstruation and in bleeding disorders, the rate of absorption is stepped up from less than 1 mg per day to 1.5 mg or more.

MOVEMENT OF GAS THROUGH THE DIGESTIVE TRACT

The movement of gas through the intestines produces the gurgling sounds known as borborygmi. In the resting state there are usually about 200 ml of gas in the gastrointestinal tract. Its composition varies: between 20 and 90 percent is nitrogen, up to 10 percent is oxygen, up to 50 percent is hydrogen, up to 10 percent is methane, and between 10 and 30 percent is carbon dioxide.

Most of the air that people swallow, while talking and eating in particular, is either regurgitated (as in belching) or absorbed in the stomach. Anxiety or eating quickly induces frequent swallowing of air with consequent belching or increased rectal flatus. Although some of the carbon dioxide in the small intestine is due to the interaction of hydrogen ions of gastric acid with bicarbonate, some is generated in the jejunum by the degradation of dietary triglycerides to fatty acids. High levels of carbon dioxide in rectal flatus reflect bacterial activity in the colon.

Methane cannot be produced by any cell and is entirely the result of bacteria's acting on fermentable dietary residues in the colon, although there appears to be a familial factor involved in this, as not everyone can generate methane. In the colon bacterial production of hydrogen is markedly elevated when the diet contains an excess of vegetable saccharides. This is particularly noticeable after consuming beans, for example. Gas is more often responsible for the buoyancy of stools than is excessive residual fat in malabsorption states.

The gradient between the partial pressures (or the pressure exerted by each gas in a mixture of gases) of particular gases in the intestinal lumen and the partial pressures of gases in the circulating blood determines the direction of movement of gases. Thus, because oxygen tends to be in low pressure in the colon, it diffuses out from the blood into the intestine. The diffusion of nitrogen from the blood into the intestine occurs because a gradient is established by the carbon dioxide, methane, and hydrogen that result from metabolic activities of the commensal bacteria. The partial pressure contributed by nitrogen in the colon is lowered, stimulating nitrogen to enter the intestine from the blood.

In areas where lactase, the enzyme that breaks down lactose (milk sugar), is missing from the group of disaccharidases of the small intestine, lactose passes into the colon undigested. In a lactase-deficient person, the unhydrolyzed lactose enters the colon, where the amount of lactose normally present in a glass of milk is capable of liberating, after bacterial fermentation, the equivalent of two to four cups (500–1,000 ml) of gas (hydrogen). About 15 percent of the gas diffuses back into the blood, with the rest passing as flatus.

Hydrogen generated in the colon is partly absorbed, passes in the circulating blood to the lungs, and diffuses into the respiratory passages, where its presence can be easily determined. The time taken for hydrogen to appear in the breath after ingestion of a standard load of glucose or lactose is used to determine whether the upper area of the gastrointestinal tract is colonized by bacteria. Hydrogen that appears within 30 minutes of the ingestion of the sugar load suggests heavy colonization of the small intestine.

THE DIGESTIVE TRACT AS AN ORGAN OF IMMUNITY

The body is continuously exposed to damage by viruses, bacteria, and parasites; ingested toxins and chemicals, including drugs and food additives; and foreign protein of plant origin. These insults are received by the skin, the respiratory system, and the digestive system, which constitute the interface between the sterile body interior and the environment.

The defense of the body is vested largely in the lymphatic system and its lymphocytes. A substantial part of the gastrointestinal tract is occupied by lymphoid tissue, which can be divided into three sectors. The first is represented by the pharyngeal tonsils, the appendix, and the large aggregates of nodules known as Peyer patches located at intervals throughout the small intestine. The second sector includes the lymphocytes and plasma cells that populate the basement membrane (lamina propria) of the small intestine, the area of loose connective tissue above the supporting tissue of the mucosal lining extending into the villi. The third sector comprises lymphocytes that lie between the epithelial cells in the mucosa. The interaction between these cells of the lymphatic system and the threatening agent is the basis of defense in the gastrointestinal tract.

Lymphocytes are of two types, B and T, according to whether they originate in the bone marrow (B) or in the thymus gland (T), located in the chest. On leaving their tissue of origin, both types end up in the peripheral lymphoid structures. These include the peripheral lymph glands, the spleen, the lymph nodes in the mesentery of the intestine, the Peyer patches, and the spaces between the epithelial cells of the mucosa.

Lymphocytes are immature until they come into contact with antigens. If foreign material is recognized as such by T cells (T lymphocytes), the lymphocytes undergo a process of maturation in which they proliferate and divide into subclasses. The first subclass comprises the "helper" T cells, which are mediators of immune function. The second class consists of "suppressor" T cells, which modulate and control immune responses. The third class comprises the "killer" T cells, which are cytotoxic (i.e., they are able to destroy other cells). Most of the lymphocytes lying between the epithelial cells of the mucosa are killer T cells.

When B cells (B lymphocytes) recognize antigen, they also mature, changing to the form known as plasma cells. These cells elaborate a highly specialized protein material, immunoglobulin (Ig), which constitutes antibodies. There are five varieties of immunoglobulin: IgA, IgM, IgG, IgD, and IgE. B cells and plasma cells are found mainly in the cells in the spaces of the basement membrane. Another group of specialized cells are known as M cells. These are stretched over and around ordinary epithelial cells of the mucosa. The M cells package antigenic material into vesicles and move it through the cell and into the surrounding spaces.

Lymphocytes of the Peyer patches pass through lymph vessels to the nodes in the mesentery and then to the thoracic duct. This is the collecting channel in the abdomen, which passes up through the thorax to drain into the venous system at the junction of the left internal jugular and left subclavian veins. The various ramifications of the abdominal lymphatics all drain into the thoracic duct. From there the lymphocytes are carried back to the intestine as well as being dispersed to other organs. It is these migrated lymphocytes that come to populate the basement membrane and to occupy the spaces between epithelial cells.

Most cells in the mesenteric nodes and the basement membrane are plasma cells that produce immunoglobulin of class IgA. IgM and, to a lesser extent, IgE are produced by other cells, and IgG is formed by cells in the spleen and peripheral lymph nodes. The IgA of plasma cells is secreted into the lumen of the intestine, where it is known as "secretory IgA" and has a different molecular structure from that of the IgA circulating in the blood. When secreted, it is accompanied by a glycoprotein that is produced by the epithelial cells of the mucosa. This substance, when attached to the IgA molecule, protects it from digestion by protein-splitting enzymes. This IgA complex can adhere to viruses and bacteria, interfering with their growth and diminishing their power to invade tissue. It is also capable of rendering toxic substances harmless. Formed by B cells, IgE coats the surface of mast cells, which are specially adapted to deal with the allergic challenge posed by parasites and worms.

The newborn infant is protected by already-matured immunoglobulin with which the colostrum, the initial secretion of the lactating breast, is richly endowed. As time passes, the gastrointestinal tract of the infant is increasingly exposed to various insults, and the lymphocytes and other cells of the immune system become adapted to deal with these. In this way, the body also develops a tolerance to potentially offending substances. If invasion of tissue occurs despite these various defenses, then a generalized systemic immune reaction is marshaled. Some of the features of this reaction, such as fever and a massive increase in the white blood cells, are the evidence of illness.

CHAPTER 6

DISEASES OF THE UPPER DIGESTIVE TRACT

Diseases of the upper digestive tract can affect the structures of the oral cavity, including the teeth and tongue, as well as the pharynx, the salivary glands, the esophagus, and the stomach. Examples of common conditions that affect these portions of the digestive system include dental caries (cavities), peptic ulcer, and gastroesophageal reflux disease. In some cases, conditions such as cracked edges of the lips, discoloration of the tongue, or inflammation of the tongue (glossitis) may arise secondary to nutritional deficiency or systemic disease. In addition, some diseases of the upper portions of the digestive tract have symptoms that involve the organs of the lower digestive tract. Thus, diseases of the upper digestive system sometimes require multiple diagnostic tests to reveal their true origins and causes.

DISEASES OF THE MOUTH AND ORAL CAVITY

Besides local disease, features characteristic of systemic disorders are often present on the mouth and in the oral cavity. For example, lips that are fissured and eroded at the corners may indicate riboflavin deficiency. Likewise, multiple brown freckles on the lips, when associated with polyps in the small intestine, are characteristic of Peutz-Jeghers syndrome. In Fordyce disease, a localized condition of the oral cavity, aggregates of small yellow spots occur on the buccal mucosa and on the mucosa behind the lips. The spots are due to the presence of enlarged sebaceous glands just below the mucosal surface.

The most common mouth ulcers are due to aphthous stomatitis. These ulcers affect one out of every five Caucasians. The manifestations of this condition range from one or two small painful vesicles rupturing to form round or oval ulcers, occurring once or twice a year and lasting seven to 10 days, to deep ulcers of one centimetre (about half an inch) or more in diameter. The ulcers are frequently multiple, occur anywhere in the mouth, and may persist for months at a time. Symptoms range from a mild local irritation to severe distressing pain that prevents talking and eating. Scarring can be seen at the sites of previous ulcers.

Aphthous ulceration is sometimes associated with stress, but it may also be a reflection of an underlying malabsorptive disease such as celiac disease. Treatment is directed to the predisposing cause. Topical and systemic corticosteroids are the most effective treatment. Local anesthetic agents and analgesics may permit easier talking and eating. In a more serious condition, Behçet syndrome, similar ulcers occur in the mouth and on the genitalia, and the eyes may become inflamed.

Discoloration of the tongue, commonly white, is due to deposits of epithelial debris, effete (or worn-out) bacteria, and food. It also occurs in circumstances in which there is reduced saliva production. This may be acute, as in fever, when water loss through the skin is excessive. Discoloration of the tongue becomes chronic following atrophy of the salivary glands and in the absence of good oral hygiene. If the person is a heavy smoker, the deposit is coloured brown. Black discoloration of the tongue with the formation in the centre of a dense pellicle of furlike filiform papillae (black hairy tongue) may be due to a fungus with pigmented filaments. Occasionally it simply represents excessive elongation of the filiform papillae.

A deeply fissured tongue (scrotal tongue) may be due to a congenital variation in the supporting tissue of the tongue, but it can be caused by syphilis, scarlet fever, or typhoid fever. There is a mild degree of inflammation in the fissures, which causes a slight burning discomfort. Other important diseases of the oral cavity include glossitis, Vincent gingivitis, oral cancer, and dental caries.

Pellagra

Pellagra is a nutritional disorder caused by a dietary deficiency of niacin (also called nicotinic acid) or by a failure of the body to absorb this vitamin or the amino acid tryptophan, which is converted to niacin in the body. Joseph Goldberger of the United States Public Health Service was the first to associate pellagra with a nutritional deficiency. In 1937 it was shown that dogs with a disorder similar to pellagra known as black tongue could be cured by the administration of niacin.

In humans pellagra is characterized by skin lesions and by gastrointestinal and neurological disturbances. The so-called classical three Ds of pellagra are dermatitis, diarrhea, and dementia. Skin lesions result from an abnormal sensitization of the skin to sunlight and tend to occur symmetrically on the exposed surfaces of the arms, legs, and neck. They may look at first like a severe sunburn, later becoming reddish brown, rough, and scaly. Gastrointestinal symptoms usually consist of diarrhea, with an accompanying inflammation of the mouth and the tongue and fissuring and dry scaling of the lips and corners of the mouth. Neurological signs appear later in most cases, when the skin and alimentary manifestations are

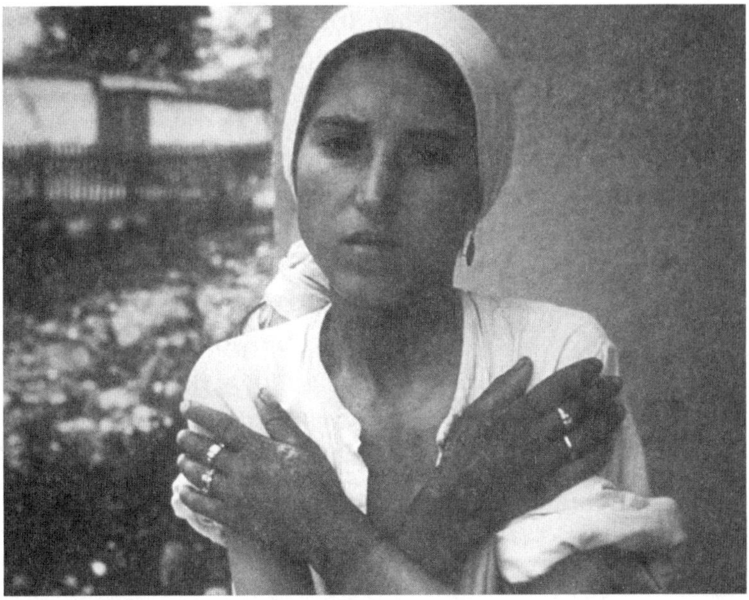

This patient exhibits dermatitis of her hands, one of the symptoms of pellagra. This disorder is caused by a lack of niacin. CDC

prominent. The dementia, or mental aberrations, may include general nervousness, confusion, depression, apathy, and delirium.

In humans, pellagra is seldom a deficiency of niacin alone. Response to niacin therapy tends to be partial, whereas the therapeutic administration of a well-balanced, high-protein diet and multivitamins commonly brings swift recovery. Mild or suspected instances of niacin deficiency can be effectively treated with a well-balanced diet alone.

Pellagra is seldom encountered in countries in which the population generally eats a well-balanced diet, but it still occurs in most countries in which people live on a diet that consists predominantly of corn (maize)—which is low in tryptophan, and contains little or no protein-rich food. Such foods as milk and eggs, although low in niacin, will protect the body from pellagra because their proteins contain sufficient tryptophan for the synthesis of niacin. Pellagra can also be a side effect of chronic alcoholism. Symptoms closely resembling those of pellagra are seen in Hartnup disease.

Glossitis

Glossitis is an inflammation of the tongue characterized by loss of the surface papillae, a condition that gives the affected area a smooth, red appearance. Glossitis may be the primary disease, or may be a symptom of one of several hereditary and acquired conditions—such as certain forms of anemia, pellagra, syphilis, or nutritional deficiencies. There may, however, be a mild burning sensation that can be controlled with topical anesthetics.

A bald tongue (atrophic glossitis), with a smooth surface due to complete atrophy of the papillae, is associated with malnutrition, severe iron deficiency anemia, pernicious anemia, and pellagra. The condition is endemic in underdeveloped countries in which there are periods of famine. Atrophic glossitis may heal spontaneously when the underlying cause is corrected.

Geographic tongue (benign migratory glossitis) refers to the chronic presence of irregularly shaped, bright red areas on the tongue, surrounded by a narrow white zone. Normal tongue epithelium may grow back in one area while new areas of glossitis develop elsewhere, making the disease seem to wander. These changes usually give rise to no symptoms or, at the most, to a mild burning sensation. The cause is unknown, and the condition may persist for years. There is no treatment.

Median rhomboid glossitis refers to a single rough, lozenge-shaped area of glossitis in the midline of the tongue. It appears to be a combination of anomalous fetal development and a yeast infection. Though some individuals fear that glossitis is cancerous, malignancy is rarely associated with the condition.

Vincent Gingivitis

Vincent gingivitis—which is also known by a variety of other names, including Vincent stomatitis, acute necrotizing ulcerative gingivitis, and trench mouth—is an acute and painful infection of the tooth margins and gums that is caused by the symbiotic microorganisms *Bacillus fusiformis* and *Borrelia vincentii*. The chief symptoms are painful, swollen, bleeding gums; small, painful ulcers covering the gums and tooth margins; and characteristic fetid breath. The ulcers may spread to the throat and tonsils. Fever and malaise may also be present.

Vincent gingivitis can occur after a prolonged failure to brush one's teeth, though there are many other predisposing factors, such as vitamin deficiencies, emotional stress, and so on. It is endemic in countries where there is severe malnutrition and poor oral hygiene. It is uncertain if it is transmitted by the exchange of saliva in kissing, but its epidemic increase in wartime and its frequency in the sexually promiscuous suggest this.

The infection is readily treated by bed rest, the administration of penicillin or other antibiotics, and the use of antiseptic mouth rinses. It may also be treated by trimming the gum margins to eliminate subgingival pockets. Regular tooth brushing is the chief preventive measure.

Oral Cancer

Oral cancer is a disease characterized by the growth of cancerous cells in the mouth, including the lips. Oral cancer is often associated with cancers of the cavity located behind the tonsils and the back of the throat (oropharyngeal cancer). It is sometimes caused by chronic thermal irritation in heavy smokers and is often preceded by leukoplakia (plaquelike patches arising on the mucous membranes of the cheeks, gum, or tongue). Similarly, oral cancer can be caused by the habit of keeping tobacco in the space between the cheek and the teeth. Cancers of the salivary glands and of the mucous membranes of the cheeks cause pain, bleeding, or difficulty in swallowing. The lymphomas and other tumours of lymphoid origin may first appear in the tonsillar or pharyngeal lymph nodes.

Most cases of oral cancer originate from the flattened cells that make up the lining of the oral cavity (squamous cell carcinomas). Oral cancers can spread into the jaw and may occur simultaneously with cancers of the larynx, esophagus, or lungs. Cancer of the tongue and of the bony structures of the hard palate or sinuses, for example, may project into the mouth or may burrow deep into the surrounding tissues.

Causes and Symptoms of Oral Cancer

Several factors have been identified that increase the risk of developing oral cancer. Tobacco and alcohol use are the leading factors, with each increasing the risk sixfold. Tobacco use includes cigarettes, cigars, pipes, and chewing tobacco. Oral cancer affects men at twice the rate of women, probably because men have generally been more likely to use tobacco and alcohol. Vitamin A deficiency is also a risk factor, and some strains of human papillomavirus can infect the mouth and may increase risk of oral cancer. Exposure to ultraviolet radiation from the sun is responsible for some cancers of the lips.

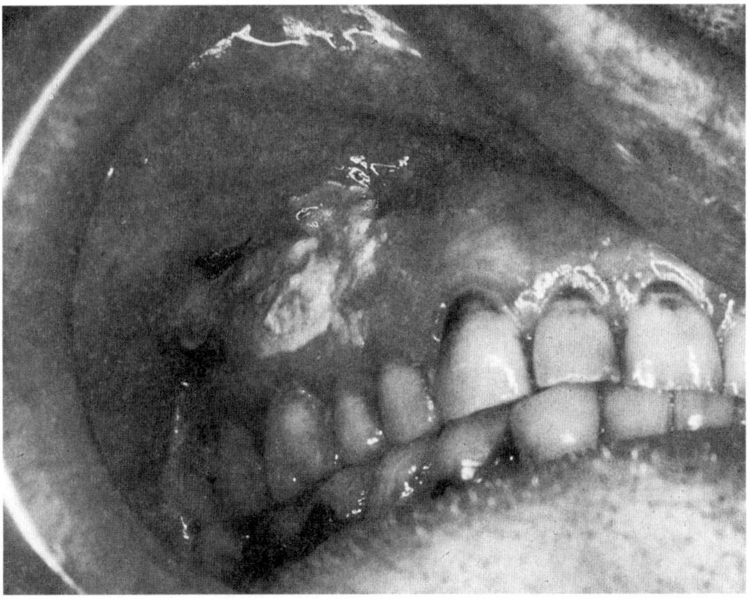

Detail of a person's mouth with leukoplakia, a precancerous lesion that develops on the tongue, gums, or the inside of the cheek. It is caused by chronic irritation, such as smoking. American Cancer Society/Getty Images

Symptoms of oral cancer vary depending on the location of the cancer. The most common symptom is a mouth sore that does not heal. Some early visual signs include white or red patches in the mouth. White patches (leukoplakia) progress to cancer in about 5 percent of cases. The red patches (erythroplakia) bleed easily, and roughly half of them become cancerous. Other symptoms of oral or oropharyngeal cancer include lumps or swelling in the cheek, neck, or jaw, difficulty swallowing or moving the tongue or jaw, and pain in the jaw or teeth. Virtually any type of continuing mouth pain may indicate oral cancer and should be investigated by a physician.

Diagnosis of Oral Cancer

Once cancer is suspected, a thorough examination is conducted to determine its type and stage. Suspected tumours are analyzed by biopsy, and the mouth, pharynx, and larynx are examined visually with small mirrors or a laryngoscope—a flexible tube that contains a light and lens at the end. In some cases a more extensive examination of the head and neck may be conducted under general anesthesia. Several imaging methods may also be used, such as chest and head X-rays, computed tomography (CT) scans, or magnetic resonance imaging (MRI). A swallowed dose of barium may be required before administering X-rays in order to provide better image contrast.

Once oral cancer has been diagnosed, its stage is determined to indicate how far the cancer has progressed. Stage 0 oropharyngeal cancer is confined to the epithelial cells that line the oral cavity or pharynx and is sometimes called carcinoma in situ. Stage I and II cancers are less than 2 cm (about 3/4 of an inch) and between 2 and 4 cm, respectively, and have not spread to nearby lymph nodes. Stage III tumours are either larger than 4 cm (1.5 inches) or are smaller cancers that have spread to one lymph node on the same side of the neck as the tumour. Stage IV tumours have spread to other regions of the neck, the lymph nodes, or other organs in the body. Survival is considerably higher when the cancer is detected early but very low once the cancer has spread to distant organs.

Treatment and Prevention of Oral Cancer

Like most cancers, oral and oropharyngeal cancers can be treated with surgery, radiation, or chemotherapy. Surgery is often the first mode of treatment. In order to minimize tissue loss, superficial cancers of the lip may be shaved off a layer at a time until no cancer is detected. Small early-stage tumours can be removed along with some surrounding tissue with minimal side effects. If the cancer has spread into the surrounding bone, part or all of the jaw may have to be removed (mandible resection) or a maxillectomy performed to remove the hard palate. Both of these procedures require subsequent reconstructive surgery. If the cancer has spread into the lymph nodes of the neck, these nodes will also be removed.

Oral and oropharyngeal cancers may be treated with radiation, using either external beams or surgically implanted radioactive pellets. For oral cancer, external radiation is the most common approach. Radiation is usually employed in conjunction with surgery to destroy small amounts of remaining cancerous tissue.

Oral cancer is almost completely preventable if the key risk factors of smoking and alcohol consumption are avoided. A healthy diet containing sufficient vitamin A is also recommended. Regular dental examinations may detect oral cancer early. Dentures should be removed and cleaned at night to avoid trapping cancer-causing agents against the gums.

Dental Caries

Dental caries, also known as cavities or tooth decay, are localized diseases of the teeth. Caries result from the destruction of the dental enamel and underlying tissues by organic acids. These acids are formed by bacteria growing in debris and food accumulated in pockets between the base of the teeth and the gum margins. Decay typically begins at the surface of the tooth and may progress through the dentine into the pulp cavity. The protein structure of the dentine is destroyed by enzymatic action and bacterial invasion. This periodontal infection ultimately leads to the involvement and inflammation of the tooth's nerve, causing toothache.

An abscess may form at the apex of the tooth and extend into the jawbone, causing osteomyelitis (inflammation of the bone), or into the soft tissues around the roots of the teeth, causing cellulitis (inflammation of the soft tissues). Halitosis (foul breath) is due to the rotting debris in the pockets under the gum margins. Eventually the teeth loosen and fall out or need to be extracted.

Malnutrition, alcoholism, and malabsorption of vitamin D (rickets) or of proteins (as in celiac disease), initiate or aggravate caries. Structural defects of the teeth and heredity can also affect one's chances of developing caries.

There are an estimated 600 species of bacteria that normally inhabit the human oral cavity. Thus, the bacterial composition of the oral cavity is suspected to play an important role in the development of caries and gum disease. In 2008 the discovery of a bacterial species named *Prevotella histicola*, which is present in both healthy and cancerous oral tissues and which generates acidic metabolites, such as acetic acid and lactic acid, that can damage tooth enamel, underlined the need to better understand oral microorganisms and their role in tooth decay.

Treatment of caries includes attention to diet, often entailing the avoidance of sweets, and care of the teeth by cleansing and by restoring teeth that have cavities. The addition of sodium fluoride to fluoride-deficient municipal water supplies has been observed to reduce the incidence of caries by as much as 65 percent. The sealing of the biting surfaces of teeth with adhesive plastics has also greatly reduced the incidence of caries. Today scientists are investigating ways to influence or alter the bacterial composition of the oral cavity for the prevention and treatment of tooth decay.

Pharyngitis

Pharyngitis is an inflammatory illness of the mucous membranes and underlying structures of the throat (pharynx).

Inflammation usually involves the nasopharynx, uvula, soft palate, and tonsils. Pharyngitis is very common, especially in young persons.

Pharyngitis can be caused by bacteria, viruses, mycoplasmas, fungi, and parasites and by recognized diseases of uncertain causes. Infection by *Streptococcus* bacteria may be a complication arising from a common cold. The symptoms of streptococcal pharyngitis (commonly known as strep throat) are generally redness and swelling of the throat, a pustulant fluid on the tonsils or discharged from the mouth, extremely sore throat that is felt during swallowing, swelling of lymph nodes, and a slight fever. Sometimes in children there are abdominal pain, nausea, headache, and irritability.

Diagnosis is established by a detailed medical history and by physical examination; the cause of pharyngeal inflammation can be determined by throat culture. Usually only the symptoms can be treated—with throat lozenges to control sore throat and acetaminophen or aspirin to control fever. If a diagnosis of streptococcal infection is established by culture, appropriate antibiotic therapy, usually with penicillin, is instituted. Within approximately three days the fever leaves. The other symptoms may persist for another two to three days.

Viral pharyngitis infections also occur. They can produce raised whitish to yellow lesions in the pharynx that are surrounded by reddened tissue. Lymphatic tissue in the upper part of the pharynx, as well as tissues at the root of the tongue, may be similarly involved. Viral pharyngitis causes fever, headache, and sore throat that lasts for 4 to 14 days. A number of other infectious diseases may cause pharyngitis, including tuberculosis, syphilis, diphtheria, and meningitis. In diphtheritic pharyngitis, the membranous exudate is more diffuse than in other types of pharyngitis, it is tougher, and it extends over a much larger part of the mucous membrane of the mouth and nose.

One of the complications of pharyngitis may be a peritonsillar abscess, also called quinsy, adjacent to one tonsil. This appears as an extremely painful bulging of the mucosa in the area. Surgical incision and draining are sometimes necessary if antibiotics are not given promptly.

Congenital Defects

There are several congenital disorders (conditions arising during fetal development) that can affect the structures of the oral cavity. Cleft lip, also known as harelip, is a congenital deformity in which the central to medial lip fails to fuse properly, resulting in a fissure in the lip beneath the nostrils. Other disorders are related to an abnormal position of the teeth and the jaws, resulting in inefficient chewing, and to the absence of one or more of the salivary glands, which may lessen the amount and quality of saliva that they produce. Neurological defects that provide inadequate stimulation to the muscles of the tongue and the pharynx can seriously impair chewing and even swallowing. Sensory-innervation defects may not allow the usual reflexes to mesh smoothly, or they may permit harmful ingestants to pass by undetected.

DISEASES OF THE SALIVARY GLANDS

The secretion of saliva is markedly diminished in states of anxiety and depression. The consequent dry mouth interferes with speech, which becomes thick and indistinct. In the absence of the cleansing action of saliva, food debris persists in the mouth and stagnates, especially around the base of the teeth. The debris is colonized by bacteria and causes foul breath (halitosis). In the absence of saliva, swallowing is impeded by the lack of lubrication for the chewing of food that is necessary to form a bolus. The condition is aggravated in states of anxiety and depression when drugs that have an anticholinergic-like activity (such as amitriptyline) are prescribed, because they further depress the production of saliva.

The salivary glands are severely damaged and atrophy in a number of autoimmune disorders such as Sjögren disease and systemic lupus erythematosus. The damage occurs partly by the formation of immune complexes (antigen-antibody associations), which are precipitated in the gland and initiate the destruction. In these circumstances, the loss of saliva is permanent. Some symptomatic relief is obtained by the use of "artificial saliva," methylcellulose mouthwashes containing herbal oils such as peppermint. As some of the salivary glands retain their function, they may be stimulated by chewing gum and by a parasympathomimetic agent such as bethanecol. The production of saliva may be also impaired by infiltration of the salivary glands by pathological lymphocytes, such as in leukemias and lymphomas. In the early stages of these diseases, the glands swell and become painful.

Excessive production of saliva may be apparent in conditions interfering with swallowing, as in Parkinson disease, or in pseudobulbar paralysis from blockage of small arteries to the midbrain regions. True salivary hypersecretion is seen in poisoning due to lead or mercury used in certain industrial processes and as a secondary response to painful conditions in the mouth, such as aphthous stomatitis (certain ulcers of the oral mucosa) and advanced dental caries.

Acute and painful swelling of salivary glands develops when salivary secretion is stimulated by the sight, smell, and taste of food, but saliva is prohibited from flowing through an obstructed salivary duct. Swelling and pain subside between meals. Diagnosis can be confirmed by X-ray. Persistent swellings may be due to infiltration by benign or malignant tumours or to infiltration by abnormal white blood cells, as in leukemia. The most common cause of acute salivary swelling is mumps.

DISEASES OF THE ESOPHAGUS

Difficulty in swallowing (dysphagia) may be the only symptom of a disorder of the esophagus. Sometimes dysphagia is accompanied by pain (odynophagia), or pain may occur spontaneously without swallowing being involved. The esophagus does nothing to alter the physical or chemical composition of the material it receives, and it is poorly equipped to reject materials that have got past the intricate sensors of the mouth and throat. Consequently, it is vulnerable to mucosal injury from ingestants as well as to materials that reflux into its lower segment from the stomach. Although the esophageal muscle coats are thick, the esophagus is not protected with a covering of serous membrane, as are neighbouring organs in the chest.

Congenital Defects

Congenital defects of the esophagus are most often seen in infancy, primarily as a failure to develop normal passageways. Infants born with openings between the esophagus and trachea cannot survive without early surgery. The lower end of the esophagus is subject to various developmental abnormalities that shorten the organ so that the stomach is pulled up into the thoracic cavity. Abnormalities of the diaphragm may contribute to a similar outcome.

Inflammatory Disorders

Inflammatory disorders of the esophagus result from a variety of causes, from the ingestion of noxious materials, the lodgment of foreign bodies, to a complex of events associated with reflux of gastric contents from the stomach into the lower esophagus. Inflammation resulting from surface injury by caustic substances is called corrosive esophagitis. The term "peptic esophagitis" is applied to inflammation that is associated with reflux and involves both the mucous membrane and the submucosal layer. A number of other diseases may cause inflammation of the esophagus—for example, scleroderma, a disease in which the smooth muscle of the organ degenerates and is eventually replaced by fibrous tissue, and generalized candidiasis, a disease in which the esophagus is often involved in a septic process characterized by many small abscesses and ulcerations.

Strictures

Fibrous (scar) tissue contracts over time. Consequently, when fibrous tissue develops around a tube, as in the esophagus, in response to inflammation, the contracting scar narrows the lumen, causing a stricture, and may eventually obstruct it completely. Strictures are readily diagnosed by X-ray or esophagoscope.

Dysphagia

Dysphagia is characterized by difficulty in swallowing caused by lesions, failure to transport a bolus through the esophagus, or mechanical obstruction by stricture, tumours, or foreign bodies in the esophagus. In persons over 50 years of age, the sensation of food "sticking" is more often caused by a disease process, frequently a tumour, involving the wall of the esophagus and providing a mechanical rather than a functional obstacle to the passage of food. The neural arc of swallowing involves the medulla of the brain stem, the vagus (10th cranial) nerves, and the glossopharyngeal, trigeminal, and facial nerves. Consequently, dysphagia may also result from interference with the function of any part of this pathway. Thus, it occurs commonly, but usually transiently, in strokes. Dysphagia may be prominent in degenerative diseases of the central nervous system, especially of the ganglia at the base of the brain. In these circumstances, the behaviour of the smooth muscle of the pharynx and the upper esophageal sphincter is disturbed.

Most individuals can locate the site of dysphagia and the distribution of the pain with accuracy. A sense of food sticking or of pain on swallowing, however, may be felt to be in the throat or upper sternum when the obstruction or disease is in fact at the lower end of the esophagus. The sensation of a "lump in the throat," or "globus hystericus," is not connected with eating or swallowing. The sensation may result from gastroesophageal reflux or from drying of the throat associated with anxiety or grief. Treatment is directed toward the cause of the disorder.

Esophageal Pain

The nerves conveying the sense of pain from the esophagus pass through the sympathetic system in the same spinal cord segments as those that convey pain sensations from the muscle and tissue coverings of the heart. As a result, episodes of pain arising from the esophagus as a result of muscle spasm or transient obstruction by a medicine tablet or other object may be experienced in the chest and posterior thorax and radiate to the arms. This pain thus mimics pain of cardiac origin (angina). The pain due to transient obstruction may be felt not only in the chest but also, through radiation to the back, between the shoulder blades. It is very similar to pain from gallstones; attacks last 10 to 30 minutes.

In middle-aged and elderly persons, spontaneous and diffuse spasm of the smooth muscle of the esophagus causes considerable discomfort as well as episodes of dysphagia. Alternative names for the condition are "corkscrew" esophagus and diffuse spasm of the esophagus. The appearance of the esophagus seen on an X-ray screen while a barium bolus is swallowed resembles that of the outline of a corkscrew because of the multiple synchronized contractions at different levels of the spirally arranged smooth muscle. The pain of esophageal spasm may be relieved by medications that relieve cardiac angina, especially nitroglycerin or nifedipine.

Disorders of Esophageal Motility

Disorders of the motility of the esophagus tend to be either caused by or aggravated during times of stress. Eating rapidly is another trigger, as this demands more precise and rapid changes in muscle activity than eating slowly. Achalasia, formerly called cardiospasm, is a primary disturbance in the peristaltic action of the esophagus that results in failure to empty the organ of its contents. The lower sphincteric portion of the esophagus does not receive its normal signal to relax and, over time, may become hypertonic, resisting stretching. A cycle occurs in which the main portion of the esophagus slowly becomes distended, holding a column of fluid and food that it cannot propel downward to a lower esophageal sphincter that stays closed because of a failure in its neural system. In most persons with this disorder, there is a shortage or disease of ganglion cells of the myenteric plexus (Auerbach plexus), or a disease of the network of nerves within the muscles of the esophagus, so that coordinated peristalsis becomes impossible.

In Chagas disease, parasites called trypanosomes invade the neural tissue and directly destroy ganglion cells. These organisms are not present in the temperate zones of the world, however, and the reason for ganglion cell degeneration in achalasia is generally unknown. Effective treatment is achieved by destroying the ability of the lower esophageal sphincter of the esophagus to contract. This may be done by forcible dilatation, using a balloon, of the esophagus in the area that is tonically contracted. The objective is to rupture the circular muscle at the site, and this is generally achieved with one or two dilatations. If this fails to overcome the contraction or if the contraction recurs, surgery is required that involves opening the abdomen and cutting through the circular muscles from the outside of the esophagus. The disadvantage of both methods of treatment is that the anti-reflux mechanism is thereby destroyed. Consequently, if precautions are not taken, the individual may lose the symptoms and risks of achalasia but may develop the symptoms and signs of reflux peptic esophagitis.

Gastroesophageal Reflux Disease

In healthy individuals, reflux of gastric contents into the esophagus occurs occasionally. This causes the burning sensation behind the sternum that is known as heartburn. Some of the refluxed material may reach the pharynx where it also may be felt as a burning sensation. Reflux is most likely to occur after large meals, especially if physical activity, including bending, stooping, or lifting, is involved. In these circumstances, the esophagus responds with peristaltic waves that sweep the gastric contents back into the stomach, with relief of the heartburn.

Persistent reflux symptoms are invariably due to inadequate functioning of the anatomical components, such as the lower esophageal sphincter, which keep the contents of the stomach below the diaphragm, delayed esophageal clearance of the refluxed material, and delayed emptying of the stomach. The disorder can also be caused by obesity. Excessive fat on the trunk is almost always accompanied by large deposits of fat within the abdomen, especially in the mesentery (the curtainlike structure on which most of the intestine is hung). Consequently, when intra-abdominal pressure is increased, such as in physical activity, there is insufficient room within the abdomen to accommodate the displacement of the organs, and the resulting pressure forces the stomach upward.

The weak point is the centre of the diaphragm at the opening (hiatus) through which the esophagus passes to join the stomach. The upper portion of the stomach is pushed through the hiatus, and the distortion of the position of the organs brings about impaired functioning of the anti-reflux mechanisms. In the early stages the stomach may slide back into the abdomen when the increase in the intra-abdominal pressure eases, but eventually, if the circumstances are unchanged, the upper part remains above the diaphragm.

A common contributory cause of gastroesophageal reflux in women is pregnancy. As the uterus containing the developing fetus comes to occupy a large part of the abdomen, the effect is the same as in obesity. Because gravity is the only force that keeps the gastric contents within the stomach, if a hernia develops, the reflux and the symptoms from it will promptly occur when the individual lies down. Persisting reflux of gastric contents with acid and digesting enzymes leads to chemical inflammation of the lining of the esophagus and ultimately to peptic ulceration. If inadequately treated, the process leads to submucosal fibrosis and stricturing, and, besides the symptoms of heartburn and regurgitation, the patient experiences pain on eating and swallowing.

The treatment of peptic reflux esophagitis includes losing weight, avoiding acidic and fatty foods and beverages, remaining upright for two to three hours after meals, giving up smoking, and raising the head of the bed high enough to discourage nocturnal gastroesophageal reflux. Antacids are effective, as are medications that reduce the secretion of acid by the stomach, such as histamine receptor antagonists and proton pump inhibitors. If a stricture has formed, it can be dilated easily. If the disorder is not overcome with these conservative measures, surgical repair is performed through either the chest or the abdomen.

Some individuals with severe peptic reflux esophagitis develop Barrett esophagus, a condition in which the damaged lining of the esophagus is relined with columnar cells. These cells are similar to those lining the upper part of the stomach and are not the usual squamous cells that line the esophageal mucosa. In some persons in whom this transformation occurs, a carcinoma develops some 10 to 20 years later. The decision as to the treatment of a hiatal hernia by conservative means or by surgery is influenced by such factors as age, occupation, and the likelihood of compliance with a strict regimen.

There is a much less common form of hiatal hernia, called a paraesophageal hernia, in which the greater curvature of the stomach is pushed up into the thorax while the esophagogastric junction remains intact below the diaphragm. Such individuals experience dysphagia caused by compression of the lower esophagus by the part of the stomach that has rolled up against it. This rarer form of hernia is more dangerous, often being complicated by hemorrhage or ulceration, and requires relief by surgery.

Diverticula of the Esophagus

Pouches in the walls of the structures in the digestive system that occur wherever weak spots exist between adjacent muscle layers are called diverticula. In the upper esophagus, diverticula may occur in the area where the striated constrictor muscles of the pharynx merge with the smooth muscle of the esophagus just below the larynx. Some males over 50 years of age show protrusion of a small sac of pharyngeal mucous membrane through the space between these muscles. As aging continues, or if there is motor disturbance in the area, this sac may become distended and may fill with food or saliva. It usually projects to the left of the midline, and its presence may become known by the bubbling and crunching sounds produced during eating. Often the patient can feel it in the left side of the neck as a lump, which can be reduced by pressure of the finger. Sometimes the sac may get so large that it compresses the esophagus adjacent to it, producing a true obstruction. Treatment is by surgery. Small diverticula just above the diaphragm sometimes are found after the introduction of surgical instruments into the esophagus.

Boerhaave syndrome is a rare spontaneous rupture to the esophagus. It can occur in patients who have been vomiting or retching and in debilitated elderly persons with chronic lung disease. Emergency surgical repair of the perforation is required. A rupture of this type confined to the mucosa only at the junction of the linings of the esophagus and stomach is called a Mallory-Weiss lesion. At this site, the mucosa is firmly tethered to the underlying structures and, when repeated retching occurs, this part of the lining is unable to slide and suffers a tear. The tear leads to immediate pain beneath the lower end of the sternum and bleeding that is often severe enough to require a transfusion. The circumstances preceding the event are commonly the consumption of a large quantity of alcohol followed by eating and then vomiting. The largest group of individuals affected are alcoholic men. Diagnosis is determined with an endoscope (a flexible, lens-containing tube). Most tears spontaneously stop bleeding and heal over the course of some days without treatment. If transfusion does not correct blood loss, surgical suture of the tear may be necessary. An alternative to surgery is the use of the drug vasopressin, which shuts down the blood vessels that supply the mucosa in the region of the tear.

Esophageal Cancer

Esophageal cancer is a disease characterized by the abnormal growth of cells in the esophagus. Esophageal tumours may be benign or malignant. Generally, benign tumours originate in the submucosal tissues and principally are leiomyomas (tumours composed of smooth muscle tissue) or lipomas (tumours composed of adipose, or fat, tissues).

Malignant tumours are either epidermal cancers (squamous cell carcinomas), made up of unorganized aggregates of surface (squamous) cells, or adenocarcinomas, in which there are glandlike formations. Approximately half of esophageal cancers are squamous cell carcinomas. Cancers arising from squamous tissues are found at all levels of the esophagus, whereas adenocarcinomas are more common at the lower end where a number of glands of gastric origin are normally present.

Worldwide, men are more than twice as likely to develop esophageal cancer than women. In the United States, blacks are three times more likely than whites to develop the disease. Tumours of the esophagus seem to vary greatly in their worldwide distribution. In North China, for example, the incidence of esophageal cancer in men is 30 times that of white men in the United States and 8 times that of black men.

Causes and Symptoms of Esophageal Cancer

The exact causes of esophageal cancer are not known. However, several risk factors have been identified that increase the likelihood of developing esophageal cancer. Some factors, such as age, sex, and race, are impossible to control. However, tobacco and alcohol use increase risk, and these behaviours can be controlled. People who accidently swallowed lye as children also have a higher risk of esophageal cancer as adults. Long-term problems with acid reflux may lead to Barrett esophagus, in which the normal squamous cells that line the esophagus are replaced with glandular cells. This condition increases cancer risk. Rare disorders such as tylosis and achalasia are also risk factors. Women may be predisposed by long-standing iron deficiency, or Plummer-Vinson (Paterson-Kelly) syndrome.

Dysphagia is the first and most prominent symptom. Later swallowing becomes painful as surrounding structures are involved. Hoarseness indicates that the nerve to the larynx is affected. Other symptoms may include pain or tightness in the chest, unexplained weight loss, or frequent hiccups.

Diagnosis of Esophageal Cancer

Esophageal cancers are usually diagnosed once symptoms have appeared, but by this time the cancer has usually developed to a relatively advanced stage. The diagnosis is suggested by X-ray, although several other imaging methods may be employed as well, including CT scans or ultrasound. There is no definitive laboratory test for esophageal cancer. However, diagnosis can be reinforced by removing quantities of cells with a nylon brush for examination under a microscope (exfoliative cytology). Indeed, endoscopy with multiple biopsies from the area of abnormality often confirms diagnosis.

Once esophageal cancer has been diagnosed, its stage is determined to indicate how far the cancer has progressed. Stage 0 esophageal cancer is also called carcinoma in situ and is confined to the inner layer of epithelial cells lining the esophagus. Stage I cancers have spread into the connective tissue layer below the epithelium but have not invaded the underlying muscle layer. Stage II cancers either have spread through the muscle layer to the outer boundaries of the esophagus or have spread only into the muscle layer but have reached nearby lymph nodes. Stage III esophageal cancers have spread through the esophageal wall to the lymph nodes or other local tissues. Stage IV cancers have metastasized, or spread, to distant organs such as the stomach, liver, bones, or brain.

The survival rate for esophageal cancer is lower than for many other cancers. When the cancer is detected before it has invaded the underlying tissue layers of the esophagus, five-year survival is high, but fewer than 25 percent of esophageal cancers are diagnosed at this stage. If the cancer has moved to the tissue immediately underlying the mucosal surface, five-year survival is reduced to about

50 percent, and the rate drops significantly once the cancer has moved from the esophagus to nearby lymph nodes or other tissues. Once the cancer has spread to distant tissues in the body, five-year survival is extremely low.

Treatment and Prevention of Esophageal Cancer

Esophageal cancers are best treated surgically when possible. If the cancer is confined to the upper region of the esophagus, an esophagectomy may be done to remove the cancerous portion, along with nearby lymph nodes, and to reconnect the remaining esophagus to the stomach. For cancers of the lower esophagus, it may be necessary to perform an esophagogastrectomy, in which a portion of the esophagus is removed along with a portion of the stomach. The stomach is then reattached directly to the remaining esophagus, or a segment of the colon is used to link the stomach and esophagus. Both of these surgeries are difficult and often result in serious complications. Other, less-drastic surgeries may be used to relieve symptoms, especially when surgical cure is not possible. In advanced cases, a tube may be inserted into the esophagus to keep it open. Where the channel is greatly narrowed, the size of the tumour can be reduced by destroying the tissue with lasers.

Radiation therapy is used to relieve symptoms. It is used for malignancies of the upper esophagus and as treatment for those at the lower end. The side effects of radiation treatment include vomiting, diarrhea, fatigue, and esophageal irritation. Chemotherapy is also used for some esophageal cancers in order to relieve symptoms. Side effects of chemotherapy resemble those of radiation therapy. Although neither chemotherapy nor radiation therapy are curative, they play important complementary roles in the overall treatment of esophageal cancer, since they not only relieve symptoms but also may be able to shrink tumours prior to surgery. Lessening the effects of the disease, with restoration of eating ability, is very important, because otherwise the inability to swallow even saliva is distressing, and starvation may result.

Esophageal cancer cannot be completely prevented, but risk can be lowered by reducing alcohol consumption and avoiding tobacco. Individuals who are at high risk should receive regular screening in order to increase the probability of early detection. Because there is no blood test available for esophageal cancer, screening requires regular biopsies and viewing of the esophagus with an endoscope.

DISEASES OF THE STOMACH

Diseases that affect the stomach can hinder the breakdown of food and the absorption of nutrients. Many disorders of the stomach involve abnormalities of acid secretion and tend to be painful and distressing to the patient. Among the most commonly occurring conditions that affect the stomach are ulcer, gastritis, and cancer.

Indigestion

Indigestion, also called dyspepsia, is any or all of the unpleasant symptoms that are associated with the malfunctioning of the digestive system. Indigestion may be caused by a disease, but it primarily occurs because of stress or improper eating habits, smoking, drinking excessive quantities of coffee or alcohol, or hypersensitivity to particular foods.

Any disorder that affects the coordination of the stomach muscles is capable of producing symptoms ranging from those that are mildly unpleasant to others that are life-threatening. Symptoms include abdominal discomfort, belching, flatulence, anorexia, nausea, vomiting, diarrhea, constipation, and heartburn. Anorexia and nausea seem to be mediated through the central nervous system, with reflex input from nerve endings in the stomach and duodenum. Sometimes the entire duration of a nausea-vomiting episode is so short that it appears to be vomiting alone, obscuring the presence of nausea. This is characteristically noted in persons with primary diseases of the brain, especially those with tumours or meningitis in which the cerebrospinal fluid is under increased pressure. In many diseases, vomiting may not be preceded by nausea at all, and in others there may be a long time lag between the two. Seasickness is the best-known example of this relationship.

The intrinsic muscles of the stomach are innervated by branches of the vagus nerves, which travel along the esophagus from their point of emergence in the brain stem. Gastric retention may result from the degeneration of these nerves that can result from diabetes mellitus. Obstruction due to scarring in the area of the gastric outlet, or to tumours encroaching on the lumen, causes the stomach to fill up with its own secretions as well as with partially digested food. In these circumstances, vomiting leads to dehydration and to electrolyte losses, which threaten life if not corrected. The ingestion of soluble alkali in this situation may aggravate the disturbance in the acid-base balance of the body. Bulimia, a nervous disorder characterized by compulsive eating followed by vomiting and purging, can cause severe dehydration and even a ruptured stomach, and it can prove fatal.

Ulcerative Diseases

Ulcers are produced when external factors reduce the ability of the mucosal lining to resist the acidic effects of gastric

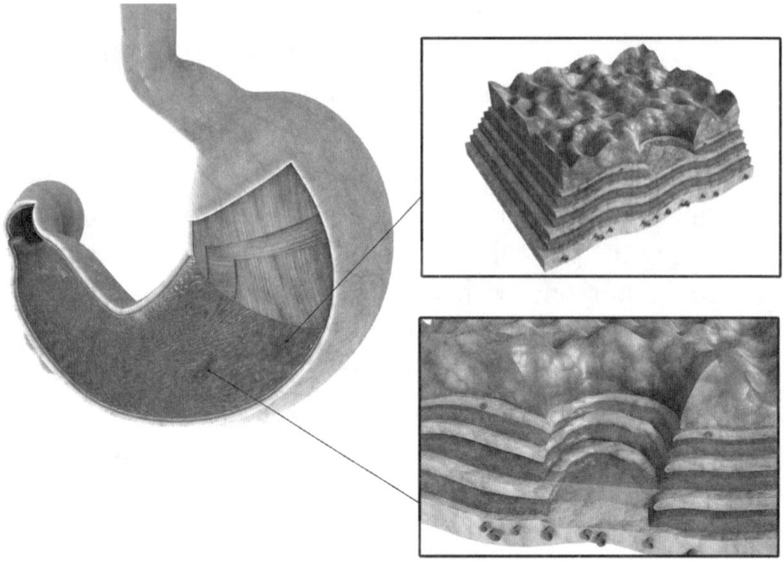

This illustration shows stages of a stomach ulcer, from erosion to a chronic ulcer. 3D4Medical.com/Getty Images

juice. The area of the stomach in which acid and pepsin are secreted has the highest resistance to peptic ulcer. The mucosa elsewhere is less well protected, and its breakdown may lead to ulceration. If the lesion is confined to the superficial layers of the mucosa, it is called an erosion. If it extends through the intrinsic layer of muscle of the mucosa into the tissues below, it is known as an ulcer.

Erosions and ulcers can be acute or chronic according to how readily they heal. Infection with the bacterium *Helicobacter pylori* and long-term use of nonsteroidal anti-inflammatory drugs (NSAIDs) are the two major causes of ulcers. In special circumstances, such as the state of shock produced by large burns, intracranial surgery, coronary occlusion, and septicemia, acute and rapidly penetrating ulcers may occur.

In the Western world, duodenal ulcer is much more common than gastric ulcer, occurs more often in men than in women, and is aggravated by stress. In Japan gastric ulcer is more common than duodenal ulcer and is thought to be related to the raw fish and acetic acid pickles of the traditional diet. Duodenal ulcer is most common between ages 25 and 35, whereas gastric ulcer is uncommon before age 40 and has a peak frequency between ages 55 and 65. Genetic factors are also involved in the development of ulcers. Inheriting blood group O may render a person more likely to develop duodenal ulceration. There are families in whom the secretion of pepsinogen I is excessive and renders them prone to duodenal ulcer since excess acid secretion is linked to excess secretion of this hormone.

Pain is the major symptom of duodenal ulcers. The pain is a burning or gnawing sensation felt in the midupper abdomen. In gastric ulcer it comes on soon after eating, whereas in duodenal ulcer it comes on when the stomach is empty—one and a half to two hours after meals and during the night hours. In the early stages of the disease, the pain is easily and immediately relieved by antacids and, in duodenal ulcer, by light food.

Gastric ulcers almost always recur in the same site within the stomach, but duodenal ulcers are often multiple, and recurrence may be anywhere in the duodenal bulb. Furthermore, duodenal ulcers are usually accompanied by an inflammation affecting the whole bulb (duodenitis). Multiple erosions varying in size between 0.5 and 5 mm (0.02 and 0.2 inch) are frequently scattered over the mucosa. With gastric ulcers the inflammation is usually confined to the immediate vicinity of the crater and, as a rule, is not accompanied by erosions. The exceptions are gastric ulcers in the antrum and prepyloric area associated with the use and abuse of analgesics and NSAIDs for arthritic disorders, in which multiple erosions are commonly present.

The most common site of gastric ulcers is halfway up the inner curvature of the stomach at the junction of the lower one-third with the upper two-thirds of the organ. This may be because blood flow to this site is more easily reduced than elsewhere. Chronic gastric ulcers at this site are strongly associated with obstructive disease of the airways (chronic bronchitis and emphysema). Smoking impairs the healing of both gastric and duodenal ulcers.

Infection with *H. pylori* is the most common bacterial infection in humans. This bacteria is pervasive in the Third World, and in the United States, it affects about a third of the population. Among those who suffer from peptic ulcers, as many as 90 percent of those with duodenal ulcers and 70 percent with gastric ulcers are believed to be infected with *H. pylori*. This bacterium converts the abundant waste product urea into carbon dioxide and ammonia. The process causes the mucosal lining to break down. In its weakened condition the lining cannot withstand the corrosive effects of gastric acid, and an ulcer can form.

The complications of peptic ulcers are hemorrhage, perforation, and obstruction of the outlet of the stomach (pyloric stenosis) by scarring of the duodenal bulb or of the pyloric channel. Scarring often leads to bouts of vomiting and accompanying malnutrition and requires surgery. Bleeding may be obscured because of oozing from the floor of the ulcer and detectable only by laboratory testing of the feces, or bleeding may be brisk, leading to the passage of tar-coloured stools (melena). Occasionally, when the ulcer erodes into a large vessel, bleeding is excessive and life-threatening. The mortality associated with bleeding is high in the elderly because of chronic changes in the lungs, heart, and blood vessels, which reduces cardiorespiratory reserves. This is further aggravated by smoking.

Brisk bleeding is usually accompanied by the vomiting of blood (hematemesis), which requires treatment by blood transfusion. In the elderly, hardening of the arteries (atherosclerosis) prevents the vessel from closing down around the lesion. If bleeding persists or recurs, surgery is necessary. Ulcers that penetrate the back wall of the stomach or duodenum erode into the pancreas, and back pain becomes prominent. If the ulcer penetrates the anterior wall, free perforation into the abdominal cavity may occur. This causes immediate, intense pain and shock, and the abdominal wall becomes rigid. In most instances this requires emergency surgery with drainage of the abdomen.

Surgery for chronic ulceration is used less frequently since the introduction of drugs that stop the secretion of stomach acid. Histamine-receptor antagonists, such as cimetidine, ranitidine, and famotidine, block the action of histamine on the acid-secreting parietal cells of the stomach. Proton pump inhibitors, such as omeprazole, lansoprazole, and rabeprozale, inhibit the ATPase enzyme inside the parietal cell and prevent acid secretion. Most peptic ulcers not caused by *H. pylori* infection result from the ingestion of large quantities of NSAIDs. Withdrawal of NSAID treatment usually allows the ulcer to heal. Treatment for *H. pylori*–induced ulcers are antibiotics and a proton pump inhibitor.

Gastritis

A diffuse inflammation of the stomach lining, gastritis is usually an acute disorder caused by contaminated food, by alcohol abuse, or by bacterial- or viral-induced inflammation of the gastrointestinal tract (gastroenteritis). Such episodes are short-lived and require no specific treatment.

Pain is generalized in the upper abdomen and is continuous, but it progressively subsides over two or three days.

Aspirin and NSAIDs taken for arthritis cause erosions in the antrum of the stomach and in some instances cause bleeding and chronic ulceration. Infection by the bacteria *H. pylori* is also a common cause of chronic gastritis. This usually responds to the withdrawal of the offending drugs and treatment with the same agents used to treat peptic ulcers of the stomach and duodenum.

Another form of gastritis is gastric atrophy, in which the thickness of the mucosa is diminished. Gastric atrophy is often the culmination of damage to the stomach over many years. Diffuse gastric atrophy leads to partial loss of the glandular and secreting cells throughout the stomach and may be associated with iron deficiency anemia. Atrophy of the mucosa confined to the body and fundic regions of the stomach is seen in pernicious anemia and is due to the formation of antibodies to intrinsic factor secreted by the parietal cells. Intrinsic factor is necessary to the absorption of vitamin B_{12}.

Stomach Cancer

Stomach cancer, also called gastric cancer, is a disease characterized by the abnormal growth of cells in the stomach. The incidence of stomach cancer has decreased dramatically since the early 20th century in countries where refrigeration has replaced other methods of food preservation such as salting, smoking, and pickling. Stomach cancer rates remain high in countries where these processes are still used extensively.

Causes and Symptoms of Stomach Cancer

Ninety-five percent of malignant stomach cancers develop from the cells that form the innermost lining, or mucosa, of the stomach. These tumours are called adenocarcinomas. Other stomach cancers can develop from the surrounding immune cells, hormone-producing cells, or connective tissue.

Multiple risk factors have been identified that increase a person's probability of developing this cancer. These include a diet high in salted, smoked, or pickled foods, tobacco and alcohol use, or a family history of stomach cancer. Infection by the bacterium *H. pylori*, which can cause significant damage to gastric tissues and is a cause of peptic ulcers, can also lead to stomach cancer. Other factors that may increase the risk of stomach cancer to varying degrees are previous stomach surgery, blood type A, advanced age (60–70 years), or chronic stomach inflammation. Males develop stomach cancer at approximately twice the rate of females.

Rare disorders such as pernicious anemia or Menetrier disease and congenital disorders that lead to increased risk for colorectal cancer may also increase stomach cancer risk. The symptoms of stomach cancer are prevalent in many other illnesses and may include abdominal pain or discomfort, unexplained weight loss, vomiting, poor digestion, or visible swelling in the abdomen.

Diagnosis of Stomach Cancer

No specific laboratory test for stomach cancer exists, and the disease is therefore usually diagnosed through a combination of visual means. A physician can inspect the lining of the stomach with an endoscope. The endoscope can also be used to take samples from potentially cancerous tissues for biopsy. These samples are examined under a microscope for signs of cancer. An endoscope may also be modified with a special probe that emits sound waves in the stomach, which allows the physician to create an image of the stomach wall. X-rays are also employed, usually after the patient has swallowed a barium compound that coats the stomach and provides better image contrast. Other imaging techniques such as CT scans and MRI are also used, especially when the cancer is believed to have spread.

Once stomach cancer has been diagnosed, its stage is determined. The stage is an indicator of how far the cancer has progressed. Staging for stomach cancer is complicated and is based on a combination of how far the cancer has grown through the stomach wall and on the number of lymph nodes affected, if any. Stage 0 stomach cancer is also called carcinoma in situ and is confined to the mucosal lining of the stomach. Stage I and stage II cancers have spread into the connective tissue or muscle layers that underlie the mucosa, but they have reached fewer than six nearby lymph nodes. Stage III and IV cancers are more advanced and may have metastasized to distant tissues.

A very high percentage of individuals survive stomach cancer for at least five years if the cancer is diagnosed very early, and many of them go on to live long, healthy lives. Unfortunately, only a small percentage of stomach cancers are identified and treated at such an early stage. At the time when most lower-stomach cancers are diagnosed, roughly half the patients survive for at least five years. Cancers of the upper stomach have a lower survival rate, and if the cancer has spread to distant tissues in the body, the survival rate is extremely low.

Treatment and Prevention of Stomach Cancer

Surgery is the only method available for curing stomach cancer, although radiation or chemotherapy may be used in conjunction with surgery or to relieve symptoms. If the cancer is localized, the cancerous portions of the stomach are removed in a procedure called a partial gastrectomy. In some cases, the entire stomach must be removed along with the spleen and nearby lymph nodes.

Repair of the stomach generally requires permanent changes in dietary habits and may demand intravenous administration of vitamin supplements. If a cancer cannot be cured, surgery may still be used to relieve symptoms or digestive discomfort. Radiation therapy is sometimes used in conjunction with surgery to destroy any remaining cancer cells. When stomach cancer has spread to distant organs, chemotherapy may be required so that as many cancer cells as possible can be sought out and destroyed. Both radiation therapy and chemotherapy may produce several side effects such as vomiting and diarrhea.

Stomach cancer cannot be completely prevented, but people can decrease their risk of disease by adopting a diet that is low in salted, smoked, and pickled foods and high in fruits and vegetables. Elimination of tobacco use and reduction in alcohol consumption also help lower risk. Research has indicated that prompt treatment of *H. pylori* infection can reverse gastric tissue damage, thereby reducing stomach cancer risk.

CHAPTER 7

DISEASES OF THE INTESTINES

Diseases that affect the small and large intestines can arise from a variety of causes and range from relatively harmless, with very little pain and requiring minimal therapeutic intervention, to severe, causing acute or chronic pain and potentially necessitating the removal of a portion of the intestinal tract. Examples of common conditions of the intestines include traveler's diarrhea, parasitic infection, and inflammation. Because the intestines play a prominent role in the absorption of nutrients during the digestive process, many chronic diseases that involve the lower digestive tract result in signs and symptoms of malnutrition.

DISEASES OF THE SMALL INTESTINE

The duodenum is often involved in the diseases of its neighbours, in particular the pancreas and the biliary tract. Primary cancer of the duodenum is an infrequent disease. Benign tumours, particularly polyps and carcinoids, are more frequent. Cancers of the common bile duct or of the pancreas may make their presence known by obstruction of the duodenum and pain. These cancers often are diagnosed by upper intestinal X-ray studies, endoscopy, ultrasound, or CT scanning. Benign anomalies of the organs of this area, like an encircling ring of pancreas, may also encroach upon the duodenum.

In countries of the Middle and Far East, where parasites are endemic, roundworms and tapeworms in particular are often found anchored in the duodenum. In inflammations of the pancreas, the motility of the neighbouring duodenum is often impaired, and occasionally ulceration with hemorrhage occurs. A protozoal parasite, *Giardia lamblia*, can contaminate drinking water and is a common cause of diarrhea and, if unrecognized, malabsorption.

A lack of coordination of the inner circular and outer longitudinal muscular layers of the intestinal wall usually results in an accumulation of excess contents in the intestinal lumen, with consequent distension. This distension may cause pain and usually results in hyperactive contractions of the normal segment next to the distended area. Such contractions may be strenuous enough to produce severe, cramping pain. The most common cause of disturbed motility in the small intestine is food that contains an unsuitable additive, organism, or component.

Traveler's Diarrhea

Traveler's diarrhea is the abnormally swift passage of watery waste material through the intestines, with consequent discharge of loose feces. Traveler's diarrhea is accompanied by cramping and lasts a few days. It is almost always caused by toxin-generating *Escherichia coli*. *Shigella* infection may occur simultaneously, however, and visitors to countries where giardiasis is endemic may suffer infection.

Contaminated salads remain the most common cause of traveler's diarrhea in countries where the climate is hot. Such diarrhea generally disappears spontaneously with abstention from food accompanied by drinking of nonalcoholic fluids. Mixtures of sodium and potassium chloride, sodium bicarbonate, and glucose reconstituted with water are one method of treatment.

Intestinal Obstruction

Intestinal obstruction is the functional or mechanical blockage of the alimentary canal. Functional blockage occurs when the muscles of the intestinal wall fail to contract normally in the wavelike sequence (peristalsis) that propels the intestinal contents. Mechanical obstructions include a narrowing of the channel (stricture), adhesions, tumours, the presence of a foreign object, pressure from outside, hernia, volvulus, and intussusception. In a hernia a loop of intestine protruding from the abdomen may be compressed at the point where it passes through the abdominal wall. A volvulus is a twisting of the intestine upon itself, and an intussusception is the telescoping of a section of intestine into an adjacent portion.

The loss of fluids and chemicals through vomiting is frequent with obstructions that are located high in the intestinal canal. Obstructions of the lower reaches of the small intestine (ileum) and of the large intestine are inaccessible to evacuation by vomiting. In such cases, the intestine above the obstruction becomes distended by accumulated material and swallowed air. The pressure in the intestinal channel may compromise the blood supply and cause death of tissue in the walls of the intestine. The walls may become abnormally permeable, allowing noxious agents to escape into the abdominal cavity and the bloodstream. The symptoms and treatment of intestinal obstruction depend on the nature of the obstruction and its location. Surgery is often necessary.

Irritable Bowel Syndrome

The common disorder known as irritable bowel syndrome (IBS) is probably due to a disturbance of the motility of the whole intestinal tract or to increased sensitivity of the large intestine. The symptoms vary from watery diarrhea to constipation and the passage of stools with difficulty. When the colon is involved, an excess of mucus is often observed in the stools. Pain and cramping are most often felt in the lower abdomen. Generalized abdominal discomfort, sometimes with nausea, may follow defecation and may last 15 to 30 minutes. Many sufferers experience high levels of stress, and some have periods of anxiety depression.

Occasionally irritable bowel syndrome may be due to an allergy to specific foods. IBS may develop following an infection such as bacillary dysentery, after which the small intestine remains irritable for many months. Treatment of IBS includes elimination of stress, psychological support, change in lifestyle, and exercise. Possible aggravating items such as lactose-containing foods, coffee, and deep-fried dishes should be eliminated from the diet, and dietary fibre should be added to help in resolving constipation. When discomfort is prominent, antispasmodic agents that relax smooth muscle, such as dicyclomine hydrochloride or mebeverine, may be prescribed. If diarrhea does not respond to dietary measures, diphenoxylate or loperamide may slow the movement of the intestinal contents, thereby increasing the potential for the reabsorption of water.

Malabsorption

Malabsorption occurs when the small intestine is unable to transport broken-down products of digestive materials from the lumen of the intestine into the lymphatics or mesenteric veins, where they are distributed to the rest of the body. Defects in transport occur either because the absorptive cells of the intestine lack certain enzymes—whether by congenital defect or by acquired disease—or because the cells are hindered in their work by other disease processes that infiltrate the tissues, disturb motility, permit bacteria to overpopulate the bowel, or block the pathways over which transport normally proceeds. Malabsorption also may result from pancreatitis, cystic fibrosis, obstruction of the bile ducts or lymphatic vessels, or surgical removal of a section of the small intestine.

Diagnosis of malabsorption is determined primarily from the patient's history, physical examination, X-ray films of the abdomen, and study of the stools under controlled dietary conditions. Motor aspects of the intestine can be studied using a variety of techniques. A biopsy of the small intestine may also be performed to detect abnormalities.

Congenital Malformations

Meckel diverticulum is a common congenital malformation that occurs when the duct leading from the navel to the small intestine in the fetus fails to atrophy and close. The duct serves as the principal channel for nourishment from the mother. The diverticulum in the child or adult may range from a small opening to a tube that is a foot or more in length. It may contain cells derived from the stomach glands that secrete acid and pepsin. If such secretions spill onto intestinal mucosa, the mucosa ulcerates and often bleeds. Thus, a peptic ulcer can develop at a site far from the stomach or duodenum. The peptic ulcer gives rise to pain, bleeding, or obstruction, and it is the most common cause of bleeding from the lower intestine in children. Meckel diverticulum must be treated surgically if complications develop.

Another congenital problem in the small intestine is the presence of multiple diverticula, or outpouchings of mucosa and serosa. Multiple diverticula are seen usually in elderly persons, although occasionally one may be the site of acute inflammation in a young adult. Bacteria flourish in these diverticula because the outpouchings have no motor activity and cannot empty themselves. The bacteria deprive the body of nutrients and may cause diarrhea and serious malabsorption. The overgrowth of bacteria also upsets the motor activity of the small intestine. Antibiotics may control the condition in the elderly, but surgical resection of diverticula is necessary in younger persons.

Bacterial Infections

Many bacterial organisms can infect the human body and cause disease. Species of *Salmonella* that cause typhoid and paratyphoid remain endemic scourges in tropical countries and, together with *Shigella*, are occasional causes of epidemics in health care institutions, especially among the elderly. Diagnosis is confirmed by the presence of the organisms in a stool culture. Antibiotics and solutions rich in electrolytes are effective therapy. Treatment is with antibiotics. Periodic vaccination is advisable for the protection of individuals exposed to areas where typhoid and paratyphoid are endemic.

Cholera, caused by *Vibrio cholerae*, is endemic to Southeast Asia and periodically becomes pandemic (widely distributed in more than one country). The oral or intravenous administration of electrolyte solutions rich in potassium has revolutionized the treatment of cholera, because deaths are due to a massive depletion of electrolytes and water. The toxin produced by *V. cholerae* attaches to the intestinal cells, the enterocytes, where it stimulates the membrane enzyme adenylate cyclase. This in turn interferes with the intracellular enzyme 3',5'-cyclic adenosine monophosphate synthetase (cyclic AMP), disrupting the sodium pump system for movement of water and allowing potassium and bicarbonate to seep out of the cell.

Parasitic Infections

In tropical countries, parasitism is endemic. Roundworms, tapeworms, amoebae, hookworms, strongyloides, threadworms, and blood flukes (schistosomiasis) are the main types of parasites. Consequently it is commonplace in these areas for multiple parasite infestation to occur in addition to other disorders. This common occurrence, reflecting poverty, lack of health education, malnutrition, contaminated drinking water, and inadequate sanitation, is a major factor in chronic illness and early death.

Roundworms

Roundworms, particularly *Ascaris lumbricoides*, may cause intestinal obstruction if present in sufficient numbers. As they mature from the larval state to the adult worm, roundworms migrate through the body, causing ascariasis, an infection characterized by fever; pneumonitis (lung inflammation); cholangitis (inflammation of the bile ducts); and pancreatitis. Roundworms interfere with the absorption of fat and protein in the intestine, causing diarrhea. They are eliminated with the administration of piperazine or other anthelmintics, but occasionally surgery is required for obstruction.

Hookworms

Hookworm, or *Ancylostoma duodenale*, infection begins when the worm is in the larval stage. It penetrates the skin, usually of the feet, migrates during its life cycle through the liver and the lungs, and attaches to the mucosa of the small intestine where it matures. Hookworms deplete the body of nutrients, and one major effect is severe chronic iron-deficiency anemia. This effect can be corrected with the oral administration of iron, and the number of worms can be controlled with tetrachloroethylene or other anthelmintics.

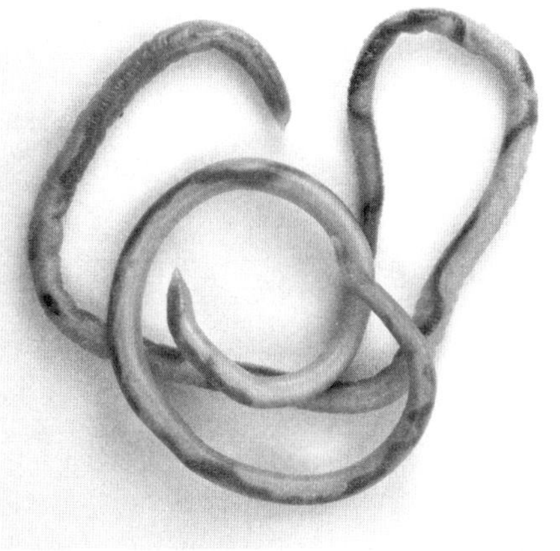

This image shows two curled up parasitic roundworm.
Kim Taylor/Dorling Kindersley/Getty Images

Pinworms

Pinworms, or *Enterobius vermicularis*, live mainly in the cecum. The adult female migrates at night to the anus and lays eggs on the perianal skin, which cause anal itching. Transmission of the pinworm occurs via a fecal-oral route, and it can affect an entire family. Pinworms can be eradicated with piperazine or vyprinium embonate.

Tapeworms

The common tapeworms are *Taenia saginata*, found in beef, and *T. solium*, found in pork. Larvae of *Echinococcus granulosus*, mature worms of the genus *Diphyllobothrium*, and some dwarf tapeworms also cause disease.

Fertilized ova are passed in feces and are ingested by an intermediary host animal, such as a cow. The embryos migrate to the bloodstream and on reaching muscle or viscera develop into larvae. When the flesh is consumed by humans, the larvae pass into the intestine, where they

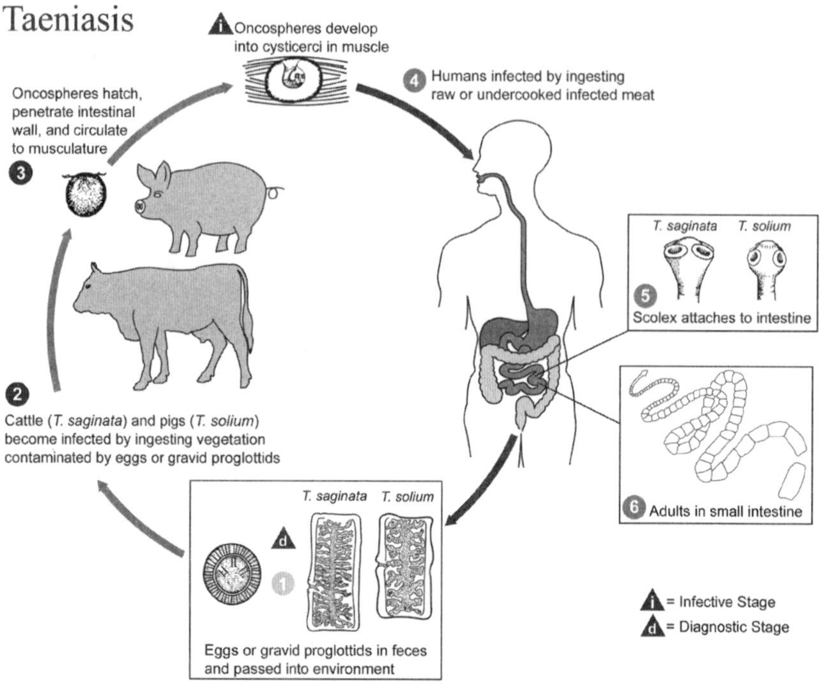
Taeniasis
Oncospheres develop into cysticerci in muscle
Humans infected by ingesting raw or undercooked infected meat
Oncospheres hatch, penetrate intestinal wall, and circulate to musculature
3
T. saginata
T. solium
5
Scolex attaches to intestine
2
Cattle (T. saginata) and pigs (T. solium) become infected by ingesting vegetation contaminated by eggs or gravid proglottids
6
Adults in small intestine
T. saginata
T. solium
1
Eggs or gravid proglottids in feces and passed into environment
= Infective Stage
= Diagnostic Stage

This is an illustration of the life cycle of Taenia saginata *(tapeworm found in beef) and* Taenia solium *(tapeworm found in pork).*
CDC/Alexander J. da Silva, PhD/Melanie Moser

attach and mature into adult worms. Thus, the most common source of infection is inadequately cooked meat. Tapeworms found in beef and pork only give rise to symptoms if their number and size cause intestinal obstruction. *Diphyllobothrium latum*, a fish tapeworm, may cause a severe anemia similar to pernicious anemia, because it consumes most of the vitamin B_{12} in the diet of the host.

Appendicitis

Appendicitis is an inflammation of the vermiform appendix that may be caused by infection or partial or total obstruction. The primary symptom of appendicitis is abdominal pain. In a person with a normally sited appendix, the pain of appendicitis is situated at a point between the navel and the front edge of the right hipbone. But many people have the appendix lying in an abnormal position and may feel the pain of an appendicitis attack in a different or misleading location, which makes their symptoms difficult to distinguish from the abdominal pain caused by a variety of other diseases.

The early pain associated with appendicitis is usually not very severe, and after one to six hours or more, the pain may become localized to the right lower abdomen. Nausea and vomiting may develop, and fever is usually present but is seldom high in the early phases of the attack. The patient's leukocytes (white blood cells) are usually increased from a normal count of 5,000–10,000 in an adult to an abnormal count of 12,000–20,000. This phenomenon can be caused by many other acute inflammatory conditions that occur in the abdomen.

Careful diagnostic examination by a physician can usually determine if acute appendicitis is indeed causing a patient's abdominal pain. Ultrasound or CT scans may also be useful in diagnosing the condition. In some cases a doctor may wait and observe the patient's symptoms for a period of 10 to 24 hours so that a definitive diagnosis can be made. This wait does slightly increase the risk that the appendix will rupture and peritonitis set in, so the patient is kept under careful medical surveillance at this time. The basic treatment of appendicitis is the surgical removal of the appendix in a minor operation called an appendectomy. The operation itself requires little more than a half hour under anesthesia and produces relatively little postoperative discomfort.

Widespread use of antibiotics for upper-respiratory and other diseases may have lessened the incidence of

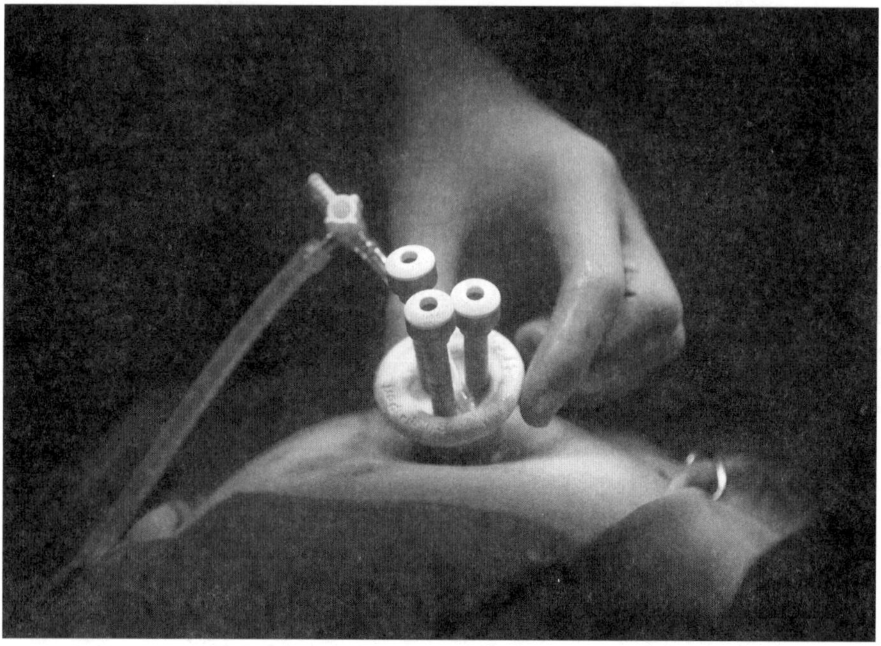

A surgeon removes an inflamed appendix in Pretoria, South Africa. Doctors can use either a classic laparotomy involving an incision into the abdomen, or less-invasive laparoscopic surgery to remove these diseased organs. In laparoscopic surgery, surgeons are guided by a laparoscope, a lit, telescope-like device introduced into the body through a tiny cut. Gallo Images/Getty Images

acute appendicitis, so that more cases of late-developing appendiceal abscess are being reported. Parasitic worms also can contribute to its incidence. Appendicitis principally occurs in persons younger than age 35; however, it does occasionally occur in elderly people.

Chronic Inflammations

Chronic inflammations of the small intestine include tuberculosis and regional enteritis (Crohn disease). These disturbances are difficult to diagnose in their early stages because their initial symptoms are often vague. General symptoms include low-grade fever, a tendency toward loose stools, weight loss, and episodes of cramping abdominal pain caused by obstruction of the lumen and interference with normal muscular activity by inflammation of the intestinal wall. Diagnosis is usually determined by X-ray or colonoscopy. A biopsy may also be performed to examine the lining of the small intestine.

Celiac Disease

Celiac disease, also called nontropical sprue or celiac sprue, is an inherited autoimmune digestive disorder in which people cannot tolerate gluten, a protein constituent of wheat, barley, malt, and rye flours. General symptoms of the disease include the passage of foul, pale-coloured stools (steatorrhea), progressive malnutrition, diarrhea, decreased appetite and weight loss, multiple vitamin deficiencies, stunting of growth, abdominal pain, skin rash, and defects in tooth enamel. Advanced disease may be characterized by anemia, osteoporosis, vision disturbances, or amenorrhea (absence of menstruation in women).

The way in which the disease manifests varies widely. For example, some people experience severe gastrointestinal symptoms, whereas others are asymptomatic, are irritable and depressed, or develop an itchy skin rash with blisters, known as dermatitis herpetiformis. If left undiagnosed or uncontrolled, celiac disease may lead to intestinal adenocarcinoma (malignant tumour of glandular tissue) or intestinal lymphoma or to miscarriage in pregnant women. Pregnant women affected by the disease and thus suffering from vitamin deficiencies are also at an increased risk for giving birth to infants with congenital disorders.

In children, celiac disease begins within several months of adding gluten-containing foods such as cereal to the diet. However, the onset of the disease is also influenced by the length of time the child was breast-fed and by the amount of gluten that the child ingests. The disease frequently is first noticed following an infection and is chronic, with periods of intestinal upset, diarrhea, and failure to grow and gain weight, interspersed with periods of apparent normality. Adult celiac disease commonly begins past the age of 30, but it may appear at an earlier age following severe stress, surgery, or childbirth.

Several gene mutations have been identified in celiac disease. However, genetic mutations themselves do not give rise to the disease. Instead, it is triggered by the combination of genetic and environmental factors; i.e., when a genetically predisposed individual eats foods containing gluten. In people with celiac disease, gluten stimulates the immune system to produce autoantibodies that damage the mucosal lining of the small intestine.

In most cases, celiac disease can be diagnosed by blood tests for anti-tissue transglutaminase antibody and anti-endomysial antibody. Diagnosis is usually confirmed by endoscopic examination and biopsy of the small intestine. Endoscopy provides visual evidence of intestinal damage, marked by flattening of the villi in the mucosal lining, which normally project into the intestinal cavity and increase the surface area available for nutrient absorption. Biopsied tissue is examined for the presence of certain lymphocytes that indicate inflammation caused by gluten.

Celiac disease is estimated to occur, on average, in about 1 in every 266 people worldwide. However, only about three percent of these people are actually diagnosed with celiac disease. This is in part because some people are asymptomatic, but it is also attributed to misdiagnosis, since many symptoms of the disease are similar to other conditions, including irritable bowel syndrome, Crohn disease, and chronic fatigue syndrome. Several autoimmune diseases have mutations in the same chromosomal region as celiac disease, and although the underlying mechanisms remain unclear, these diseases often develop in association with celiac disease. As a result, the longer a person with celiac disease remains undiagnosed or misdiagnosed, the more likely he or she is to develop an associated autoimmune disease, such as a thyroid disorder, type I diabetes, or autoimmune hepatitis.

The symptoms of most patients are relieved by strict adherence to a gluten-free diet. In children the intestinal mucosa is usually healed within several months to one year of initiating the diet, and in adults, it is usually healed within two years. In rare cases, symptoms and destruction of the mucosal lining may progress despite a gluten-free diet; these individuals generally receive intravenous vitamin therapy.

Tropical Sprue

Tropical sprue is an acquired disease characterized by the small intestine's impaired absorption of fats, vitamins, and minerals. While its cause is unknown, infection, parasite infestation, vitamin deficiency, and food toxins have been suggested as possible causes. It is found primarily in the Caribbean, Southeast Asia, India, and areas in which polished rice is a staple food. Sprue often attacks middle-aged adults and is commonly caused by bacterial contamination of the small intestine, which in turn is responsible for inadequate fat digestion and absorption.

The onset of the disease is insidious. In the initial phase, complaints include fatigue, weakness, loss of appetite, severe vomiting, dehydration, and numerous bulky, frothy, greasy, light-coloured stools. In infants and children, sometimes weeks or months elapse before a typical pattern is revealed. Often profound behavioral changes occur, as temper and irritability alternate with timidity and withdrawal signs. Notable is the sad, fretful facial expression of youngsters so afflicted.

The second stage of tropical sprue follows in three to six months with prominent weight loss, inflamed and painfully fissured tongue, fissures of the mouth lining, and swelling and scaling of the lips accompanied by changes in the cornea (hyperkeratosis). If the disease progresses to the third stage, severe anemia and imbalance of protein (e.g., albumins, globulins) and electrolytes (e.g., sodium, potassium, and chlorine in solution) may precipitate total debilitation. Dramatic improvement occurs after administering folic acid, a chemical of the vitamin B complex found in leafy vegetables and liver and also produced synthetically.

DISEASES OF THE LARGE INTESTINE

A wide variety of diseases and disorders occur in the large intestine. Abnormal rotation of the colon is fairly frequent and occasionally leads to disorders. Unusually long mesenteries (the supporting tissues of the large intestine) may permit recurrent twisting, cutting off the blood supply to the involved loop. The loop itself may be completely obstructed by rotation. Such complications are usually seen in elderly patients and particularly in those with a long history of constipation.

Constipation

Constipation is the delayed passage of waste through the lower portion of the large intestine, with the possible discharge of relatively dry, hardened feces from the anus. Among the causes cited for the disorder are lack of regularity in one's eating habits; spasms of the large intestine; metabolic diseases such as hypothyroidism or diabetes mellitus; neurological disorders such as a stroke; certain medications including morphine, codeine, antidepressants, and antispasmodics; lack of sufficient fibre in one's food; and excessive use of laxatives.

Constipation may also be caused by intestinal obstruction by tumours or polyps or by weakness of the abdominal muscles. Temporary constipation most often occurs in conjunction with a change or interruption in one's usual activities, as in travel, temporary confinement to bed, or a change in eating or sleeping habits. In most cases, dietary and lifestyle changes can help relieve constipation.

Megacolon

Aganglionic megacolon, or Hirschsprung disease, is a condition of unknown cause that is characterized by the absence of ganglion cells and normal nerve fibres from the distal (or lower) 3 to 40 cm (1 to 16 inches) of the large intestine. Neuromuscular transmission is absent from this segment, and peristalsis cannot occur. It is thus a functional obstruction. In 10 percent of cases, a larger segment is involved and, on rare occasions, the whole colon. The area of normal intestine above the obstruction works harder to push on the fecal contents, and eventually the muscle of the normal segment thickens. The entire colon thus slowly becomes more and more distended and thick-walled. Diagnosis is made by the examination of the microscopic appearance of a deep biopsy of the lower rectum. Various surgical procedures are used to correct the condition.

Acquired megacolon is commonly caused by a combination of faulty toilet training and emotional disorders during childhood, in which the child withholds defecation. The administration of increasing amounts of laxatives fails to solve the problem permanently, and over time the intrinsic innervation in the intestinal wall is damaged. A dilated rectum full of feces develops over the years. The impacted feces act as an obstruction, and further fecal material piles up behind, with voluminus dilatation of the whole colon in some cases.

Evacuation of the contents of the bowel prior to surgery, if it is required, may require hospitalization for up to three months. Acquired megacolon is occasionally encountered in those with schizophrenia and severe depression. It may be related to neurological disorders such as paraplegia, to unrecognized rectal strictures, and to some metabolic disorders. Severe degrees of constipation, often running in families and leading to megacolon, occur, but the cause has not been discovered. Resection of the colon and uniting the ileum to the rectum is effective treatment.

Diarrhea

Diarrhea is the abnormally swift passage of waste material through the large intestine, with consequent discharge of loose feces from the anus. Because water is normally absorbed from the colonic content, principally in the ascending, or right, colon, diarrhea can be caused by any inflammatory, neoplastic, or vascular disturbance of that part of the colon. Diarrhea can also be caused by bacterial, viral, or parasitic infection. Most cases of diarrhea are not serious and do not require treatment.

Diarrhea is common in those who are deficient in lactase, the enzyme that splits lactose (milk sugar) into its component parts, glucose and galactose. Shortly after drinking milk, such persons usually have severe intestinal cramping, followed later by watery diarrhea. The lactose in the milk is not broken down, and it stays in the lumen of the small intestine, drawing water to it. The increased bulk of fluid and sugar distends the intestine, which then contracts actively. The rapid contractions drive the material along the intestine into the colon, which cannot absorb the water rapidly enough. The resultant watery, unformed stools are frequently acidic.

Intestinal Gas

Intestinal gas consists principally of swallowed air and partly of by-products of digestion. When a person is in an upright position, gas diffuses to the uppermost portions of the colon. There it is compressed by the contraction of adjacent segments, giving rise to pain that is localized either near the liver and gallbladder or under the diaphragm and heart. This pain can be incorrectly thought to be associated with diseases of these organs, whereas it is actually caused by increased gas in the colon. Eating slower to reduce the amount of air ingested, decreasing the intake of carbonated beverages and whipped foods that contain air bubbles, and avoiding certain gas-producing foods, such as most beans, onions, sprouts, nuts, and raisins, usually help to reduce flatulence.

Diverticula of the Large Intestine

Diverticula of the large intestine arise in the wall as small pouches or sacs. Arteries penetrate the muscular walls of the colon from its outside covering, the serosa, and distribute themselves in the submucosa. With aging, and perhaps in persons predisposed to the disorder, the channels in which these arteries lie become larger. If the peristaltic activity of the colon maintains a high pressure within its lumen, as in persons straining to defecate, the mucous membrane of the colon may be driven slowly into these channels and eventually may follow the arteries back to their site of colonic entrance in the serosa. At this time, the outward-pushing mucosa becomes a budding sac, or diverticulum, on the antimesenteric border of the colon with a connection to the lumen.

In the Western world, multiple colonic diverticula occur in as many as 30 percent of persons over age 50. Diverticula are particularly common in those whose diets are deficient in fibre. Hypertrophy (increase in size and mass) of the muscle fibre of the colon, especially in the sigmoid region, precedes or accompanies diverticulosis. This is especially apparent in the diverticulosis in middle-aged persons as opposed to that in the elderly.

The principal dangers of diverticulosis are hemorrhage and inflammation. Hemorrhage results from the action of hard stools against the small arteries of the colon that are exposed and unsupported because of diverticula. As the arteries age, they become less elastic, less able to contract after bleeding begins, and more susceptible to damage. Diverticulitis occurs when the narrow necks of the diverticula become plugged with debris or undigestible foodstuff and when bacteria—uninhibited by the usual motor activity that keeps the intestine clean—proliferate in the blind sacs. When the sacs enlarge, the adjacent intestinal wall becomes inflamed and irritable, muscle spasms occur, and the patient experiences abdominal pain and fever. If the sacs continue to enlarge, they may rupture into the peritoneum, giving rise to peritonitis, an inflammation of the peritoneum. More commonly they fix themselves to neighbouring organs and produce localized abscesses, which may prove difficult to treat surgically.

Mild diverticulitis responds well to antibiotics. Massive hemorrhages often require emergency surgery. Recurrent diverticulitis requires resection of the affected area of the colon.

Abscesses of the Large Intestine

Abscesses (cavities of pus formed from disintegrating tissue) in the perianal area are common complicating features of many diseases and disorders of the large intestine. Fungal infections of the moist and sometimes poorly cleansed area around the anus are common and permit the maceration (or gradual breaking down) of tissue and invasion by bacteria from the skin and colon. In diabetics, who are susceptible to skin infection, perianal hygiene is very important.

Bacterial Infections of the Colon

The colon may become inflamed because of invasion by pathogenic, or disease-causing, bacteria or parasites. A variety of species of *Shigella*, for example, attack the mucous membrane of the colon and produce an intense but rather superficial hemorrhage. In infants and in the elderly, the amount of fluid and protein lost by the intense inflammatory response may be fatal, but ordinarily such symptoms are less serious in otherwise healthy persons. *Salmonella* species, responsible for severe generalized infections originating from invasion of the small intestine, may damage the lymph follicles of the colon, but they do not produce a generalized inflammation of the colon (colitis). The cytomegalic virus, on the other hand, can cause a severe colitis, producing ulcerations. *Lymphopathia venereum* causes a more generalized and superficial colitis.

Food residues provide an excellent culture medium for bacteria, and the interior of the colon is a nearly ideal environment for their growth. The most widely distributed parasite producing disease in the colon is the protozoan *Entamoeba histolytica*. This parasite enters the digestive tract via the mouth and lodges in the cecum and ascending colon. This usually results in irritability of the ascending colon and failure to absorb water properly, so that intermittent, watery diarrhea ensues. The amoebas undermine the mucosal coat and may create large ulcerations that bleed excessively. Stools contain blood, but there is little pus or other evidence of reaction by the colon to the invading organism.

In more generalized amoebic colitis, the rectum and sigmoid colon are invaded by *E. histolytica*, which manifest their presence by numerous discrete ulcerations separated from each other by a relatively normal-appearing mucous membrane. The amoebas may enter the portal circulation and be carried to the liver, where abscesses form and sometimes rupture into the chest or the abdominal cavity. Immunologic tests of the blood may help in diagnosis. After identification of the parasites by direct smear tests from the margin of the ulcers or from the stools, a combination of amoebicidal drugs and a broad-spectrum antibiotic—i.e., an antibiotic that is toxic to a wide variety of parasites, usually metronidazole and tetracycline—is administered.

Inflammatory Bowel Disease

Inflammatory bowel disease (IBD) is a chronic inflammation of the intestines that results in impaired absorption of nutrients. IBD encompasses two disorders: Crohn disease (regional ileitis) and ulcerative colitis. The onset of IBD typically occurs between the ages of 15 and 35, and the disease tends to run in families.

The factors that trigger intestinal inflammation and onset of IBD remain unknown. Symptoms of IBD may develop suddenly or gradually and include constipation, diarrhea, fever, rectal bleeding, and abdominal discomfort. In both Crohn disease and ulcerative colitis, patients may experience periods of symptom remission and relapse. IBD is particularly difficult to diagnose in children, and affected children may fail to grow properly. In addition to physical examination, blood tests, and stool analysis, IBD may be diagnosed by colonoscopy, in which the entire colon is investigated, or sigmoidoscopy, in which only the rectum and sigmoid colon are investigated. Individuals with a family history of IBD may undergo genetic testing for specific gene mutations to determine their susceptibility to the disease.

Research has indicated that IBD is polygenic, meaning that variations in multiple genes combine to give rise to the disease. While the exact combinations of genetic variants that cause IBD have not been identified, individual genetic variations associated with the disease have been discovered. For example, mutation of a gene called *TNFRSF6B* (tumour necrosis factor receptor superfamily, member 6b, decoy), which is involved in suppressing inflammation in the gastrointestinal tract, has been linked with the onset of IBD in childhood. In addition, variation of a gene called *GLI1* (glioma-associated oncogene homolog 1), identified in patients in northern Europe, results in reduced activity of the anti-inflammatory GLI1 protein, and dampened activity of this protein has been associated with increased inflammation in the intestines.

Furthermore, some genetic variations are associated with increased risk for both ulcerative colitis and Crohn disease, whereas other variations are disorder-specific. For example, variation of a gene called *ECM1* (extracellular matrix protein 1) has been linked to ulcerative colitis, whereas variation of a gene called *NOD2* (nucleotide-binding oligomerization domain containing 2) has been linked to Crohn disease. The discovery of genetic mutations that lead to specific abnormalities in immune function in IBD has facilitated research into the development of unique treatment strategies. For example, there is potential for the development of an agent that targets the GLI1 protein to restore the protein's activity to normal levels, thereby reducing intestinal inflammation and relieving symptoms.

Treatment generally includes a diet low in fat, high in protein and easily digestible carbohydrates, and free of lactose (milk sugar). Increased intakes of certain nutrients, such as iron, calcium, and magnesium, and supplementation with fat-soluble vitamins may also be recommended, along with additional fluid and electrolytes to replace losses due to diarrhea. Anti-inflammatory agents, such as corticosteroids (e.g., prednisone) and mesalamine, and immunosuppressive agents, such as cyclosporine and methotrexate, may be prescribed for patients with moderate to severe IBD.

Ulcerative Colitis

The most common form of chronic colitis (inflammation of the colon) in the Western world is ulcerative colitis. This condition varies from a mild inflammation of the mucosa of the rectum—giving rise to excessive mucus and some spotting of blood in the stools—to a severe, sudden illness, with destruction of a large part of the colonic mucosa, considerable blood loss, toxemia and, less commonly, perforation. The most common variety affects only the rectum and sigmoid colon and is characterized by diarrhea and the passage of mucus. Ulcerative colitis tends to follow a remitting-relapsing course. Diagnosis is determined by performing a colonoscopy or a biopsy.

Another type of colitis arises when antibiotic use causes the abnormal proliferation of certain types of bacteria in the colon, leading to inflammation. This disorder is treated by stopping the use of the causal antibiotic and administering others such as vancomycin or mexronidazole. About 15 percent of all cases of colitis involve extension of the disease beyond the area initially affected, with an increase in severity. Where the destruction has been extensive, there is a risk of malignancy 10 to 20 years after the onset of the disease.

Crohn Disease

Crohn disease, also called regional enteritis or regional ileitis, is characterized by chronic inflammation of the digestive tract, usually occurring in the terminal portion of the ileum. Crohn disease was first described in 1904 by Polish surgeon Antoni Leśniowski. It was later named for American gastroenterologist Burrill Bernard Crohn, who in 1932, in collaboration with fellow physicians Leon Ginzburg and Gordon D. Oppenheimer, published a thorough description of a then-unknown intestinal disorder they called regional ileitis.

Today, Crohn disease is characterized as a type of inflammatory bowel disease (IBD) and has been associated with abnormal function of the immune system and genetic variations. The disease also has been linked to abnormal changes in populations of intestinal bacteria. For example, *Faecalibacterium prausnitzii*, a normal inhabitant of the human intestinal tract, is found in decreased levels in people with Crohn disease. *Mycobacterium avium paratuberculosis*, found in the intestinal tracts of ruminants affected by Johne disease, which is similar to Crohn

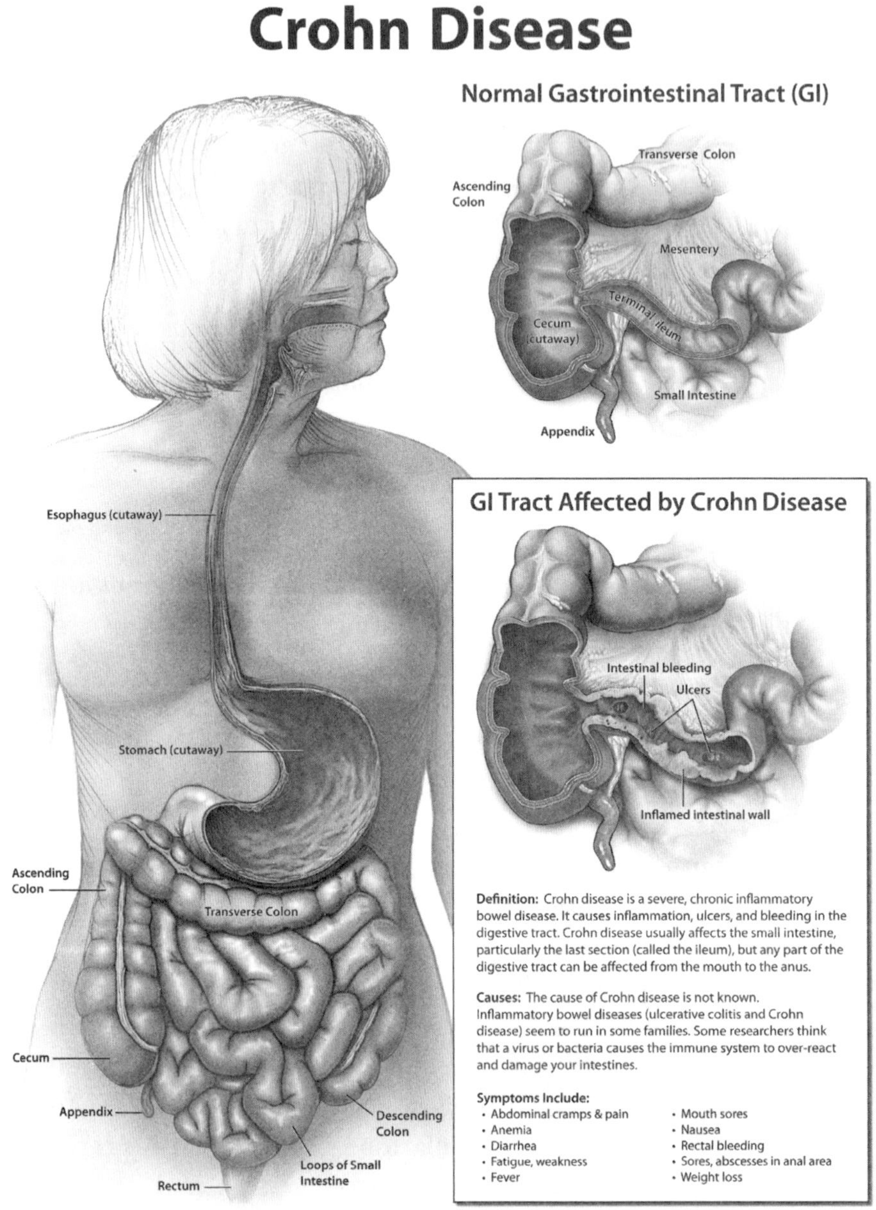
Crohn Disease
Normal Gastrointestinal Tract (GI)
Transverse Colon
Ascending Colon
Mesentery
Terminal ileum
Cecum (cutaway)
Small Intestine
Appendix
GI Tract Affected by Crohn Disease
Intestinal bleeding
Ulcers
Inflamed intestinal wall
Definition: Crohn disease is a severe, chronic inflammatory bowel disease. It causes inflammation, ulcers, and bleeding in the digestive tract. Crohn disease usually affects the small intestine, particularly the last section (called the ileum), but any part of the digestive tract can be affected from the mouth to the anus.
Causes: The cause of Crohn disease is not known. Inflammatory bowel diseases (ulcerative colitis and Crohn disease) seem to run in some families. Some researchers think that a virus or bacteria causes the immune system to over-react and damage your intestines.
Symptoms Include:
• Abdominal cramps & pain
• Anemia
• Diarrhea
• Fatigue, weakness
• Fever
• Mouth sores
• Nausea
• Rectal bleeding
• Sores, abscesses in anal area
• Weight loss
Esophagus (cutaway)
Stomach (cutaway)
Ascending Colon
Transverse Colon
Cecum
Appendix
Descending Colon
Loops of Small Intestine
Rectum

This medical exhibit portrays Crohn disease. It shows the healthy gastrointestinal tract and the gastrointestinal tract with Crohn disease. Nucleus Medical Art, Inc./Getty Images

disease in humans, has been isolated from the blood of some patients. However, despite these associations, the cause of Crohn disease remains unknown.

The most common symptoms of Crohn disease include diarrhea and abdominal pain. Rectal bleeding, fever, weight loss, arthritis, and anemia are indications of moderate to severe disease. Some patients develop fistulas, or abnormal passages connecting the bowel to other organs, such as the bladder or the vagina. These often lead to abscesses (pus-filled cavities within tissues). The formation of fistulas and the thickening of the intestinal wall—to the point of obstruction—are the only microscopic findings that distinguish Crohn disease from ulcerative colitis, the other type of IBD.

In Crohn disease the maximum damage to the intestine occurs beneath the mucosa, and lymphoid conglomerations, known as granulomata, are formed in the submucosa. In addition, Crohn disease attacks the perianal tissues more often than does ulcerative colitis. Crohn disease is diagnosed by a combination of methods, including blood and stool analysis and colonoscopy. Diagnosis may be confirmed by other methods, such as barium enema, which uses X-rays to examine the intestine following rectal insertion of a liquid barium contrast agent. Another method, capsule endoscopy, examines the intestines via a pill-sized video camera that is swallowed by the patient and transmits images to sensors attached to the patient's body as it passes through the digestive tract.

A combination of immunosuppressive and anti-inflammatory drugs, including corticosteroids and aminosalicylic acid compounds, are used to treat Crohn disease. The drugs are effective both in treating acute episodes and in suppressing the disease over the long term. Depending on the circumstances, hematinics, vitamins, high-protein diets, and blood transfusions are also used. Surgical resection of the portion of the large bowel affected is often performed. The entire colon may need to be removed and the small intestine brought out to the skin as an ileostomy, an opening to serve as a substitute for the anus.

Colorectal Cancer

Colorectal cancer is a disease characterized by uncontrolled growth of cells within the large intestine (colon) or rectum (terminal portion of the large intestine). Colon cancer (or bowel cancer) and rectal cancer are sometimes referred to separately. Colorectal cancer develops slowly but can spread to surrounding and distant tissues of the body.

Causes and Symptoms of Colorectal Cancer

Like most cancers, colorectal cancers have multiple causes, many of which remain unknown. Some cases appear to be inherited, whereas others seem to occur randomly or to have nongenetic causes. Approximately 95 percent of colorectal cancers involve the glandular cells in the wall of the colon and are called adenocarcinomas. Other colorectal cancers may begin among hormone-producing cells, immune cells, or underlying connective tissue.

Several factors increase the risk of developing the disease. Colorectal cancer becomes more common with increasing age. Ninety percent of cases are diagnosed in people age 50 or older. A family history of colorectal cancer—specifically forms such as familial adenomatous polyposis (FAP), Gardner syndrome, and hereditary non-polyposis colon cancer (HNPCC)—can predispose an individual to developing colorectal cancer. Each of these conditions is caused in part by a known genetic mutation. In addition, Ashkenazi Jews have a slightly higher incidence of colorectal cancer due to a mutated gene, and there exists a gene mutation that increases risk of colorectal cancer in people of European descent but does not increase risk in people of Japanese descent. This latter mutation, discovered in 2008, was the first to provide evidence of ethnic differences in genetic susceptibility to colorectal cancer.

Chronic inflammatory bowel diseases such as Crohn disease or ulcerative colitis are associated with colorectal cancer, as is the presence of a large number of noncancerous polyps along the wall of the colon or rectum. Other risk factors include physical inactivity and a diet high in fats. Those who have previously been treated for colorectal cancer are also at increased risk of recurrence.

Because colorectal cancer is a disease of the digestive tract, many of the symptoms are associated with abnormal digestion and elimination. Symptoms include episodes of diarrhea or constipation that extend for days, blood in the stool, rectal bleeding, jaundice, abdominal pain, loss of appetite, and fatigue. Because these symptoms accompany a variety of different illnesses, a physician should be consulted to determine their cause.

Diagnosis of Colorectal Cancer

Diagnoses of colon and rectal cancers are made by means of several techniques. During a digital rectal exam, the physician inserts a gloved finger into the rectum and feels its surface for abnormalities. A fecal test may also be used to detect the presence of blood in the stool. In order to examine the rectum more carefully, a physician may use a narrow, flexible tube called a sigmoidoscope to look at the lining of the rectum and the end of the colon. Colonoscopy uses a similar device to examine the entire colon. A biopsy may also be conducted in which abnormal tissue is removed by using the colonoscope and then examined under a microscope for signs of cancer. An X-ray procedure called a double-contrast barium enema may be used. Barium sulfate is used to coat the colon, and the colon is filled with air. A series of X-rays are then taken, and the resulting high-contrast images indicate any abnormalities present.

If cancer is found, the degree to which it has spread (metastasized) from the colon or rectum is determined. Biopsies may be conducted of surrounding tissues, or one of several imaging techniques may be used to detect metastasis. Techniques include rectal ultrasound, MRI, and X-ray or CT scans.

Once colorectal cancer has been diagnosed, its stage is then determined to indicate how far the cancer has progressed. Stage 0 colorectal cancer is also called carcinoma in situ and is confined to the lining of the colon or rectum. Stage I cancers have spread into the connective tissue beneath the lining or into the underlying muscle layer. Stage II cancers have spread completely through the wall of the colon or rectum but have not invaded nearby lymph nodes. Stage III colorectal cancer has reached nearby lymph nodes, and stage IV cancers have spread to distant structures such as the lungs, liver, bones, or reproductive organs.

Colorectal cancer patients have an excellent five-year survival rate when the disease is detected early, and those who reach this stage often go on to live long, healthy lives. Approximately two-thirds of patients with local metastases survive for five or more years, but in cases where cancer is detected late and has spread to distant regions of the body, the five-year survival rate is very low.

Treatment and Prevention of Colorectal Cancer

Colorectal cancer is treated by surgery, chemotherapy, or radiation. The method used depends on the site of the cancer and the degree to which it has spread. For cancers localized to the colon or rectum, surgery is usually all that is required. For early-stage colon cancer, a colonoscope may be used to remove the cancerous tissue. Other early cancers require a surgical resection, whereby the portion of the colon containing the cancerous tissue is removed along with surrounding tissue and nearby lymph nodes and the remainder of the colon is repaired.

Rectal cancers may be treated by removing only the cancerous polyp or polyps, the cancer plus surrounding tissues, or larger sections of the rectum. Some cancers may be removed by burning them in a procedure called electrofulguration. In cases where the lower portion of the rectum is involved, a colostomy may be required, whereby the surgeon creates an artificial opening for the removal of waste. If colorectal cancer has spread to surrounding tissues such as those of the uterus, prostate, liver, kidneys, or bladder, more extensive surgery may be required to remove all or part of these organs.

Both colon and rectal cancers may be treated with radiation, using either external beams or surgically implanted radioactive pellets. Radiation is usually used in conjunction with surgery—either before the surgery to shrink tumours or following surgery to destroy small amounts of remaining cancerous tissue. Chemotherapy may also be indicated for treatment of colorectal cancers, especially when cancer has spread to other parts of the body but also as an adjuvant therapy to primary surgery and radiation. Side effects of both radiation and chemotherapy may include vomiting, diarrhea, and fatigue.

A lifestyle that includes regular exercise and a diet low in fats and high in fruits and vegetables helps to prevent colorectal cancer. Early detection is important in preventing the development of advanced colorectal cancer. Some medical societies recommend regular screening by a physician after age 50.

Hemorrhoids

A hemorrhoid, or pile, is formed by distension of the network of veins under the mucous membrane that lines the anal channel or under the skin lining the external portion of the anus. A form of varicose vein, a hemorrhoid may develop from anal infection or from increase in intra-abdominal pressure, such as occurs during pregnancy, while lifting a heavy object, or while straining at stool. It may be a complication of chronic liver disease or tumours.

The weakness in the vessel wall that permits the defect to develop may be inherited. Mild hemorrhoids may be treated by such methods as the use of suppositories, nonirritating laxatives, and baths. If clots have formed, or in the presence of other complications, the hemorrhoids may require surgical removal.

CHAPTER 8

DISEASES OF THE LIVER AND PANCREAS

A variety of agents, including viruses, drugs, environmental pollutants, genetic disorders, and systemic diseases, can affect the liver and the pancreas. In the liver the resulting disorders usually affect one of the three functional components: the hepatocyte (liver cell), the bile secretory (cholangiolar) apparatus, or the blood vascular system. Diseases of the pancreas typically affect one of the organ's two primary glandular tissues: the exocrine tissue or the endocrine tissue. Both the liver and the pancreas can also be affected by inflammation or dysfunction of the gallbladder or other components of the biliary tract.

DISEASES OF THE LIVER

Diseases of the liver—though generally limited to the hepatocytes, the bile secretory apparatus, or the blood vascular system—may in time also involve other components. Thus, although viral hepatitis (inflammation of the liver) predominantly affects hepatocytes, it commonly leads to damaged canaliculi, small channels that transport bile from hepatocytes.

Most acute liver diseases are self-limiting, and liver function returns to normal once the causes are removed or eliminated. In some cases, however, the acute disease process destroys massive areas of liver tissue in a short time, leading to extensive death (necrosis) of hepatic cells. For example, when acute hepatitis lasts for six months or more, a slow but progressive destruction of the surrounding liver cells and bile ducts occurs, a stage called chronic active hepatitis. If hepatocellular damage is severe enough to destroy entire acini (clusters of lobules), healthy tissue is often replaced with fibrous scar tissue. Bile canaliculi and hepatocytes regenerate in an irregular fashion adjacent to the scar tissue and result in a chronic condition called cirrhosis of the liver. Where inflammatory activity continues after the onset of cirrhosis, the disorderly regeneration of hepatocytes and cholangioles may lead to the development of hepatocellular or cholangiolar cancer.

Benign cysts (tissue swellings filled with fluid) in the liver may occur as congenital defects or as the result of infections from infestation of the dog tapeworm (*Echinococcus granulosus*). Abscesses on the liver result from the spread of infection from the biliary tract or from other parts of the body, especially the appendix and the pelvic organs. Specific liver abscesses also result from infections with the intestinal parasite *Entamoeba histolytica*. Abscesses usually respond well to treatment with specific antibiotics, although surgical drainage is required in some cases.

ACUTE HEPATOCELLULAR HEPATITIS

Although a number of viruses affect the liver—including cytomegalovirus and Epstein-Barr virus, which causes infectious mononucleosis—there are three distinctive transmissible viruses that are specifically known to cause acute damage to liver cells. These viruses are hepatitis A virus (HAV), hepatitis B virus (HBV), and hepatitis C virus (HCV). The hepatitis A virus is transmitted almost exclusively via the fecal–oral route, and it thrives in areas where sanitation and food handling are poor and hand washing is infrequent. HAV proliferates in the intestinal tract during the two weeks following the onset of symptoms, but it then disappears. Many infected persons are unaware of being ill, since their disease remains asymptomatic or quite mild.

The incubation period of HAV infections, from viral ingestion to the onset of symptoms, averages four to five weeks. Acute illness in an otherwise healthy pregnant woman does not appear to have adverse effects upon the fetus. Persons can become passively immunized against HAV for several months with either the hepatitis A vaccine or a single injection of immunoglobulin. Persons can be actively immunized to HAV by acquiring the virus subsequent to becoming passively immunized, but such infections are either inapparent or very mild.

Hepatitis B virus is present throughout the world in asymptomatic human carriers who may or may not have ongoing liver disease. Formerly, the disease was widely spread by the transfusion of whole blood or blood products, such as the cryoprecipitate used in the treatment of hemophilia. Since the signs of infection have become so readily identifiable, this mode of transmission is much less common, comprising only about 10 percent of cases, compared with 60 percent in the past. Virus particles in carriers are found in bodily secretions, especially saliva and sexual emissions, as well as in blood. The incidence of B antigens is high among persons engaging in promiscuous sexual activity, drug addicts who share syringes, health care workers, and infants of mothers who are carriers. Many newly infected persons develop the acute disease within three weeks to six months after exposure, while some develop an asymptomatic form of hepatitis that may appear only as chronic disease years later. Others eliminate the virus completely without any symptoms beyond the appearance of antibodies to surface antigen, while still others become carriers of surface antigen and thus presumably are infective to others.

There are two methods of preventing hepatitis B: passive immunization, through the use of a specific immunoglobulin derived from patients who have successfully overcome an acute HBV infection; and active immunization, through the injection of noninfective, purified HBV surface antigen. The first method is used following specific exposures that carry a high risk of infection, such as using needles contaminated with HBV particles, the ingestion of body secretions likely to be infected, or the birth of an infant to a surface-antigen-positive mother. The second method, active immunization, is used for those who belong to groups with a high risk of HBV infection, such as children living in endemic areas, medical personnel in high-risk specialties, drug addicts, sexually promiscuous persons, and family groups living close to known carriers. Active immunization, involving a series of three injections of vaccine over a period of three to six months, has been shown to confer a high degree of resistance to infection.

Hepatitis C appears to be transmitted in a manner similar to HBV transmission. The incidence for HCV is high among persons engaging in promiscuous sexual activity, intravenous drug users, homosexual males, children living in endemic areas, infants born to infected mothers, health care workers, and hemodialysis patients. The average incubation period of the disease is about seven weeks, and an acute attack of hepatitis C is usually less severe than acute hepatitis B. Hepatitis C, however, is more likely to become chronic than is hepatitis B, and it may recur episodically with acute flares. The two approved treatments for hepatitis C are alpha interferon and ribavirin, but only about half of those receiving the drugs respond to them.

The symptoms characteristic of acute hepatitis caused by HAV, HBV, and HCV are essentially similar. Patients often complain of a flulike illness for several days, with chills, fever, headache, cough, nausea, occasional diarrhea, and malaise. Abdominal pain caused by swelling of the liver is a common complaint. As many as half of the infected patients develop only mild symptoms or none at all. A small percentage of patients, especially those with HBV infections, may develop hives, painful skin nodules, acute arthritis, or urinary bleeding caused by the deposition of large immune antigen-antibody complexes in the small blood vessels of adjacent organs. After several days of such symptoms, jaundice commonly develops. At times the jaundice is so mild that it is not noticed by patients, although they often do note that the urine has become dark amber in colour because of the high levels of water-soluble bilirubin transmitted to the kidneys by the bloodstream.

The onset of jaundice usually brings with it a marked improvement in other symptoms. Jaundice lasts about two weeks but may continue for several months, even in those who have complete recovery. Some patients complain of itching during this period, and they notice the light colour of their stools. These symptoms probably result from the compression of bile canaliculi and intralobular bile ducts by the swelling of hepatocytes and Kupffer cells. The changes result in the reduced secretion of bile pigments into the biliary system, their reflux into the bloodstream, and the deposition of bile salts and other biliary constituents in the skin and subcutaneous tissues—a condition called obstructive jaundice. After the phase of jaundice subsides, almost all patients with hepatitis A, and at least 90 percent of those with hepatitis B, recover completely.

Aside from jaundice, the physical examination of patients with acute viral hepatitis may reveal nothing more than a detectable enlargement and, at times, tenderness of the liver. Some also show an enlarged spleen. Signs of confusion or disorientation indicate severe damage to the liver. The diagnosis of hepatitis is confirmed by blood tests that show marked elevations of enzymes (aminotransferases) released from damaged liver cells and by the presence of viral antigens or acute viral antibodies (IgM).

A small number, perhaps 1 percent, of patients with viral hepatitis, especially the elderly, develop a sudden, severe (fulminant) form of hepatic necrosis that can lead to death. In this form of the disease, jaundice increases to high levels during the first 7 to 10 days; spontaneous bleeding occurs because of reductions of blood-clotting proteins; and irrational behaviour, confusion, or coma follow, caused by the accumulation in the central nervous system of the breakdown products of protein normally metabolized by the liver. Beyond supportive measures there is no effective treatment of fulminant hepatic failure except liver transplantation.

Acute hepatitis also may be caused by the overconsumption of alcohol or other poisons, such as commercial solvents (e.g., carbon tetrachloride), acetaminophen, and certain fungi. Such agents are believed to cause hepatitis when the formation of their toxic intermediate metabolites in the liver cell is beyond the capacity of the hepatocyte to conjugate, or join them with another substance for detoxification and excretion.

Acute Canalicular (Cholestatic) Hepatitis

Acute canalicular (cholestatic) hepatitis is most commonly caused by certain drugs, such as psychopharmacologics, antibiotics, and anabolic steroids or, at times, by hepatitis viruses. The symptoms are generally those of biliary obstruction and include itching, jaundice, and light-coloured stools. Drug-induced cholestasis almost invariably disappears within days or weeks after exposure to the agent is discontinued.

Acute congestive liver disease usually results from the sudden engorgement of the liver by fluids after congestive heart failure. The liver may enlarge and become tender. The levels of hepatocytic enzymes in the blood are often greatly increased, and recovery is rapid once the heart failure improves. Jaundice is uncommon in acute hepatic congestion.

Chronic Active Hepatitis

Chronic hepatitis is the result of unresolved acute injury and is associated with ongoing liver damage. The course of the disease is usually slow but relentlessly progressive. A milder form of chronic disease, called persistent hepatitis, does not appear to lead to progressive liver damage despite evidence of a continuing mild inflammation. These conditions may result from viral hepatitis, drug-induced hepatitis, autoimmune liver diseases (lupoid hepatitis), or congenital abnormalities. A prominent autoimmune liver disease is Wilson disease, which is caused by abnormal deposits of large amounts of copper in the liver. Granulomatous hepatitis—a condition in which localized areas of inflammation (granulomas) appear in a portion of the liver lobule—is a type of inflammatory disorder associated with many systemic diseases, including tuberculosis, sarcoidosis, schistosomiasis, and certain drug reactions. Granulomatous hepatitis rarely leads to serious interference with hepatic function, although it is often chronic.

Chronic viral hepatitis B and C can be treated with interferon. Cirrhosis of the liver, and occasionally liver cancer, usually result from a gradual loss of liver function. Chronic hepatitis that is the result of autoimmune disorders usually responds to the administration of immunosuppressive medications and adrenal corticosteroids, which moderate the inflammatory reaction.

Cirrhosis

The end result of many forms of chronic liver injury is cirrhosis, or scarring of liver tissue in response to previous acinar necrosis and irregular regeneration of liver nodules and bile ducts. Among the congenital disorders producing cirrhosis are Wilson disease, hemochromatosis (over-deposition of iron pigment), cystic fibrosis, biliary atresia (congenital absence of a part of the bile ducts), and $alpha_1$-antitrypsin deficiency, or the congenital absence of a proteolytic enzyme inhibitor that results in the accumulation of abnormal forms of carbohydrate in hepatocytes.

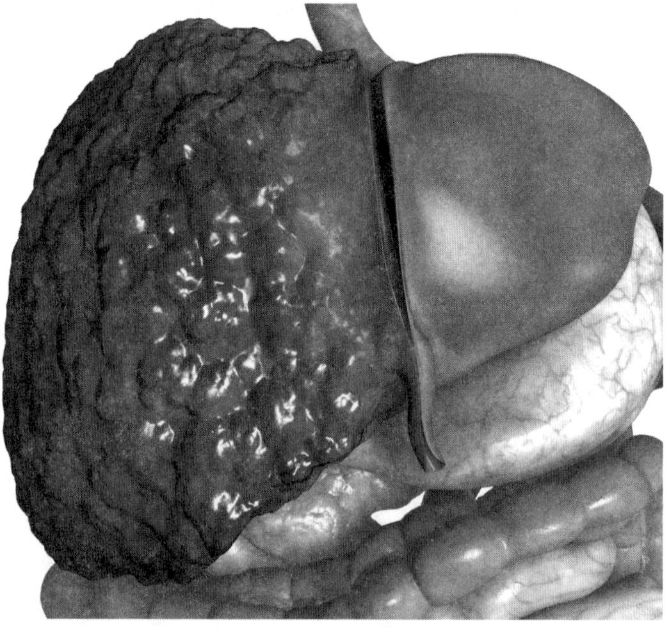

A close-up of a human liver. The right lobe displays severe cirrhosis. 3D4Medical.com/Getty Images

In the Western world, cirrhosis of the liver most commonly results from chronic heavy intake of alcohol. This type of cirrhosis is known as Laënnec, or portal, cirrhosis. Chronic viral hepatitis is probably the leading cause of cirrhosis in underdeveloped countries. Primary biliary cirrhosis—a geographically widespread, though uncommon, autoimmune inflammatory disease of bile ducts—is a disorder primarily affecting middle-aged and older women. The inflammation leads to necrosis and gradual disappearance of bile ducts over a period of one or more decades. Secondary biliary cirrhosis results from chronic obstruction or recurrent infection in the extrahepatic bile ducts caused by strictures, gallstones, or tumours. Infestation of the biliary tract with a liver fluke, *Clonorchis sinensis*, is a cause of secondary biliary cirrhosis in Asia. Cirrhosis occasionally is the result of chronic vascular congestion of the liver in persons with prolonged heart failure and in those with chronic obstruction of the hepatic veins caused by benign blood clots or metastatic cancer.

Symptoms of cirrhosis are usually absent during the early stages of the disease. Occasionally, cirrhosis is detected during a physical examination when an enlargement of the liver, spleen, or veins in the upper abdominal wall is found. More often, patients develop symptoms related either to the failure of the liver to perform its functions or to complications caused by the circulatory changes that a cirrhotic liver imposes on the venous blood flow from the intestinal tract (portal hypertension). Thus, common symptoms of cirrhosis include jaundice, resulting from reduced passage of conjugated bilirubin into the biliary tract; increased bleeding, from sequestration of blood platelets in a congested spleen; or deficient production of short-lived coagulation proteins by the liver. There may be certain changes in the skin, such as the appearance of small spiderlike vascular lesions on the hands, arms, or face, a marked reddening of portions of the palms, or enlargement of the breast in females or reduction in testicular size in males. These symptoms are believed to occur because of the liver's inability to metabolize the female sex hormones normally produced by the body.

The gradual accumulation of fluid in the abdominal cavity (ascites), sometimes accompanied by swelling of the ankles, is attributable to portal hypertension and to reduced hepatic production of albumin. Failure of the liver to metabolize amino acids and other products of protein digestion may lead to the state of confusion called hepatic encephalopathy. Loss of appetite, reduction of muscle mass, nausea, vomiting, abdominal pain, and weakness are other symptoms of hepatic cirrhosis. Diabetes in a patient with cirrhosis is frequently caused by hemochromatosis (excessive deposition of iron in tissues, especially in the liver and pancreas), since iron deposits compromise the production of insulin by the islets of Langerhans in the pancreas. Severe spastic disorders of the muscles in the limbs, head, and face suggest the presence of Wilson disease, especially if there is a family history, since the copper deposits characteristic of that disorder are toxic to the liver and to structures in the base of the brain. A history of chronic lung infections or of progressive obstructive lung disease may be present in patients with cystic fibrosis or a deficiency of $alpha_1$-antitrypsin.

A diagnosis of cirrhosis is confirmed by blood tests that show an elevated concentration of hepatocytic enzymes, reduced levels of coagulation proteins, elevated levels of bilirubin, and, most importantly, reduced amounts of serum albumin (a major protein of human blood plasma) and increases in serum globulin (a specific group of proteins found in blood plasma and including immunoglobulins). Although other tests may also be abnormal in patients with acute liver disease, serum albumin levels are usually not reduced in the acute stage of the disease because that protein is rather long-lived (up to one month) and levels do not decrease until the liver disease becomes chronic.

Elevated levels of serum iron or copper support a diagnosis of hemochromatosis or Wilson disease, respectively, while a positive test for serum antibodies to cellular mitochondria is associated almost solely with primary biliary cirrhosis. The presence of HBV surface antigen or of delta agent suggests viral cirrhosis. A biopsy of the liver is the most valuable diagnostic test, since this procedure makes available an actual specimen of liver tissue for microscopic examination. Treatment of cirrhosis of the liver never results in a completely normal organ, since the process of scarring and nodular regeneration is permanent. The process itself, however, can be prevented or its progress halted by managing the precipitating factors of the disease.

Hepatic Encephalopathy

Hepatic encephalopathy refers to changes in the brain that occur in patients with advanced acute or chronic liver disease. If liver cells are damaged, certain substances that are normally cleansed from the blood by the healthy liver are not removed. These products of cell metabolism are primarily nitrogenous substances derived from protein, especially ammonia, or possibly certain short-chain fatty acids. They pass to the brain where they damage functioning nervous tissue or subvert the actions of neurotransmitters—chemical messengers that carry impulses from one brain cell to another.

In acute cases, the brain becomes swollen to the point where normal breathing may cease. Chronic exposure can lead to destruction of nerve cells with replacement by scar tissue (gliosis). A patient with chronic hepatic encephalopathy may develop progressive loss of memory, disorientation, and muscular tremors, leading to a form of chronic dementia. The ingestion of protein invariably aggravates these symptoms. Patients with gastrointestinal bleeding, infection, kidney failure, and constipation and those who are taking certain medications are all at risk of worsened episodes of hepatic encephalopathy.

The treatment of hepatic encephalopathy involves, first, the removal of all drugs that require detoxification in the liver and, second, the reduction of protein intake. Ammonia is a potentially harmful by-product of digestion, and its concentration in the blood can be lowered in one of two ways. The first is through the reduction of intestinal bacteria by administration of enteric antibiotics, which reduce the production of ammonia in the colon. The other is by administration of lactulose, a nonabsorbable carbohydrate whose by-products make the contents of the colon more acidic, creating an environment that reduces the diffusion of ammonia from the intestinal lumen to the portal blood vessels.

Portal Hypertension

Portal hypertension is the increased pressure in the portal vein and its tributaries. It is the result of impediments to venous flow into the liver, and is brought about by the scarring characteristic of the cirrhotic process. The increased pressure causes feeders of the portal vein to distend markedly, producing varices, or dilations of the veins. When varices are located in superficial tissues, they may rupture and bleed profusely. Varices most commonly occur in the lower esophagus, the stomach, and the perianal region. Esophageal varices are likely to bleed most heavily, and, because of the reduced blood flow in the liver that results and the large amount of protein contained in the blood that is shed into the intestines, profuse bleeding from esophageal varices is frequently associated with the onset of hepatic encephalopathy or coma. Because of their location at the lower end of the esophagus or the upper portion of the stomach, bleeding from varices is often difficult to control. It may stop spontaneously, but it is likely to recur.

Considerable success in stemming such hemorrhage and preventing its recurrence has been achieved by using rubber bands to block the blood supply to each varix or by the injection of sclerosing (hardening) agents into varices during endoscopic visualization. If variceal bleeding persists and if the patient can withstand a long and complex operative procedure, surgical formation of a shunt, or artificial passageway, may be performed. The shunt may go from the portal vein or one of its feeders to a systemic abdominal vein, such as the vena cava or the left renal vein, or from the hepatic vein to the portal vein.

Ascites

The accumulation of fluid in the abdominal cavity, or ascites, is related to portal hypertension, significant reduction in serum albumin, and renal retention of sodium. When albumin levels in the blood are lower than normal, there is a marked reduction in the force that holds plasma water within the blood vessels and normally resists the effects of the intravascular pressure. The resulting increase in intravascular pressure, coupled with the increased internal pressure caused by the portal venous obstruction in the liver, leads to massive losses of plasma water into the abdominal cavity. The associated reduction of blood flow to the kidneys causes increased elaboration of the hormone aldosterone, which, in turn, causes the retention of sodium and water and a reduction in urinary output. In addition, because the movement of intestinal lymph into the liver is blocked by the cirrhotic process in the liver, the backflow of this fluid into the abdominal cavity is greatly increased.

The volume of abdominal ascites in adults with cirrhosis may reach levels as great as 10 to 12 litres (11 to 13 quarts). Ascitic fluid may accumulate in the scrotum and in the chest cavity, where its presence, combined with the upward pressure on the diaphragm from the abdominal fluid, may severely affect breathing. Appetite also is often reduced by the abdominal distention.

The treatment of cirrhotic ascites begins with the removal of enough fluid directly from the abdomen by needle puncture to ease discomfort and breathing. Patients are placed on diets low in salt (sodium chloride), and they are given diuretic drugs to increase the output of water by the kidneys. If these measures do not control massive ascites, ascites can be drained internally into the general venous blood system by running a plastic tube from the abdominal cavity, under the skin of the chest, into the right internal jugular vein of the neck (peritoneovenous shunt of LeVeen) or from the hepatic vein to the portal vein.

Hepatorenal Syndrome

Hepatorenal syndrome, a progressive reduction in kidney function that often occurs in persons with advanced acute or chronic liver disease, probably results from an inadequate flow of blood through the cortical (outer) portions of the kidneys, where most removal of waste products occurs. In some instances, hepatorenal syndrome is caused by marked reductions in blood volume that result from a low concentration of water in the blood. Hemorrhages also can reduce kidney function by leading to damage of renal tubules.

With advanced hepatocytic dysfunction, a spasm of blood vessels in the renal cortex can occur, which results in progressive failure in kidney function and often leads to death. The kidneys themselves are frequently undamaged structurally. Treatment of patients with volume depletion and tubular damage often may lead to significant improvement in kidney function. Dialysis may improve symptoms.

Liver Cancer

Liver cancer refers to any of several forms of disease that are characterized by tumours in the liver. Benign liver tumours remain in the liver, whereas malignant tumours are, by definition, cancerous and thus capable of invading tissues outside the liver. Most malignant liver tumours are hepatomas, also called hepatocellular carcinomas (HCCs). HCCs account for fewer than 1 percent of U.S. cancers but are common in Africa, Southeast Asia, and China. These tumours begin in the functional cells of the liver and account for 85 percent of all liver cancers. The remaining cancers develop from blood vessels (hemangiosarcomas), small bile ducts, (cholangiocarcinomas), or immature liver cells (hepatoblastomas). Hepatoblastomas occur primarily in children. Treatment and prognosis for liver cancers vary, depending on the type and stage, or degree, of advancement.

Causes and Symptoms of Liver Cancer

The causes of liver cancer vary and in many cases remain unknown, but several factors have been identified that increase the risk of developing the disease. Previous infection with hepatitis B or hepatitis C viruses is clearly linked to liver cancer, as is cirrhosis of the liver. Exposure to several chemicals also increases cancer risk. These chemicals include vinyl chloride (commonly used in plastics manufacturing), thorium dioxide (once used with certain X-ray procedures), aflatoxin (a poison produced by a fungus of spoiled peanuts and certain grain products), and arsenic. Use of anabolic steroids and oral contraceptives may increase the risk of certain types of liver cancer. Other illnesses such as gallstones, chronic inflammation of the colon or gallbladder, and certain parasitic infections are also risk factors.

Symptoms of liver cancer often remain undetected until the disease has progressed to an advanced stage. Symptoms include abdominal pain or swelling, loss of appetite, unexplained weight loss, an early sense of fullness during meals, or jaundice. Individuals with chronic liver diseases may experience a sudden worsening of their overall condition. Laboratory tests may reveal elevated levels of calcium in the blood, low blood sugar, or other signs of liver dysfunction.

Diagnosis and Prognosis of Liver Cancer

Early diagnosis of liver disorders usually involves a blood test for abnormal liver function. Special tests for two specific antigens in the blood may also indicate liver cancer. If cancer is suspected, a biopsy will be done either during exploratory surgery or by inserting a thin needle into the liver.

The cancer is further diagnosed by means of imaging techniques such as CT scans, MRI, and ultrasound. In some cases an X-ray procedure called angiography will be used to examine blood vessels in and around the liver. A physician can also directly examine the liver with a laparoscope, a flexible tube with a lens on the end that is inserted through an incision in the abdomen.

Once liver cancer has been diagnosed, its stage is then determined to indicate how far the cancer has progressed. Some tumours that are localized, or found in a confined area of the liver, may be completely removed. Other localized cancers cannot be completely removed, as the resultant loss of remaining liver function would be fatal. Advanced cancer has either invaded a large portion of the liver or spread (metastasized) to distant tissues in the body.

Whereas survivability of most cancers is expressed in terms of a five-year survival rate, the rapid course of this disease following appearance of symptoms has resulted in use of a three-year survival rate. This rate is fairly high if the cancer is localized and can be completely removed by surgery. If the cancer is localized but inoperable, the rate is lower, and in more advanced stages of liver cancer the three-year survival is low. Unfortunately, overall survival from liver cancer is lower than that for many other types of cancer because it is not usually detected in its early stages.

Treatment and Prevention of Liver Cancer

Surgery can cure liver cancer, but only when the cancer is limited to a region small enough to permit its removal while leaving enough of the liver behind to perform normal functions. Surgery is not curative for cancers that have spread beyond the liver and is not usually recommended for patients with cirrhosis. When surgery is not an option, some local tumours can be destroyed either by being frozen or by being injected with alcohol. Other cancers may be starved by blocking nearby blood vessels. This procedure, however, carries inherent risks because it also blocks blood flow to healthy liver tissue.

Radiation therapy is rarely used to treat liver cancer owing to the high sensitivity of healthy liver cells to radiation. Chemotherapy may be used, especially if the cancer has spread to distant tissues, to seek out and destroy as many cancer cells as possible. A chemotherapeutic agent may, in some cases, be administered directly into the main artery that feeds the liver. This allows direct delivery of cancer-destroying drugs to the liver while minimizing systemic exposure.

The risk of liver cancer can be greatly reduced by taking steps to eliminate key risk factors. Hepatitis B infection can be prevented by vaccination against the virus and by avoiding unprotected sexual contact or contact with human blood. Hepatitis C can also be avoided by eliminating direct exposure to blood. Alcohol consumption should be limited; anabolic steroids should never be used without the advice of a physician; and guidelines regarding vinyl chloride exposure should be followed.

DISEASES OF THE BILIARY TRACT

There are several important diseases of the biliary tract that affect the function not only of the biliary system but also of the organs and tissues associated with it. Disorders of the biliary tract can lead to an excess accumulation of bile pigments in the bloodstream, giving rise to jaundice, in which the skin, the whites of the eyes, and the mucous membranes acquire a yellow to orange and sometimes even greenish discoloration. Examples of biliary diseases include gallstones and cancer.

Gallstones

Cholelithiasis, or the formation of gallstones in the gallbladder, is the most common disease of the biliary tract. Gallstones are of three types: stones containing primarily calcium bilirubinate (pigment stones); stones containing

25 percent or more of cholesterol (cholesterol stones); and stones composed of variable mixtures of both bilirubin and cholesterol (mixed gallstones).

Pigment stones are more common in certain parts of Asia than in the Western world, and they usually occur in persons who have forms of anemia caused by the rapid destruction of red blood cells (hemolysis). Hemolytic disease results from the hereditary or acquired acquisition of abnormal forms of hemoglobin or from abnormalities of the red blood cell membrane in disorders such as sickle cell anemia, thalassemia, or acquired hemolytic anemias. Increased destruction of red blood cells leads to abnormally large amounts of bilirubin, the hemoglobin derivative, in the liver and the consequent secretion into the biliary tract of increased amounts of the water-soluble conjugate, bilirubin diglucuronide, a pigment that is normally secreted in the urine. In the biliary tract, particularly in the gallbladder, some of this bilirubin diglucuronide is broken down by enzymes into water-insoluble bilirubin, which then tends to form stones.

There are two types of pigment stones, black and brown. Black stones tend to form mainly in the gallbladder and occur in sterile bile, while brown stones may occur in any part of the biliary tract in patients with chronic biliary infections and stasis (stagnation of blood). The reasons for the increased incidence of pigment stones among persons with cirrhosis of the liver and the elderly are not clear, although increased red blood cell destruction may play a part. The occurrence of pigment stones is slightly more common in women.

Cholesterol and mixed stones occur when the proportion of cholesterol in bile exceeds the capacity of bile acids and the phospholipid lecithin to contain the total amount of cholesterol in micellar colloidal solution. When this critical micellar concentration is surpassed and the solution is saturated, crystalline particles of cholesterol are formed. The resulting gallstones contain large amounts of crystalline cholesterol and smaller quantities of calcium bilirubinate. Pure cholesterol gallstones are rare.

Cholesterol gallstones occur about twice as frequently in women as they do in men, and at younger ages. Those at increased risk of cholesterol gallstones include persons who are obese, on diets high in caloric content or in cholesterol, diabetic, or taking female sex hormones. Each of these factors favours increased concentrations of cholesterol in bile. In addition, some persons are unable, for genetic reasons, to convert sufficient amounts of cholesterol to bile acids, thus favouring the increased formation of stones.

Some illnesses, such as Crohn disease, reduce the capacity of the lower small intestine to reabsorb bile acids, leading to deficits of bile acids that cannot be overcome by hepatic synthesis alone. During pregnancy, the ratio of chenodeoxycholic acid to cholic acid in hepatic bile is reduced, thus making bile more prone to produce stones. Decreased flow of bile in the gallbladder, a condition that occurs late in pregnancy, in persons on diets low in fat, and among diabetics, also appears to favour the formation of cholesterol stones. Occasionally, some persons produce lithogenic bile, which results from reduced concentrations of phospholipids.

Symptoms are likely to be absent in about half of all patients who have gallstones. When they do appear, symptoms are caused by obstruction of a portion of the biliary tract, most commonly the cystic duct at the point where it emerges from the gallbladder. This obstruction leads to painful contraction of the gallbladder, swelling of its wall, and acute inflammation (cholecystitis). During an attack of cholecystitis, patients are often found to have fever, sharp pain in the upper abdomen (which also may be felt in the right shoulder region), tenderness over the region of the gallbladder, and elevations of the white blood cell count. If the obstruction of the neck of the gallbladder is prolonged, bacterial infections may appear, leading to formation of an abscess.

Patients with bacterial infections in the gallbladder or bile ducts commonly have severe shaking chills, with high, spiking fevers. Jaundice does not occur with gallstone complications unless the stones become impacted and obstruct the common bile duct, thus slowing or interrupting the free passage of bile from the liver to the intestine. This jaundice is associated with a marked lightening of stool colour, caused by the absence of bile pigments in the intestine, and a change in the colour of urine to a dark amber, caused by large quantities of conjugated bilirubin.

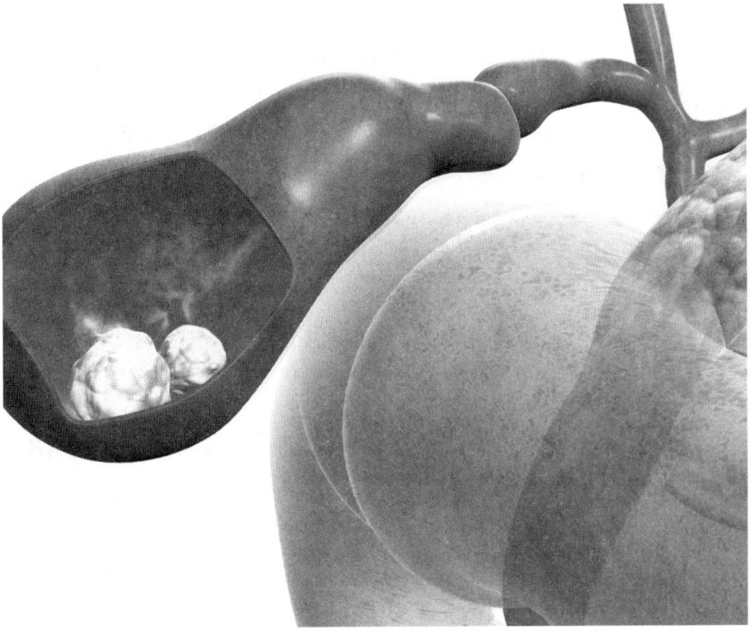

Illustration of a gallbladder that has been sectioned to reveal the gallstones contained within it. 3D4Medical.com/Getty Images

Gallstones are easy to diagnose since canaliculi, small channels in the gallbladder, can be easily detected by ultrasonography. Enlargement of the gallbladder and bile ducts (resulting from obstruction) also can be detected by this method. If gallstones are discovered on routine examination or during abdominal surgery for other reasons, and if the patient has no history of gallstone symptoms, nothing probably needs to be done. The situation is different, however, in persons who are clearly symptomatic or who are suffering acute complications, such as cholecystitis or abscesses. The traditional treatment in these cases is surgical removal of the diseased gallbladder and exploration of the bile ducts by X-rays at the time of surgery for stones. Once the gallbladder and ductal stones are removed, there is little likelihood that cholesterol or black pigment stones will recur, although brown pigment stones may occasionally recur in the bile ducts after cholecystectomy.

Cholesterol gallstones can be dissolved without surgery as long as the gallbladder has retained its ability to concentrate bile and the cystic duct is unobstructed. This is accomplished by regular oral administration of drugs made from bile acids called urosodiol and chenodiol. The ingestion of these medications increases the amount of bile acids in hepatic bile and increases the ratio of bile acids to cholesterol, thus changing the bile from lithogenic to nonlithogenic. This medication must be continued for more than one year for the cholesterol gallstones to be completely dissolved and then continued permanently at reduced doses to prevent the reappearance of stones. Only a small percentage of patients are willing to undergo this permanent treatment, and the use of bile acids is confined either to those who strongly oppose surgery or those for whom surgery imposes great risk. Pigment stones do not respond to bile acid therapy.

Other Biliary Tract Disorders

Cancer of the biliary tract is rare but may occur in almost any structure, including the gallbladder, the hepatic ducts, the common bile duct, or the hepatopancreatic ampulla (ampulla of Vater). About 90 percent of persons with primary cancer of the gallbladder also have gallstones. The risk of cancer in persons with gallstones, however, is very low (about 1 percent or less).

Congenital cysts and parasitic infections, such as liver flukes, seem to lead to increased risk of cancer of the bile duct. Persons with extensive chronic ulcerative colitis or primary sclerosing cholangitis also show a greater than normal incidence of bile duct carcinoma. Obstructive jaundice is usually the first sign of biliary tract cancer. Surgery is the only treatment, and the cure rate is low. Because most biliary duct cancers grow very slowly, physicians often try to relieve the obstructive jaundice by passing tubular stents (supporting devices) through the obstruction, using endoscopic or radiologic techniques.

Postcholecystectomy syndrome is characterized by painful attacks, often resembling preoperative symptoms, that occasionally occur following the surgical removal of gallstones and the gallbladder. These attacks may be related to biliary stricture, gallstones, or intermittent muscular spasms of the sphincter of Oddi (hepatopancreatic sphincter). Drugs are used to help prevent or reduce symptoms.

Jaundice

Jaundice, or yellowing of the skin, sclera (outer layer of the eyeball), and mucous membranes, occurs whenever the level of bilirubin in the blood is significantly above normal. This condition is evident in three different types of disorders, more than one of which may be present simultaneously in a single person.

The first type, unconjugated, or hemolytic, jaundice, appears when the amount of bilirubin produced from hemoglobin by the destruction of red blood cells or muscle tissue (myoglobin) exceeds the normal capacity of the liver to transport it. This can also happen when the ability of the liver to conjugate normal amounts of bilirubin into bilirubin diglucuronide is significantly reduced by inadequate intracellular transport or enzyme systems. The second type, hepatocellular jaundice, arises when liver cells are damaged so severely that their ability to transport bilirubin diglucuronide into the biliary system is reduced, allowing some of this yellow pigment to regurgitate into the bloodstream. The third type, cholestatic, or obstructive jaundice, occurs when essentially normal liver cells are unable to transport bilirubin either through the capillary membrane of the liver, because of damage in that area, or through the biliary tract, because of anatomical obstructions (closure or absence of an opening, gallstones, cancer).

Unconjugated Jaundice

Unconjugated, or hemolytic, jaundice is characterized by the absence of bile pigments in the urine and by normal stool color. The colour of the urine is normal because the bilirubin in the blood is unconjugated to glucuronic acid and therefore bound to blood albumin and insoluble in water. Thus the bilirubin is not filtered by the kidneys. The color of stools remains normal because much of the bilirubin in the blood is filtered normally by the liver and enters the intestine promptly by way of the biliary system.

Hemolytic diseases in newborns may lead to serious brain damage (kernicterus) if the unconjugated bilirubin crosses into the brain stem and destroys vital nuclei. Exposing infants at risk for kernicterus to blue light converts the bilirubin to harmless and colourless degradation products. Unconjugated hyperbilirubinemia also occurs in many newborns, especially if they are premature, when the bilirubin transport enzyme systems are not fully developed. This disorder is self-limited, may require occasional exposures to blue light, and usually disappears within the first two weeks of extrauterine life. Gilbert disease, a fairly common hereditary deficiency in the hepatic transport protein ligandin and the conjugating enzyme glucuronyl transferase, results in a harmless lifelong tendency to mild degrees of unconjugated jaundice, especially during periods of fasting or fatigue.

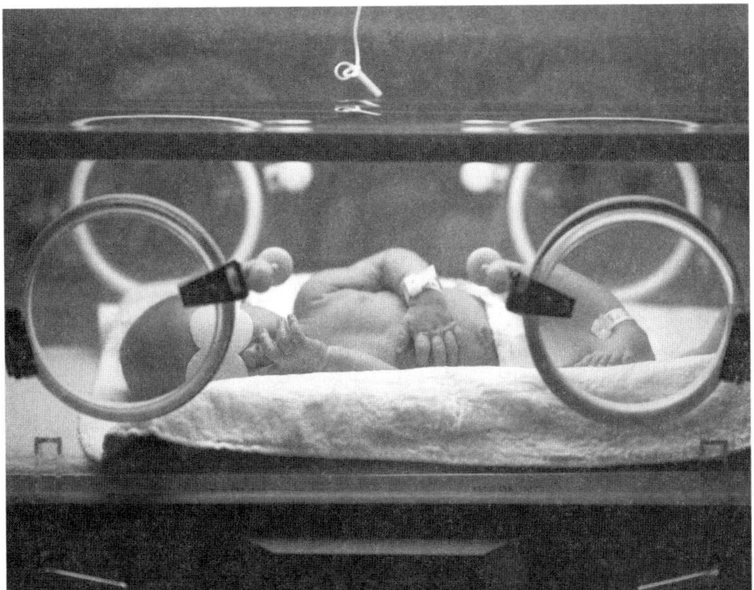

This newborn baby is being treated for jaundice by being placed under bili lights. Roderick Chen/First Light/Getty Images

Hepatocellular Jaundice

Hepatocellular jaundice, present in all types of hepatitis and cirrhosis and in congestive liver disease, is characterized by dark amber urine and normal or slightly paler than normal stools. Because much of the bilirubin in the blood already has been conjugated by the endoplasmic reticulum of the hepatocyte, it is water-soluble and can be filtered by the kidneys. Stools are usually normal because some bile pigment also manages to be excreted into the biliary tract and intestine.

Cholestatic Jaundice

Cholestatic jaundice is also distinguished by amber-coloured urine, but the colour of the stools is likely to be very pale (clay-coloured) due to the failure of bile pigments to pass into the intestine. Itching of the skin is commonly associated with this condition. Cholestasis occurs in many types of hepatitis, especially those caused by certain drugs, and in diseases that primarily damage small bile passages in the liver (intraheptic cholestasis). Cholestatic jaundice also occurs in patients with obstructive disorders of the biliary tract outside of the liver (extrahepatic cholestasis). It is often impossible to determine the level of obstruction by means of examination alone, and more sophisticated imaging techniques are required to locate the site of damage.

DISEASES OF THE PANCREAS

Diseases of the pancreas can have severe impacts on digestion and on the utilization of carbohydrates by the body. Examples of common conditions affecting the digestive functions of this organ are pancreatitis, in which inflammation causes the digestive enzymes produced by the organ to break down the tissues of the pancreas itself, and pancreatic cancer, in which the abnormal growth of cells causes severe dysregulation in the production and secretion of pancreatic hormones and enzymes. Pancreatic disease also occurs as a complication of cystic fibrosis, in which thick mucus plugs block the normal secretory functions of the organ.

Pancreatitis

Inflammation of the pancreas, or pancreatitis, is probably the most common disease of this organ. The disorder may be confined to either singular or repeated acute episodes, or it may become a chronic disease. There are many factors associated with the onset of pancreatitis, including direct injury to the pancreas, certain drugs, viral infections, heredity, hyperlipidemia (increased levels of blood fats), and congenital deformities of the ductal system.

In the Western world, most cases are related either to alcoholism or to gallstones, especially when stones pass spontaneously into the hepatopancreatic ampulla (ampulla of Vater). Although the immediate cause of acute pancreatitis is not always clear, it seems to involve one or more of the following factors: heavy stimulation of pancreatic acini; increased pressure within the duct because of partial obstruction (gallstones) or edema (alcohol); and damage to the fine ductal network in the pancreas, which allows the escape of activated and destructive digestive enzymes into the substance of the pancreas itself and into surrounding tissues.

Overstimulation of secretory enzyme production mechanisms in the acinar cell may also lead to the activation of intracellular (lysosomal) enzyme systems, resulting in the conversion of proenzymes to active forms that begin to digest cellular organelles. The gland thus begins to self-destruct. Similar damage may appear in other organs, such as the lungs, kidneys, and blood vessels, which receive these activated enzymes by way of the bloodstream. It is not clear how the proenzyme trypsinogen is converted to trypsin in the damaged acinar cell, but it is known that the activation of the other proenzymes proceeds from this conversion. The extent of acinar destruction appears to depend on the strength of the causative factors.

Localized, severe abdominal and midback pain resulting from enzyme leakage, tissue damage, and nerve irritation is the most common symptom of acute pancreatitis. In severe cases, respiratory failure, shock, and even death may occur. The severity of the symptoms generally depends on the extent of the damage to the pancreas. The diagnosis is confirmed by the detection of elevated levels of pancreatic enzymes (amylase and lipase) in the blood and, if islet cell function is disturbed by the inflammatory process, elevated blood glucose levels. Ultrasonographic or CT scans of the upper abdomen usually reveal an enlarged and swollen pancreas. Sustained pain, often with fever, suggests the presence of a pseudocyst or abscess caused by localized areas of destruction and infections in the pancreas.

Acute pancreatitis is treated primarily by supportive therapy, with replacement of fluid and sodium and control of pain. In severe cases, washing necrotic material and active enzymes from the abdominal cavity during surgery may be beneficial. Following recovery from an acute attack, the prevention of further attacks should be the primary goal. Thus, the removal of gallstones, cessation of alcohol consumption, a low-fat diet, and discontinuation of toxic drugs (thiazide diuretics, immunosuppressives, and corticosteroids, for example) can be helpful measures. In instances where repeated attacks of acute pancreatitis have resulted in strictures (scars) of the main pancreatic duct, surgical repair may decrease the number of further attacks.

Chronic Pancreatitis

Chronic pancreatitis rarely follows repeated acute attacks. It seems instead to be a separate disorder that can result from mucus plugs and precipitation of calcium salts in the smaller pancreatic ducts. The progressive loss of acinar and islet cell function follows, presumably as a consequence of continuous inflammation resulting from the ductal blockage. Progressive calcification, which at times results in the formation of stones in the major pancreatic ducts, has been attributed to diminished production of an acinar protein that normally holds calcium in solution.

Alcoholism and certain hereditary factors account for almost all of the cases of chronic pancreatitis seen in the Western world. Chronic protein malnutrition is a primary cause in underdeveloped countries. Recurrent abdominal pain, diabetes, and intestinal malabsorption of dietary nutrients are the main symptoms of chronic pancreatitis. Weight loss and deficiencies of fat-soluble vitamins (A, D, E, and K) are common. Treatment includes abstinence from alcohol, management of diabetes with insulin, and ingestion of oral pancreatic enzyme supplements to correct dietary malabsorption.

Cystic Fibrosis

Cystic fibrosis is inherited, but it is not expressed unless both members of a pair of homologous, or corresponding, chromosomes carry the trait. The major functional abnormality in persons with the disease appears to be the elaboration by mucous glands throughout the body of secretions containing greater than normal concentrations of protein and calcium. This imbalance leads to increased viscosity of the secretions of mucus and organic constituents in gland ducts. The resulting plugging process in the pancreas almost invariably causes destruction and scarring of the acinar tissue, usually without damaging the islets of Langerhans. A similar process in the hepatic biliary system produces a form of cirrhosis. In cystic fibrosis, the resulting pancreatic insufficiency usually can be treated by the oral replacement of pancreatic enzymes.

Pancreatic Cancer

Pancreatic cancer is a disease characterized by abnormal growth of cells in the pancreas. The pancreas is primarily made up of two different tissues with separate functions. The first tissue, the exocrine pancreas, secretes enzymes into the digestive tract, aiding the breakdown of fats and proteins. The other is the endocrine pancreas, which secretes glucagon and insulin into the bloodstream to control blood sugar levels. Ninety-five percent of pancreatic cancers develop from the exocrine pancreas. The remaining 5 percent are often called neuroendocrine tumours or islet cell cancers; these develop from endocrine cells.

Causes and Symptoms of Pancreatic Cancer

As is the case with many cancers, symptoms of pancreatic cancer are shared with those of many other illnesses. Symptoms often do not appear until the cancer has advanced to a late stage. They include abdominal pain, unexplained weight loss, problems with sugar metabolism, and difficulty digesting fatty foods. As a pancreatic tumour grows, it may block the common bile duct, which leads to a buildup of bilirubin in the blood and causes jaundice (a yellowing of the skin and eyes). Blockage of the bile duct may also cause the gallbladder to become enlarged.

The causes of pancreatic cancer vary and in many cases remain unknown. However, several factors have been identified that increase the risk of developing pancreatic cancer. The two most important of these factors are smoking, which is associated with about 30 percent of pancreatic tumours, and central obesity (accumulation of fat primarily around the abdomen), which can increase risk of pancreatic cancer by as much as 70 percent in some postmenopausal women. In both men and women, central obesity is associated with increased levels of insulin and with disruption of normal endocrine and metabolic functions. However, the mechanism by which abnormally high insulin levels and dysfunctional metabolism in centrally obese individuals give rise to pancreatic cancer is unclear. Furthermore, a diet high in animal products, particularly animal fat, also increases cancer risk.

Environmental factors, such as exposure to certain dyes, pesticides, and petroleum products, may increase the probability of developing pancreatic cancer. Uncontrollable risk factors include age, sex—males are 30 percent more likely to develop cancers of the pancreas than are females—and illnesses such as diabetes mellitus and chronic pancreatitis. An estimated 10 percent of cases of pancreatic cancer are the result of inherited defects. Some of these cases arise in association with known genetic syndromes, such as Peutz-Jeghers syndrome and hereditary nonpolyposis colon cancer. Other cases are associated with familial pancreatic cancer, generally defined as the occurrence of pancreatic cancer in at least one pair of first-degree relatives. Mutations in a gene designated *PALLD* (palladin, or cytoskeletal associated protein) have been linked to familial pancreatic cancer.

Diagnosis of Pancreatic Cancer

Blood tests that assess various pancreatic and liver functions may suggest pancreatic cancer. If cancer is suspected, a needle biopsy or an endoscopy procedure is usually conducted to examine pancreatic cells or the pancreas itself for signs of cancer. However, these procedures are invasive and are associated with an increased risk for serious complications, including pancreatitis.

In order to make a correct diagnosis and to determine the stage of the cancer, multiple imaging techniques may be employed that allow doctors to see the pancreas, despite its location deep within the abdominal cavity. Imaging techniques commonly used include CT scans, MRI, and different types of ultrasound, including transabdominal ultrasound (imaging performed on the external surface of the abdomen) and endoscopic ultrasound (EUS; an ultrasound device is sent through an endoscope to take images of internal tissues). Various techniques that combine contrast agents (dyes) with X-ray imaging are also used to determine whether the bile duct or other ducts within the pancreas are blocked. One example is called percutaneous transhepatic cholangiography (PTC), in which a needle is used to inject a dye directly into the liver, followed by X-ray imaging. Other X-ray imaging techniques include angiography, in which X-rays are used to view blood vessels to determine if the cancer has spread through the walls of the vessels feeding into the pancreas.

Because early detection of pancreatic cancer is critical for patient survival, research is becoming increasingly focused on specific markers (subtle, identifiable cellular changes) that are detectable in precancerous pancreatic lesions. One method of early detection employs special light-scattering spectroscopy techniques in combination with existing endoscope technology. This light-scattering imaging technology is extremely sensitive and is aimed at detecting specific markers in cells in the first part of the small intestine (the duodenum) that are indicative of very early precancerous pancreatic lesions. It is also much less invasive than needle biopsy and traditional endoscopy procedures for pancreatic lesion detection because doctors need only examine an easily accessible region in the small intestine.

Once pancreatic cancer has been diagnosed, its stage is then determined to indicate how far the cancer has progressed. Stage I cancers are confined to the pancreas and have not spread to nearby lymph nodes. Stage II cancers have spread locally to the bile duct or small intestine but have not reached the lymph nodes, whereas stage III tumours have reached these nodes. Stage IV cancers have spread to other organs such as the lungs, liver, spleen, or colon.

The survival rate from pancreatic cancer is lower than that seen with many other cancers because the symptoms of pancreatic cancer often do not become obvious until the later stages of the disease. The average five-year survival rate from all stages of pancreatic cancer is extremely low, as is the one-year survival rate. However, survival rates are higher for patients who have their cancer diagnosed early in the course of the disease.

Treatment and Prevention of Pancreatic Cancer

Surgery can be used to treat pancreatic cancer, but, given the poor prognosis of the disease and the unusually high number of complications associated with pancreatic surgery, surgery is usually reserved for cases in which there is a reasonable possibility of curing the disease. If the cancer is considered to be incurable, major surgery is done mainly to relieve symptoms or digestive problems. Islet cell tumours are often localized to the tail of the pancreas, and a distal pancreatectomy may be conducted to remove this portion of the pancreas along with the spleen.

Exocrine cancers are often treated with the Whipple procedure, a complicated surgical approach that removes all or part of the pancreas and nearby lymph nodes, the gallbladder, and portions of the stomach, small intestine, and bile duct. Serious complications often arise following this procedure, which requires an extensive hospital stay and considerable experience on the part of the surgeon. Other exocrine tumours are sometimes treated by complete removal of the pancreas (total pancreatectomy). Surgery can also be used to relieve complications of pancreatic cancers, such as obstruction of the bile duct. The bile duct may be redirected around the tumour, or a tube may be placed in the bile duct to keep it open.

Radiation therapy is sometimes used in conjunction with surgery—often prior to surgery to reduce a tumour to a more manageable size but also after surgery to destroy any remaining cancer cells. The position of the pancreas in the abdominal cavity makes it a difficult target for focused radiotherapy, but a procedure using radiotherapy simultaneously with surgery permits the surgeon to focus radiation directly onto the pancreas by moving obstructing organs aside. Side effects of this radiation therapy may include vomiting, diarrhea, fatigue, or skin irritations resembling a sunburn.

Chemotherapy is generally used when pancreatic cancers have spread to distant organs and may be required so that as many cancer cells as possible can be sought out and destroyed. Endocrine or islet cell tumours may be treated with hormone therapy, in which specific hormones are used to stop or slow the growth of the cancer in the endocrine cells. Targeted drug therapies that block cellular processes driving cancer cell proliferation have been used in combination with chemotherapy in some pancreatic cancer patients. For example, a drug called erlotinib (Tarceva) blocks the activity of a kinase (a type of enzyme) associated with the epidermal growth factor receptor (EGFR), which stimulates unregulated cell division when mutated in cancer cells. When erlotinib is given in combination with the chemotherapeutic agent gemcitabine (Gemzar), an antimetabolite that inhibits the synthesis of genetic material in dividing cells, patient survival is improved, although only modestly. Several other targeted drugs such as cetuximab (Erbitux), a monoclonal antibody that binds to EGFR and thus prevents kinase activation and cell division, are being developed and tested in clinical trials for pancreatic cancer.

In most cases, pancreatic cancer cannot be completely prevented, but risk can be decreased by reducing or eliminating cigarette smoking and following a diet low in animal products and high in fruits and vegetables. Researchers are also investigating anti-inflammatory therapeutic agents that inhibit an enzyme called cyclooxygenase-2 (COX-2). Because COX-2 plays a role in inflammation and mediates tumour growth and development, it is a valuable target for the development of drugs used in the prevention and treatment of several cancers, including breast cancer, colorectal cancer, and pancreatic cancer. In people at risk for familial pancreatic cancer, routine endoscopy can be used to monitor changes in pancreatic tissue. If tissue abnormalities arise, the pancreas can be removed before cancer develops.

Conclusion

The digestive system is relatively simple in anatomic terms—it is a tube through which food passes and is broken down into useful components. The physical and chemical processes that underlie the passage of food and the extraction and absorption of nutrients are relatively recent discoveries, having been made primarily in the 20th century. As a result, there remains much to be understood about the digestive system—especially concerning the function of certain digestive substances such as hormones and the characterization of diseases of the digestive tissues.

One major area of modern research into the digestive system involves understanding how the stomach and intestines relay signals conveying information about satiety, hunger, and cravings to the brain. Many animals are known to seek out and eat specific types of foods to fulfill their nutrient needs. Humans living in the modern world, however, have access to a large variety of foods, and understanding what compels a person to choose to eat an apple rather than a banana when given the opportunity to have either, combines information about human behaviour as well as about the basic physiology of the human digestive system.

Advancements in molecular biology, biochemistry, and genetics have proven invaluable to expanding upon existing knowledge of the digestive system. In 2009, for example, scientists overturned the once long-held theory that the human tongue contains distinct areas of taste reception. Scientists studying the molecular and biochemical properties of taste receptors on the tongue found that individual receptors capable of detecting sensations of salty, sweet, bitter, sour, and umami (meaty) are actually widely distributed and intermingled with one another, rather than isolated as populations of one receptor type in separate areas of the tongue.

Investigations into the causes of digestive system disease have focused primarily on identifying genetic abnormalities that either cause disease directly or place a person at increased risk for disease. In many instances, scientists have discovered that genetic variations associated with complex conditions such as Crohn disease appear to predispose an individual to disease, meaning that having a particular genetic variation cannot alone cause the disorder. Thus, scientists are also working to identify the environmental factors that interact with these genetic variations and thereby contribute to the development of disease. A deeper understanding of the causes and processes underlying digestive disease promises to facilitate the development of new preventative, diagnostic, and therapeutic approaches for these conditions.

Glossary

alveolar mucosa The loosely attached mucous membrane covering the basal part of the jaw and continuing into the floor of the mouth inwardly and into the cheek vestibule outwardly.

benign Noncancerous.

bicarbonate Liquid secreted by the epithelial cells lining ducts in the pancreas. Bicarbonate helps neutralize the acid going from the stomach to the small intestine.

bolus Food that has been chewed and mixed in the mouth with saliva.

canaliculi Small channels that transport bile from hepatocytes.

cecum Pouch or large tubelike structure in the lower abdominal cavity that receives undigested food material from the small intestine and is considered the first region of the large intestine.

cellulose A complex carbohydrate, or polysaccharide, consisting of 3,000 or more glucose units.

cementum Thin layer of bonelike material covering the roots and sometimes other parts of the teeth.

chylomicrons Lipoproteins that transport dietary lipids from the intestines to other locations in the body.

chyme A thick semifluid mass of partially digested food and digestive secretions that is formed in the stomach and intestine during digestion.

diuretic A substance that decreases the amount of fluid reabsorbed by the tubules of the kidneys when the fluid passes back into the blood, increasing urine flow.

epidermis The outermost protective portion of the skin.

epilepsy Chronic neurological disorder characterized by sudden and recurrent seizures that are caused by excessive signaling of nerve cells in the brain.

folic acid Water-soluble vitamin of the B complex that is essential in animals and plants for the synthesis of nucleic acids.

frenulum linguae Elevated fold of mucous membrane that binds each lip to the gums.

gastric mucosa Mucous membrane lining the inside of the stomach that works to lubricate the food masses in order to facilitate movement and to provide a protective layer over the lining epithelium of the stomach cavity.

gastritis Acute or chronic inflammation of the mucosal layers of the stomach.

gingivae More commonly known as "gums," connective tissue covered with mucous membrane, attached to and surrounding the necks of the teeth and adjacent alveolar bone.

Golgi apparatus Membrane-bound organelle of eukaryotic cells responsible for transporting, modifying, and packaging proteins and lipids into vesicles for delivery to targeted destinations.

halitosis Bad breath, most commonly caused by bacteria.

ileum The final and longest segment of the small intestine specifically responsible for the absorption of vitamin B_{12} and the reabsorption of conjugated bile salts.

jaundice Excess accumulation of bile pigments in the bloodstream and bodily tissues that causes a yellow to orange and sometimes even greenish discoloration of the skin, the whites of the eyes, and the mucous membranes.

lacteals The lymphatic vessels that serve the small intestine.

leukoplakia Precancerous tumour of the mucous membranes, most common in older men and usually seen on the lips or tongue.

lymphocytes Type of white blood cell that determines the specificity of the immune response to infectious microorganisms and other foreign substances.

lysosome Subcellular organelle that is found in all eukaryotic cells and is responsible for the cell's digestion of macromolecules, old cell parts, and microorganisms.

malignant Cancerous.

mastication Up-and-down and side-to-side movements of the lower jaw that assist in reducing particles of solid food, making them more easily swallowed; chewing.

papillae Projections on the upper surface of the tongue that contain taste buds.

sigmoidoscope Flexible fibre-optic endoscope to examine the rectum and the terminal section of the large intestine, known as the sigmoid colon.

triglycerides Any one of an important group of naturally occurring lipids that can be broken down for energy.

Bibliography

Textbooks on the digestive system include Tadataka Yamada et al. (eds.), *Textbook of Gastroenterology*, 3rd ed., 2 vol. (1999); Leonard R. Johnson (ed.), *Physiology of the Gastrointestinal Tract*, 3rd ed., 2 vol. (1994); and Marvin H. Sleisenger and John S. Fordtran, *Sleisenger & Fordtran's Gastrointestinal and Liver Disease: Pathophysiology, Diagnosis, Management*, 6th ed., ed. by Mark Feldman, Marvin H. Sleisenger, and Bruce F. Scharschmidt, 2 vol. (1998).

James L. Gould, William T. Keeton, and Carol Grant Gould, *Biological Science*, 6th ed. (1996), is a comprehensive study that includes an examination of digestion. Specialized studies include H.J. Vonk and J.R.H. Western, *Comparative Biochemistry and Physiology of Enzymatic Digestion* (1984); Leonard R. Johnson (ed.), *Physiology of the Gastrointestinal Tract*, 3rd ed., 2 vol. (1994); Horace W. Davenport, *Physiology of the Digestive Tract: An Introductory Text*, 5th ed. (1982); Charles F. Code (ed.), *Alimentary Canal*, 5 vol. (1967–68); John Morton, *Guts: The Form and Function of the Digestive System*, 2nd ed. (1979); J.B. Jennings, *Feeding, Digestion, and Assimilation in Animals*, 2nd ed. (1972); and B.I. Balinsky and B.C. Fabian, *An Introduction to Embryology*, 5th ed. (1981).

Anatomical description and illustration can be found in such comprehensive texts as Henry Gray, *Anatomy of the Human Body*, 30th American ed., ed. by Carmine D. Clemente (1985); Leslie Brainerd Arey, *Developmental Anatomy: A Textbook and Laboratory Manual of Embryology*, rev. 7th ed. (1974); Frank H. Netter, *A Compilation of Paintings on the Normal and Pathologic Anatomy of the Digestive System*, ed. by Ernst Oppenheimer, 3 vol. in 1

(1957–62; reissued 1997), vol. 3 of *The Ciba Collection of Medical Illustrations*; R.J. Last, *Last's Anatomy: Regional and Applied*, 8th ed., ed. by R.M.H. McMinn (1990); and Alfred Sherwood Romer and Thomas S. Parsons, *The Vertebrate Body*, 6th ed. (1986).

Gastrointestinal diseases are discussed in such works as Eugene R. Schiff, Michael F. Sorrell, and Willis C. Maddrey (eds.), *Schiff's Diseases of the Liver*, 8th ed., 2 vol. (1999); Robert F. Service, "Stalking the Start of Colon Cancer," *Science*, 263(5153):1559–60 (March 18, 1994); Martin J. Blaser, "The Bacteria behind Ulcers," *Scientific American*, 274(2):104–107 (February 1996); Joseph Alper, "Ulcers as an Infectious Disease," *Science*, 260(5105):159–160 (April 9, 1993); Charles Herbert Best and Norman Burke Taylor, *Best and Taylor's Physiological Basis of Medical Practice*, 12th ed., edited by John B. West (1991); and E.J. Holborow and W.G. Reeves (eds.), *Immunology in Medicine: A Comprehensive Guide to Clinical Immunology*, 2nd ed. (1983). Specialized studies include Harvey J. Dworken, *Gastroenterology: Pathophysiology and Clinical Applications* (1982); Marvin H. Sleisenger and John S. Fordtran, *Sleisenger & Fordtran's Gastrointestinal and Liver Disease: Pathophysiology, Diagnosis, Management*, 6th ed., edited by Mark Feldman, Marvin H. Sleisenger, and Bruce F. Scharschmidt, 2 vol. (1998); David J.C. Shearman, Niall Finlayson, and Michael Camilleri (eds.), *Diseases of the Gastrointestinal Tract and Liver*, 3rd ed. (1997); H.L. Duthie (ed.), *Gastrointestinal Motility in Health and Disease* (1978); William S. Haubrich and Fenton Schaffner, *Bockus Gastroenterology*, 5th ed., edited by J. Edward Berk, 4 vol. (1994); and Franklin Bicknell, *Vitamins in Medicine*, 4th ed., edited by Brian M. Barker and David A. Bender, 2 vol. (1980–82). Information on current research is available in Fred Kern and A.L. Blum (eds.), *Gastroenterology Annual*.

INDEX

T

U

V

W

Z